Learning Libgdx Game Development

Walk through a complete game development cycle
with practical examples and build cross-platform
games with Libgdx

Andreas Oehlke

[PACKT] open source *
PUBLISHING   community experience distilled

BIRMINGHAM - MUMBAI

Learning Libgdx Game Development

First published: September 2013

Production Reference: 1190913

Published by Packt Publishing Ltd.
Livery Place
35 Livery Street
Birmingham B3 2PB, UK.

ISBN 978-1-78216-604-7

www.packtpub.com

Cover Image by Aniket Sawant (aniket_sawant_photography@hotmail.com)

Credits

Author
Andreas Oehlke

Reviewers
Ebenezer Edelman
Matthias Markowski
David Saltares Márquez
Chris Moeller

Acquisition Editors
Kartikey Pandey
Julian Ursell

Lead Technical Editor
Mayur Hule

Technical Editors
Menza Mathew
Amit Shetty
Harshad Vairat

Copy Editors
Mradula Hegde
Gladson Monteiro
Sayanee Mukherjee
Kirti Pai
Adithi Shetty

Project Coordinator
Apeksha Chitnis

Proofreaders
Paul Hindle
Mario Cecere

Indexer
Rekha Nair

Graphics
Abhinash Sahu

Production Coordinator
Shantanu Zagade

Cover Work
Shantanu Zagade

About the Author

Andreas Oehlke is a professional software engineer and a computer scientist who feels very much at home on any Linux/Unix machine. He holds a Bachelor's degree in Computer Science and loves to assemble and disassemble software and hardware alike. An exorbitant affinity for electronics and computers has always been his trademark. His hobbies include game and web development, programming in general (software design and new languages), programming embedded systems with microcontrollers, playing sports, and making music.

He currently works full-time as a software engineer for a German financial institution. Furthermore, he has worked as a consultant and a game developer in San Francisco, CA. In his spare time, he provides his expertise to a German startup called Gamerald (http://www.gamerald.com/).

I want to thank my parents, Michael and Sigrid, and my brother Dennis for their constant and invaluable support, which definitely kept me on the go while writing this book. I also want to thank my close friends for giving me lots of helpful feedback, notably Sascha Björn Bolz with regard to providing the artwork for Canyon Bunny. Last but not least, I want to thank Klaus "keith303" Spang for providing the music track as well as the whole team from Packt Publishing, including all the numerous reviewers involved, for their great work in producing a high quality book.

About the Reviewers

Ebenezer Edelman is a British computer programmer currently living in South Africa. He has an eclectic and diverse set of interests ranging from technology, engineering, and science to literature, photography, videography, and music. His hobbies include playing the piano, designing rocket engines, and occasionally a game of chess.

He started game development by learning C from the manual of a C compiler and developing simple text-based games. Then, after getting to grips with C++ and the DirectX SDK, he attempted to develop a 3D physics sandbox game, which never got past the beta stage. After that, he learned C# and the XNA framework and made several 2D games before deciding to get involved in mobile game development. He did this using Java and the LibGDX framework, which he used to get some of his old 2D games to Android. He is constantly looking to broaden his knowledge, and he now uses Research In Motion's open source C++ game engine gameplay3d.

In addition, he has experience of Windows Forms (C#), the GTK+ toolkit (Vala), the Qt toolkit (C++), the Android SDK (Java), as well as the x86 Assembly language, Python, PHP, JavaScript, and HTML/CSS.

His personal website and blog is located at `http://EbenezerEdelman.tk/`, and he is on Twitter (`@EbenezerEdelman`) and Google Plus (`+EbenezerEdelman`).

Matthias Markowski is a passionate game developer and video game enthusiast who focuses on the field of Graphics Programming. He began his professional career in 2005 through his involvement in the demoscene. He has contributed to the development of the fast-paced action MMOG (Massively Multiplayer Online Game) "Black Prophecy" and the Wii U casual game "Your Shape Fitness Evolved 2013". He is currently employed at Ubisoft Blue Byte, known as a creator of excellent strategy games, located in Düsseldorf, Germany.

You can view his portfolio and contact details at `http://mmarkowski.carbonmade.com`.

David Saltares Márquez works at the award-winning developer Crytek as a games programmer. The Nottingham-based studio of the company behind the Crysis series was his jump into the AAA industry in 2012. Since then, he has been part of the Artificial Intelligence team, developing behaviors, pushing character fidelity forward, and developing systems that are now part of CryENGINE.

He obtained his BSc in Computing Science from Cádiz University (Spain) where he founded the games development society (ADVUCA) in collaboration with other passionate classmates. Through the society, he organized several talks and workshops with a strong focus on open source software, all of which were a great success.

By always working on side projects, he the joined the Libgdx community, attracted by the richness of its features, open source nature, multiplatform capabilities, and the hospitality of its developers. Libgdx allowed him to create various games such as Freegemas (`https://github.com/siondream/freegemas-gdx`) and Math Maze (`http://siondream.com/blog/games/math-maze/`). In return, he contributed to the maps' API and is very active on the forums.

Further information is available on his blog (`http://siondream.com`), where he talks in depth about Libgdx, programming, personal projects, and his experience in game jams such as Ludum Dare (`http://siondream.com/blog/game-jams/`).

Chris Moeller is a founder of the game studio Ackmi Design and Engineering. He has been building computers since the age of nine and has been programming for more than 10 years. He had the opportunity to work for software companies as a PHP developer, Java QA engineer, and Flash developer, and he currently works primarily for Android. He has been an enthusiastic gamer for most of his life and has created many game prototypes as well as several finished games. He writes game tutorials on his blog at `www.chrismweb.com`, and most of his new games can be found through his company website at `www.ackmi.com`, which he runs with his wife, Megan.

www.PacktPub.com

Support files, eBooks, discount offers and more

You might want to visit www.PacktPub.com for support files and downloads related to your book.

Did you know that Packt offers eBook versions of every book published, with PDF and ePub files available? You can upgrade to the eBook version at www.PacktPub.com and as a print book customer, you are entitled to a discount on the eBook copy. Get in touch with us at service@packtpub.com for more details.

At www.PacktPub.com, you can also read a collection of free technical articles, sign up for a range of free newsletters and receive exclusive discounts and offers on Packt books and eBooks.

http://PacktLib.PacktPub.com

Do you need instant solutions to your IT questions? PacktLib is Packt's online digital book library. Here, you can access, read and search across Packt's entire library of books.

Why Subscribe?

- Fully searchable across every book published by Packt
- Copy and paste, print and bookmark content
- On demand and accessible via web browser

Free Access for Packt account holders

If you have an account with Packt at www.PacktPub.com, you can use this to access PacktLib today and view nine entirely free books. Simply use your login credentials for immediate access.

Table of Contents

Preface

Since personal computers have conquered our private homes, video games have become more and more popular and eventually a multimillion dollar business for big video game companies. With the introduction of mobile devices such as smartphones and tablets, the market for video games has experienced another significant increase; in particular, it has now become open to independent game developers with small budgets.

For game developers, it is essential to have tools at hand that provide fundamentals which allow rapid prototyping and cost-effective implementation of their creative ideas. This is where Libgdx comes into play.

Libgdx, as a Java-based game development framework, provides a unified access layer to handle all the supported platforms. Libgdx also makes use of C/C++ to achieve cross-platform support as well as to boost the application performance for mission critical tasks.

This book will show you how easy it is to develop cross-platform games by walking you through a complete game development cycle using the free and open source library Libgdx. Besides this, you will also learn about common game structure and the involved requirements.

You will be introduced to the key features of Libgdx and you will learn how to develop a game with ease and speed up your development cycles. In ten easy-to-follow chapters, you are going to develop your first Libgdx cross-platform game and add more and more game functionalities as you progress further through this book.

The special features will also make you acquainted with advanced programming techniques such as animations, physics simulations, and shader programs that enhance your games in both their gameplay and visual presentation.

By the end of this book, you will have a fully working 2D game that will run on Windows, Linux, Mac OS X, WebGL-capable browsers, and Android. You will also have all the skills required to extend the game further or to start developing your own cross-platform games.

What this book covers

Chapter 1, Introduction to Libgdx and Project Setup, covers how to install and configure the development environment and introduces you to the project setup tool that comes with Libgdx. Then, we will take a first look at the basics of what a game needs to come alive.

Chapter 2, Cross-platform Development – Build Once, Deploy Anywhere, explains the supported target platforms and how to deploy and run our application on each platform using a demo application. For the first overview of Libgdx's API, we will take a glance at each module. Then, the Application Cycle will be introduced, and we will take a look at how to debug and manipulate our code at runtime.

Chapter 3, Configuring the Game, brings us from our demo application to a real game by setting up a new project called Canyon Bunny. We will work on this project throughout the rest of the book and extend it from chapter to chapter with new features. Since Libgdx is a framework, we will first have to build our program architecture by using UML class diagrams to structure our game engine.

Chapter 4, Gathering Resources, describes how to gather all the resources (assets) needed for Canyon Bunny including graphics, audio files, level data, and so on. We will also find out how to load, track, and organize assets efficiently. Finally, it is time to think about how level data is going to be handled so that we are able to populate our game world with objects.

Chapter 5, Making a Scene, covers how to start implementing the first game objects such as rocks, mountains, and clouds, and how to use the assets that we added in *Chapter 4, Gathering Resources.* In order to visualize the game scene, a level loader is needed to put our game objects in their right places in the game world. Typically, games have a user interface to give feedback about their current status, so we will add a game GUI to Canyon Bunny that displays the player's high score, remaining extra lives, and so on.

Chapter 6, Adding the Actors, explains how to add the remaining game objects for Canyon Bunny, including the player character and collectible items to complete our game. We will also add simple physics for player movement and basic collision detection. Additionally, the game logic will be extended so that it is able to detect the "life lost" and "game over" conditions.

Chapter 7, Menus and Options, describes how to create a menu system with widgets such as buttons, labels, and checkboxes to enrich the overall game experience. Furthermore, we will add an Options window where the player can adjust the game settings.

Chapter 8, Special Effects, covers how to make use of particle systems and how to apply interpolation algorithms to create impressive effects such as dust clouds; a smooth, following camera; floating rocks; and parallax scrolling for mountains in the background. Using special effects will spice up the appearance of your game.

Chapter 9, Screen Transitions, introduces screen transitions. We will dive into enhanced visual effects using OpenGL's Framebuffer Objects for offscreen rendering into video memory. This will allow us to create seamless transitions for an improved user experience when switching from one screen to another. For Canyon Bunny, we will create a variety of transition effects.

Chapter 10, Managing Music and Sound Effects, will walk you through a list of recommended sound generators and discuss their differences. Then, we will take a look at Libgdx's Audio API and demonstrate how to use it by creating an audio manager. We do this so that handling all our audio playback needs become a breeze.

Chapter 11, Advanced Programming Techniques, introduces you to some advanced programming techniques that will guide you to the next level of game programming. We will build up basic knowledge about the Box2D API that enables us to create believable physics simulations in games. Additionally, we will discuss the topic of shader programs using the example of a monochrome image filter effect. Lastly, we will show you how to make use of the accelerometer hardware commonly available in modern smartphones and tablets, which allows controlling the game by tilting the device.

Chapter 12, Animations, explains how to polish up the game by adding animations. We will cover two different approaches to animate the game menu and the game world. Finally, we will implement a state machine to allow event-based animations for the player character.

What you need for this book

Libgdx is a cross-platform game development framework. For development, you will need a computer running either Windows (Vista/7/8), Linux (for example, Ubuntu), or Mac OS X (10.5+).

Additionally, you will need to download the Libgdx framework for game development. You can download Libgdx from `https://code.google.com/p/libgdx/downloads/list`. Please download Version 0.9.7 of Libgdx, as this is the version that is used in this book.

The Integrated Development Environment (IDE) used in this book is Eclipse. You can download the Eclipse IDE from `http://www.eclipse.org/`.

To develop games for the Android platform, you will need an Android device running Android 2.2 (Froyo) or higher and the official Android Software Development Kit (SDK) that can be downloaded from `http://developer.android.com/sdk/index.html`.

Who this book is for

This book is written for software developers who are new to game development and to Libgdx in particular. It is assumed that you have some experience in Java to be able to follow the discussed code in this book.

Conventions

In this book, you will find a number of styles of text that distinguish between different kinds of information. Here are some examples of these styles, and an explanation of their meaning.

Code words in text are shown as follows: "The main class of the demo application is `MyDemo.java`."

A block of code is set as follows:

```
@Override
public void dispose() {
  batch.dispose();
  texture.dispose();
}
```

When we wish to draw your attention to a particular part of a code block, the relevant lines or items are set in bold:

```
public void update (float deltaTime) {
  updateMotionX(deltaTime);
  updateMotionY(deltaTime);

  // Move to new position
```

```
    position.x += velocity.x * deltaTime;
    position.y += velocity.y * deltaTime;
}
```

New terms and **important words** are shown in bold. Words that you see on the screen, in menus or dialog boxes for example, appear in the text like this: "A new tab titled **Development Mode** should open at the bottom."

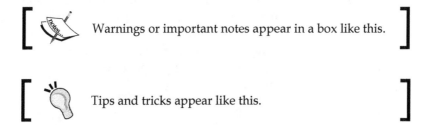

Warnings or important notes appear in a box like this.

Tips and tricks appear like this.

Reader feedback

Feedback from our readers is always welcome. Let us know what you think about this book—what you liked or may have disliked. Reader feedback is important for us to develop titles that you really get the most out of.

To send us general feedback, simply send an e-mail to feedback@packtpub.com, and mention the book title via the subject of your message.

If there is a topic that you have expertise in and you are interested in either writing or contributing to a book, see our author guide on www.packtpub.com/authors.

Customer support

Now that you are the proud owner of a Packt book, we have a number of things to help you to get the most from your purchase.

Downloading the example code

You can download the example code files for all Packt books you have purchased from your account at http://www.packtpub.com. If you purchased this book elsewhere, you can visit http://www.packtpub.com/support and register to have the files e-mailed directly to you.

Errata

Although we have taken every care to ensure the accuracy of our content, mistakes do happen. If you find a mistake in one of our books—maybe a mistake in the text or the code—we would be grateful if you would report this to us. By doing so, you can save other readers from frustration and help us improve subsequent versions of this book. If you find any errata, please report them by visiting http://www.packtpub.com/submit-errata, selecting your book, clicking on the **errata submission form** link, and entering the details of your errata. Once your errata are verified, your submission will be accepted and the errata will be uploaded on our website, or added to any list of existing errata, under the Errata section of that title. Any existing errata can be viewed by selecting your title from http://www.packtpub.com/support.

Piracy

Piracy of copyright material on the Internet is an ongoing problem across all media. At Packt, we take the protection of our copyright and licenses very seriously. If you come across any illegal copies of our works, in any form, on the Internet, please provide us with the location address or website name immediately so that we can pursue a remedy.

Please contact us at copyright@packtpub.com with a link to the suspected pirated material.

We appreciate your help in protecting our authors, and our ability to bring you valuable content.

Questions

You can contact us at questions@packtpub.com if you are having a problem with any aspect of the book, and we will do our best to address it.

1
Introduction to Libgdx and Project Setup

This book will take you on an exciting tour to show and teach you about game development using the open source Libgdx framework. Actually, you have chosen just the right time to read about game development as the game industry is in a remarkable state of change. With the advent of increasingly powerful smartphones and tablets as well as the ever-growing application stores for desktop computers and mobile platforms serving millions of users a day, it has never been easier for **Independent Game Developers** (also known as **Indies**) to enter the market with virtually no risks and very low budgets.

In this chapter you will learn about what Libgdx is and what the advantages are to use it for developing your own games. You will also get a brief overview of the feature set that Libgdx provides.

Before you can start developing games with Libgdx, you have to install and set up your development environment accordingly. You will be using the freely available and open source software **Eclipse** as your **Integrated Development Environment (IDE)** and set up a basic project that uses Libgdx. It will feature a runnable example application for each currently supported target platform. These platforms are as follows:

- Windows
- Linux
- Mac OS X
- Android (Version 1.5 and above)
- HTML5 (Using JavaScript and WebGL)

The target platforms Windows, Linux, and Mac OS X will from now on be referred to as Desktop and also share a project in our development environment.

An alert reader may have noticed that iOS is missing in the list of supported target platforms. Fortunately, it is very likely that Libgdx will support the iOS platform soon as the developers have already put great effort into this feature. At the time of writing of this book, it is said that iOS, starting from Version 5.0 and above, will be supported.

Furthermore, you are going to explore what a game needs by looking at it from a technical standpoint, and why it is so important to plan a game project before the development starts.

At the end of this chapter, you will be introduced to the game project that is going to be developed and enhanced throughout this book.

Diving into Libgdx

Libgdx is an open source, cross-platform development framework, which is designed mainly, but not exclusively, to create games using the Java programming language. Besides Java, Libgdx also makes heavy use of the C programming language for performance-critical tasks, to incorporate other C-based libraries and to enable cross-platform capabilities. Moreover, the framework abstracts the complex nature of all its supported target platforms by combining them into one common **Application Programming Interface (API)**. One of the highlights of Libgdx is the ability to run and debug your code on the desktop as a native application. This enables you to use very comfortable functions of the **Java Virtual Machine (JVM)**, such as Code Hot Swapping, which in turn lets you immediately see the effect of your changed code at runtime. Therefore, it will significantly reduce your time to iterate through different ideas or even to find and fix nasty bugs more quickly.

Another critical point is to understand that Libgdx is a framework and not a game engine that usually comes with lots of tools, such as a full-blown level editor and a completely predefined workflow. This might sound like a disadvantage at first but actually it turns out to be an advantage that enables you to freely define your own workflow for each project. For example, Libgdx allows you to go low-level so you could add your own OpenGL calls if that really became necessary at some point. However, most of the time it should be sufficient enough to stay high-level and use the already built-in functionalities of Libgdx to realize your ideas.

Features of Libgdx 0.97

Since the release of Libgdx Version 0.1 back in March 2010, a lot of work has been contributed in order to improve this library. The latest stable release of Libgdx is version 0.97 from November 2012, which we are going to use throughout this book.

Here is the list of features taken from the official website (`http://libgdx.badlogicgames.com/features.html`):

Graphics

- Rendering through OpenGL ES 1.x and 2.0 on all platforms
- Custom OpenGL ES 2.0 bindings for Android 2.0 and above
- Low-level OpenGL helpers:
  - Vertex arrays and vertex buffer objects
  - Meshes
  - Textures
  - Framebuffer objects (GLES 2.0 only)
  - Shaders, integrating easily with meshes
  - Immediate mode rendering emulation
  - Simple shape rendering
  - Automatic software or hardware mipmap generation
  - ETC1 support (not available in JavaScript backend)
  - Automatic handling of OpenGL ES context loss that restores all textures, shaders, and other OpenGL resources
- High-level 2D APIs:
  - Custom CPU side bitmap manipulation library
  - Orthographic camera
  - High-performance sprite batching and caching, and handling OpenGL ES 1.x and 2.0 differences transparently
  - Texture atlases with whitespace stripping support, which are either generated offline or online

- Bitmap fonts (does not support complex scripts like Arabic or Chinese), which are either generated offline or loaded from TTF files (unsupported in JavaScript backend)
- 2D Particle system
- TMX tile map support
- 2D scene-graph API
- 2D UI library, based on scene-graph API, and fully skinable

- High-level 3D APIs:

  - Perspective camera
  - Decal batching for 3D billboards or particle systems
  - Basic loaders for Wavefront OBJ and MD5
  - Work in progress: MD2, Ogre XML and FBX support, and 3D rendering API with materials and lighting system

Audio

- Streaming music and sound effect playback for WAV, MP3, and OGG
- Direct access to audio device for PCM sample playback and recording (unsupported in JavaScript backend)
- Decoders for OGG and MPG3 formats (unsupported in JavaScript backend)
- Pitch shifting, time stretching, and playback rate modification (unsupported in JavaScript backend)

Input Handling

- Using abstractions for mouse and touchscreen, keyboard, accelerometer, and compass.
- Gesture detector: detects taps, panning, flinging, and pinch zooming.
- Gdx remote: to control your desktop application via your Android phone. Useful to test multi-touch gestures while debugging your desktop application.

File I/O

- Filesystem abstraction for all platforms
- Read-only filesystem emulation for JavaScript backend
- Binary file support for JavaScript backend
- Preferences for lightweight setting storage

Math and Physics

- Matrix, vector, and quaternion classes. Matrix and vector operations are accelerated via native C code where possible.
- Bounding shapes and volumes.
- Frustum class, for picking and culling.
- Catmull-Rom splines.
- Common interpolators.
- Concave polygon triangulation.
- Intersection and overlap testing.
- JNI wrapper for Box2D physics. It is so awesome that other engines use it as well.
- Experimental JNI Wrapper for bullet physics.

Utilities

- Custom collections with primitive support
- JSON writer and reader with POJO (de-)serialization support
- XML writer and reader

Tools

- Gdx Setup UI for easy project setup
- Particle editor
- Texture packer
- Bitmap font generator

Getting in touch with the community

The Libgdx project enjoys a steadily growing and active community. If you ever find yourself being stuck with a problem and you just cannot figure out how to solve it, check out the official forum at http://badlogicgames.com/forum/. There is a great chance someone else has already asked your question and has even found a solution with the help of the community. Otherwise, do not hesitate to ask your question on the forums.

There is also an official IRC channel (#libgdx) on Freenode (irc.freenode.net) where you can find some of the users and developers to talk about Libgdx.

If you want to read about the latest news in development of Libgdx, visit the blog of *Mario Zechner* who is the founder of the Libgdx project or follow him on Twitter.

Libgdx website: http://libgdx.badlogicgames.com/

Blog: http://www.badlogicgames.com/

Twitter: http://www.twitter.com/badlogicgames/

Also check out the following links for more in-depth information:

Wiki: http://code.google.com/p/libgdx/wiki/TableOfContents

API overview: http://libgdx.badlogicgames.com/nightlies/docs/api/

Prerequisites for installing and configuring

Before you can start writing any application or game with Libgdx, you need to download and install the library and also some additional software.

Java Development Kit (JDK)

Due to the fact that Libgdx is a framework based on Java, it is necessary to download the JDK. The software is freely available on Oracle's website at http://www.oracle.com/technetwork/java/javase/downloads/index.html.

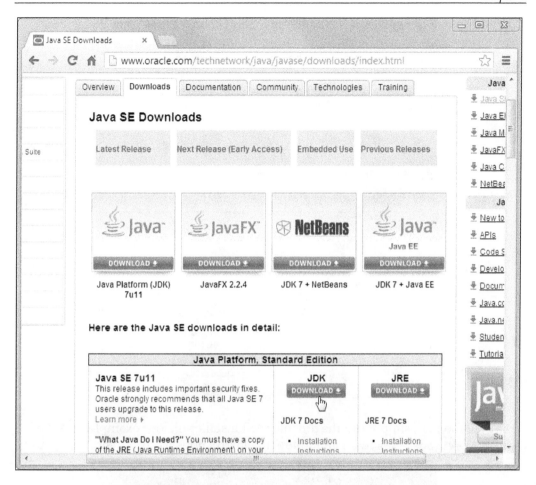

Click on the **DOWNLOAD** button to start downloading the latest JDK.

 It is important to choose the JDK instead of the JRE package. The reason is that the JDK package contains both, the **Java Runtime Environment (JRE)** to run java applications and everything else that is required to develop them.

You will have to accept the license agreement and choose the version that is appropriate for your platform. For example, if you are using a 64-bit version of Windows, choose the download labeled as **Windows x64**.

To install the JDK, simply run the downloaded installer file (for example, `jdk-7u11-windows-x64.exe`) and follow the instructions on the screen.

In the welcome screen of the installer, click on **Next >** to continue.

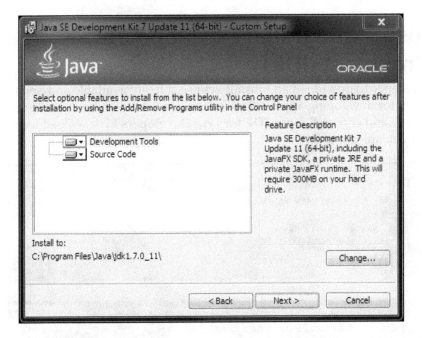

Then, keep all features selected as to be installed and click on **Next >** again to continue.

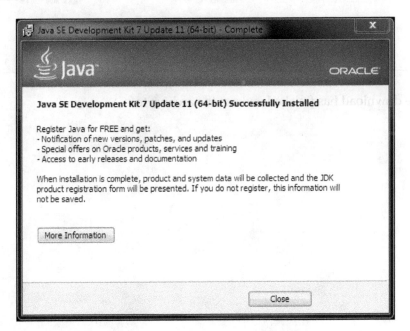

Once the installation has been completed, click on the **Close** button to exit the installer.

Eclipse – Integrated Development Environment (IDE)

The next step is to download and install Eclipse, a freely available and open source IDE for developing applications in Java. Go to `http://www.eclipse.org/downloads/` and choose **Eclipse IDE for Java Developers** to download for the platform you are using.

Once the download has finished, extract the archive to `C:\eclipse\`.

Downloading Libgdx

Next, go to `http://code.google.com/p/libgdx/downloads/list` and choose the file `libgdx-0.9.7.zip` to download Libgdx.

 At the time of writing this book, the latest stable version of Libgdx is 0.9.7. It is recommended to use the same version while working with this book.

In the meanwhile, create a new folder in the root folder of your C drive with the name `libgdx`. Once the download has finished, move the archive to `C:\libgdx\`. Then, open the archive and extract the `.jar`-File `gdx-setup-ui` to `C:\libgdx\`. The extracted program will help you later with creating new game projects in an easy to use GUI.

Installing Android SDK

The Android mobile OS is one of Libgdx's supported target platforms. Before you can create Android applications, you have to download and install the Android SDK. Go to http://developer.android.com/sdk/index.html and click on the **Download the SDK Tools for Windows** button. Should you be using an OS other than Windows, you will have to scroll down a bit further, click on **Download for other platforms** and choose the appropriate platform.

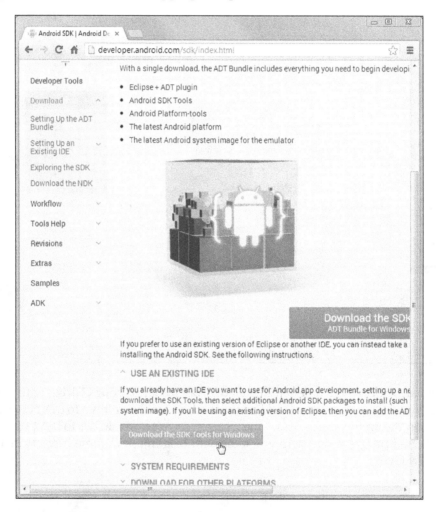

Once the download has finished, run the installer (for example, installer_ r22.0.4-windows.exe) and follow the instructions on the screen.

You may see the following screen when you try to install the Android SDK. The installer cannot find the JDK although you have already installed it.

You need to set the value of the environment variable JAVA_HOME to the installation path of the JDK. To find the correct path go to C:\Program Files\Java\. You should see a folder starting with jdk in its name. Take the full name of this folder (here, jdk1.7.0_11) and append it to its path.

The complete path should now look similar to this: C:\Program Files\Java\ jdk1.7.0_11.

Now you have to set the environment variable. Click on the **Windows Start** button and right-click on **Computer**. Then click on **Properties** to open the control panel system window.

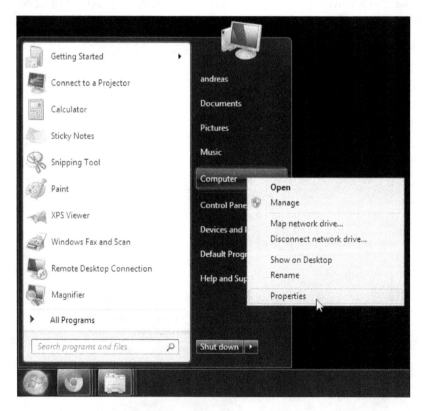

Click on **Advanced system settings** on the left side of the window.

The **System Properties** window will appear. Next, click on the **Environment Variables ...** button.

The **Environment Variables** window will appear. Click on the upper **New ...** button that corresponds to User variables for <USERNAME>. A window with the title **New User Variable** will appear.

Now, fill in the two text fields. Use JAVA_HOME in the **Variable name:** field and the JDK's path you found out earlier in the **Variable value:** field.

Great! Now your system is prepared for the Android SDK installer. Please make sure to exit the Android SDK installer in case it is still running to let the change take effect. You should be presented with the following screen after the installer has restarted.

Now, back in the Android SDK setup, click on **Next >** to continue the installation.

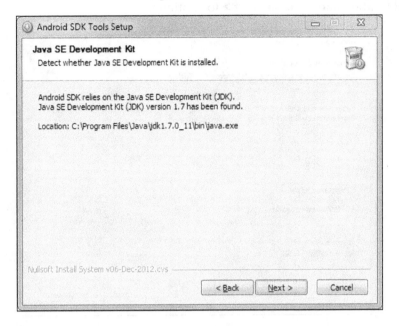

The following screen will ask you to choose the users for which the Android SDK should be installed. Usually, the suggested selection **Install just for me** is perfectly fine, so just click on **Next >** to continue.

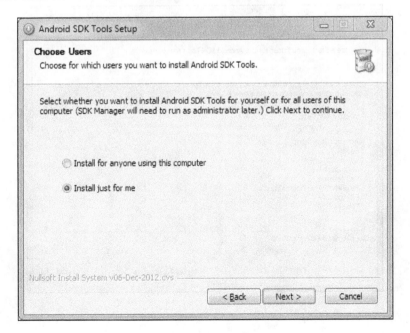

Now, choose the installation location on your computer. You can safely keep the suggested location and click on **Next >** to continue.

After that, you will be asked to choose a start menu folder. Again, you can safely keep the suggestion and click on **Install** to start the installation process.

After the installation is complete, click on **Next >** to continue.

Once the installation has finished, you can choose to start the Android SDK Manager. Leave the checkbox **Start SDK Manager (to download system images, etc.)** enabled and click on **Finish** to start the manager.

The **Android SDK Manager** enables you to download system images for the specific API levels you want to be able to develop applications for. For up-to-date and detailed information about Android API levels, check out the following link at `http://developer.android.com/guide/topics/manifest/uses-sdk-element.html#ApiLevels`.

Now, choose at least **Android 2.2 (API 8)** and/or any other higher API levels you may need and click on the **Install packages ...** button to automatically download and install all relevant files. The reason why we want to use at least API level 8 is that earlier versions before Android 2.2 do not support OpenGL ES 2.0, which we will need in later chapters. Using a certain API level also allows you to control the range of devices that will be able to see and install on your application via the Google Play Store.

Once the download and installation process has finished, close the **Android SDK Manager** window.

Running Eclipse and installing plugins

Great! You are almost done setting everything up. The remaining steps involve
running Eclipse for the first time and installing two important plugins, which are
required to develop applications for Android and HTML5/GWT with Eclipse.

Open Windows Explorer and go to the location where you extracted Eclipse
(here, `C:\eclipse\`) and simply run the program by double-clicking on the
executable called `eclipse`.

Eclipse will ask you to select a so-called workspace. This is the folder where all
your projects will be saved in. We want to use the folder `C:\libgdx\` we created
a bit earlier.

Select the **Use this as the default and do not ask again** checkbox, if you do not want
to see this dialog every time you start Eclipse. To proceed, confirm the dialog by
clicking on the **OK** button.

The first time Eclipse is started with a new workspace, it will greet you with a
welcome screen. Simply click on the small cross (**x**) of the **Welcome** tab to close it.

You should see the standard view of Eclipse now, which is also called the **Java Perspective**. On the left-hand side you can see the **Package Explorer** section. This is where you will see and manage your different projects. That is all you need to know about Eclipse for the moment.

In case you have never worked with Eclipse before, it may seem quite overwhelming with all these windows, toolbars, huge context menus, and so on. However, rest assured that all steps will be discussed in detail as required to make it easy for you to follow.

To install new plugins, go to the menu bar and click on **Help**, and then **Install New Software...**. This will open the **Install** window where you can type special repository URLs to browse for new plugins. Google provides a list with such URLs at https://developers.google.com/eclipse/docs/getting_started. You have to choose the correct URL that corresponds with your Eclipse installation.

At the time of writing this book, Eclipse 4.2.1 (Juno) was the most current version available. According to Google's website, their suggested URL for our version is http://dl.google.com/eclipse/plugin/4.2.

Type the URL into the text field that is labeled **Work with:** and press return to let Eclipse request a list of available downloads. Select everything in the list that is shown in **Developer Tools** to add support for Android applications. Then, select everything in **Google Plugin for Eclipse (required)** to install the required Eclipse plugin. Lastly, select **Google Web Toolkit SDK 2.5.1** in **SDKs** to add support for HTML5/GWT applications and click on **Next >** to continue.

Now, click on **Next >** to start the installation.

You will now be prompted to accept the terms of the license agreements by selecting the option **I accept the terms of the license agreements**. You have to do this before you can click on **Finish** to continue, as shown in the following screenshot:

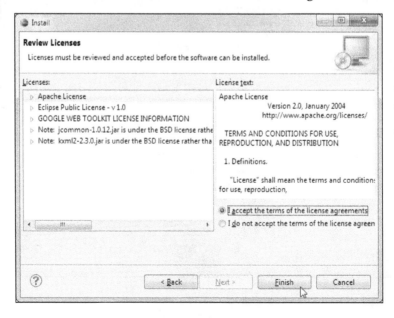

The download process should only take a couple of minutes, depending on the speed of your network connection. When downloading has finished, Eclipse will show a security warning that you are about to install unsigned content and wants to know whether it should continue or abort. There is always a potential risk of installing malicious software. However, in this case the download is provided by Google, a well-known company, which should be trustworthy enough. Click on the **OK** button to accept the warning and continue the installation, as shown in the following screenshot:

After the installation has finished, a final restart of Eclipse is required. Click on the **Yes** button to confirm the restart, as shown in the following screenshot:

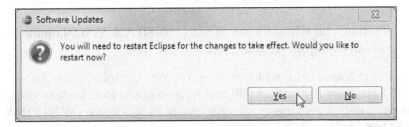

Congratulations! You have just finished the installation of everything you will need to develop and build your own games with Libgdx.

Creating a new application

The next step is to create a new application. Usually, you would have to create several projects in Eclipse: one project for the shared game code, another one for the desktop launcher, and two more for the Android and HTML5/GWT launchers. Furthermore, the projects would also have to be configured and linked together in a certain way. This is quite a time-consuming and more or less an error-prone process for inexperienced users.

Luckily, Libgdx comes with a nice tool called **Libgdx Project Setup**, which can do all of the things described previously. It is able to generate preconfigured projects for a new application, which can be directly imported into Eclipse.

To run the tool, open the Windows Explorer, go to C:\libgdx\, and double-click on the gdx-setup-ui file. When the program starts, click on the big **Create** button as shown in the following screenshot:

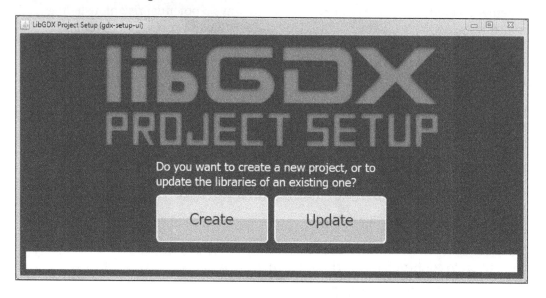

In the next window, you will see a box called **CONFIGURATION** on the left-hand side. Here you can configure what the tool will generate.

Enter demo in the **Name** field, which defines a common project name for your application. Each launcher project will add its own suffix to it, such as -desktop, -android, or -html. A preview of the outcome is shown in the **OVERVIEW** box on the right-hand side.

The **Package** field defines the name of your Java package. This needs to be a unique identifier written in lowercase, which is usually derived from a reversed domain name. You do not have to own a domain name nor does it have to really exist, but it helps in choosing non-conflicting namespaces for Java applications. This is especially important on Android, as identical package names for two separate applications would mean that the already installed application is going to be overwritten by the second one while trying to install it. For this demo application, use com.packtpub. libgdx.demo as the package name for now.

The **Game class** field defines the name of the main class in the shared game code project. Enter MyDemo as the game class name.

The **Destination** field defines the destination folder where all the projects will be generated. Click on the blue folder button and set the destination folder to C:\libgdx\.

In another box called **LIBRARY SELECTION**, the status of required libraries is shown. If there is any item listed in red color, it needs to be fixed before any project can be generated. You should see **LibGDX** being listed in red in the **Required** section. Click on the blue folder icon next to it as shown in the following screenshot:

Then, choose the downloaded archive file libgdx-0.9.7.zip from C:\libgdx\ and click on **Open**, as shown in the following screenshot:

The text color of the **LibGDX** label should have changed from red to green by now. Click on the **Open the generation screen** button to continue as shown in the following screenshot:

Click on the **Launch!** button to generate all projects as shown in the following screenshot:

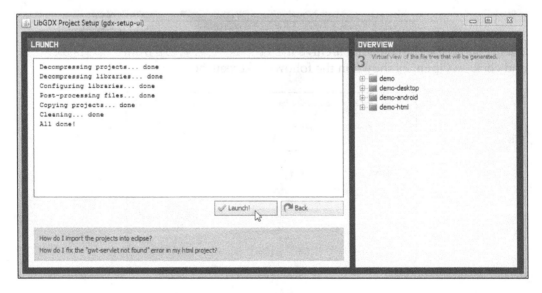

All done! You can now go to Eclipse and start importing the generated projects into your workspace. To do this, simply navigate to **File** | **Import**, as shown in the following screenshot:

In the **Import** dialog, open the **General** category, select **Existing Projects into Workspace**, and click on the **Next >** button as shown in the following screenshot:

Click on the radio button **Select root directory** and enter C:\libgdx into the text field. This is the directory where all your generated projects were created. You need to confirm your text input by pressing the return key once. Eclipse will start to scan the directory for projects and list them. Leave all checkboxes selected and click on the **Finish** button, as shown in the following screenshot:

Eclipse will automatically try to build (compile) all four newly imported projects in your workspace and probably fail. There are two issues that need to be resolved manually after the import. The first one is reported directly to the **Console** window in Eclipse. It complains about being unable to resolve the target android-15.

You have to open the project properties of the demo-android project. First, select it in the **Package Explorer** box on the left-hand side. Then go to the menu bar and navigate to **Project | Properties**, as shown in the following screenshot:

The title of the window should say **Properties for demo-android**. If this is not the case, close the window and make sure you have selected the correct project and try again. Next, select **Android** from the list on the left-hand side. You will see a list of targets that are available on your system. Select **Android 2.2**, which uses API Level 8, and click on the **OK** Button.

Eclipse should recognize the change and successfully build the Android project this time.

The second issue requires you to click on the **Problems** tab in Eclipse. Open the **Errors** list and right-click on the reported problem, which should say **The GWT SDK JAR gwt-servlet.jar is missing in the WEB-INF/lib directory**. Choose **Quick Fix** from the context menu as shown in the following screenshot:

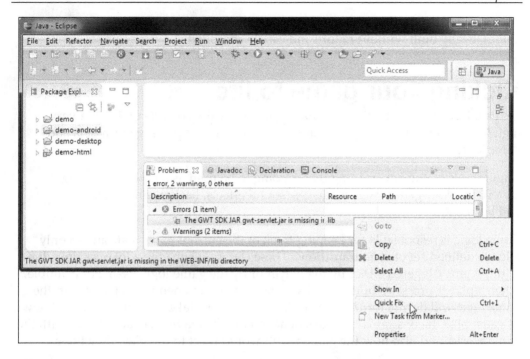

In the **Quick Fix** dialog, select **Synchronize <WAR>/WEB-INF/lib with SDK libraries** as the desired fix and click on the **Finish** button, as shown in the following screenshot:

The two issues should be solved by now, which means all projects now are automatically built without failure and can be compiled.

Kicking your game to life

Let us take a moment to discuss what a game basically consists of. From a very high level point of view, a game can be split up into two parts: game assets and game logic.

Game assets include everything that is going to be used as a kind of working material in your game, such as images, sound effects, background music, and level data.

Game logic is responsible for keeping track of the current game state and to only allow a defined set of state transitions. These states will change a lot over time due to the events triggered either by the player or by the game logic itself. For example, when a player presses a button, picks up an item, or an enemy hits the player, the game logic will decide for the appropriate action to be taken. All this is better known as game play. It constrains the ways of action in which a player can interact with the game world, and also how the game world would react to the player's actions.

To give you a better idea of this, take a look at the following diagram:

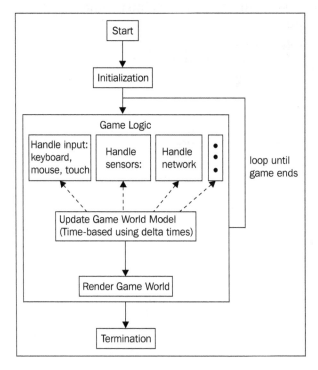

The very first step is to initialize the game, that is, loading assets into memory, creating the initial state of the game world, and registering with a couple of subsystems such as input handlers for keyboard, mouse and touch input, audio for playback and recording, sensors, and network communication.

When everything is up and running, the game logic is ready to take over and will loop for the rest of the time until the game ends and will then be terminated. This kind of looping is also referred to as the game loop. Inside the game loop, the game logic accumulates all (new) data it is interested in and updates the game world model accordingly.

It is very important to consider the speed at which updates will occur in the game world. Currently, the game would just run at the maximum speed of the available hardware. In most cases this is not a desirable effect because it makes your game dependent on the processing power and the complexity of the scene to be rendered, which will vary from computer to computer. This implies that your game world will also progress at different speeds on different computers with an almost always negative impact on the game play.

The key to tackle this issue is to use delta times to calculate the fractional progress of the game world. Now every update to the game world will occur in relation to real time that has passed since the last frame was rendered. You will see how this actually works with Libgdx in later examples.

What you have just read was an overview of the basic concept for creating games. Yes, it is that simple! Frankly speaking, there is a lot more to learn before your application becomes a real game. There are lots of topics and concepts waiting to be discovered in this book. For instance, you will need to understand how to use and manage different images in an efficient manner. Efficiency becomes even more important if you plan to target mobile devices such as Android smartphones, where available resources are constantly scarce.

Key to success lies in planning

Great! Now you have a basic understanding of what a game is and may need. It appears to be a good idea to dedicate some additional time to think about your first game project and create a plan for it. In general, planning your game projects is what you should always do in the first place before any actual work is done. For novice game developers it might be very tempting to skip this planning phase, which admittedly is a lot more fun in the beginning, but this approach is very likely to fall short in the long run. You will need some sort of outline of what you want to achieve. It does not have to be a very long and detailed description.

A simple and brief feature list of your design goals will do just fine for this purpose. The reason behind this is that you will make yourself aware of each single feature that is part of your game. In addition, this list will also serve you as a great tool to measure and compare your progress in the game during the development phase. Please bear in mind that game development is a very dynamic and iterative process. Although you should try to adhere to your list of design goals for most of the time, there should always be room to adapt to shifting requirements. Just keep in mind that adhering to the list will make sure that you are going to push development in the right direction. Conversely, it will let you focus on the important parts first, while also protecting you from running out of time and taking too many detours that prevent you from reaching the finish line due to unclear goals.

Game project – Canyon Bunny

To make this guide both easy and fun to read, it makes perfect sense to show how to plan and develop a whole game project throughout this book. As we now know, planning should be the first step to take on the journey of any new game project.

So, let us begin with the outline:

Name or Working Title: Canyon Bunny

Genre: 2D Side-Scrolling Jump and Run

List of actors:

- Player character (can jump and move forward; controlled by player)
- Rocks, serving as platforms for the player character and items
- Canyons in the background (level decoration)
- Clouds in the sky (level decoration)
- Water at the bottom of the level (deadly for player character)
- Collectible items for the player: gold coins, feather power-up

Next, it is always helpful to write down some supporting text to further describe the overall behavior of the game and how features should be implemented.

Description of the game

The game world is presented in 2D side view to the player. The view is scrolling horizontally to the right when the player character moves forward. The background shows distant canyons and clouds in the sky. The bottom of the level is filled with water and will instantly kill the player character if both get into contact with each other.

The player character will move on and jump over to random rocks, sticking out of the water. The width and height will be different to make the game more challenging. The player is only in control of a jump button, which will keep the automatically forward-moving player character from falling down into the deadly water.

The level will be randomly populated with collectible items consisting of gold coins and feather power-ups. Collecting the gold coins will increase the player's high score. The feather power-up grants the player character the ability to fly for a limited time and can be used by repeatedly pressing the jump button. The player's goal is to beat the last high score.

Since a picture is worth a thousand words, creating a sketch based on our outline can help us even more to get a better idea of the resulting game. Moreover, changing a sketch is usually a lot easier than having to change (complex) game code. So you really want to keep it very simple like just grabbing your pen and paper and starting to draw. If you feel lucky or have some time to spend, you can do something more elaborate, of course.

Here is a sketch for Canyon Bunny:

The previous sketch has been created entirely by using vector graphics. Using vector graphics in favor of raster graphics for your sketches can be an advantage as they are infinitely scalable to any size without losing image quality. However, the final graphics used in games are almost, always, rasterized graphics, simply because vector graphics are costly to render in real time. So, the common approach is to create vector graphics and later on export them choosing an appropriate rasterized graphics file format, such as .png (Portable Network Graphics) for lossless compression with alpha channel support, or .jpg (JPEG) for lossy but high compression without alpha channel support.

For more details, check out the following Wikipedia articles:

- For information on raster graphics go to http://en.wikipedia.org/wiki/Raster_graphics
- For information on vector graphics go to http://en.wikipedia.org/wiki/Vector_graphics
- For information on PNG file format go to http://en.wikipedia.org/wiki/.png
- For information on JPEG file format go to http://en.wikipedia.org/wiki/.jpg

There is a free and open source tool called **Inkscape**. It allows you to easily create your own drawings as vector graphics, and is available for Windows, Linux, and Mac OS X. Check out the project's website at http://inkscape.org/.

Summary

We learned a lot in this chapter about Libgdx and all the other bits and bobs to prepare your system for multi-platform game development, specifically on the following points:

- We discussed every step in great detail to successfully download, install, and configure all required software components: JDK, Eclipse, Libgdx, Android SDK, and two additional Eclipse plugins for Android and HTML5/GWT

- We learned how to use the project setup tool that comes with Libgdx to easily generate all required Eclipse projects for a new application, and how to import them into Eclipse including minor troubleshooting

- We also learned what a game needs to come alive

- We found out why planning game projects is so important

- We have seen how to plan a game project by writing an outline

In *Chapter 2, Cross-platform Development – Build Once, Deploy Anywhere*, you will learn more about how to deploy and run a Libgdx application on all supported target platforms. Building on this knowledge, we will finally jump to the first code examples where the magic happens and take a closer look at it to find out how it works.

2
Cross-platform Development – Build Once, Deploy Anywhere

In this chapter you will learn more about the generated Eclipse projects and how they work together. Also, you will learn more about the following components of the Libgdx framework:

- Backends
- Modules
- Application Life-Cycle and Interface
- Starter Classes

At the end of this chapter, you will take a closer look at the demo application and inspect the generated code of the Main class in great detail. You will learn how to set breakpoints, run the application in debug mode, and speed up your overall productivity with the awesome **JVM Code Hot Swapping** feature. The discussion on the demo application ends with some simple and fun modifications to the code accompanied by a demonstration of the JVM Code Hot Swapping feature.

After completing this chapter you will be able to deploy, run, and debug the demo application from *Chapter 1, Introduction to Libgdx and Project Setup* on a desktop (including Windows, Linux, and Mac OS X), on Android, and in a WebGL-capable web browser such as Google Chrome.

The demo application – how the projects work together

In *Chapter 1, Introduction to Libgdx and Project Setup*, we successfully created our demo application, but we did not look at how all the Eclipse projects work together. Take a look at the following diagram to understand and familiarize yourself with the configuration pattern that all of your Libgdx applications will have in common:

What you see here is a compact view of four projects. The **demo** project to the very left contains the shared code that is referenced (that is, added to the build path) by all the other platform-specific projects. The main class of the demo application is MyDemo.java. However, looking at it from a more technical view, the main class where an application gets started by the operating system, which will be referred to as **Starter Classes** from now on. Notice that Libgdx uses the term "Starter Class" to distinguish between these two types of main classes in order to avoid confusion. We will cover everything related to the topic of Starter Classes in a moment.

While taking a closer look at all these directories in the preceding screenshot, you may have spotted that there are two assets folders: one in the **demo-desktop** project and another one in **demo-android**. This brings us to the question, where should you put all the application's assets? The **demo-android** project plays a special role in this case. In the preceding screenshot, you see a subfolder called **data**, which contains an image named libgdx.png, and it also appears in the **demo-desktop** project in the same place.

Just remember to always put all of your assets into the assets folder under the **demo-android** project. The reason behind this is that the Android build process requires direct access to the application's assets folder. During its build process, a Java source file, R.java, will automatically be generated under the gen folder. It contains special information for Android about the available assets. It would be the usual way to access assets through Java code if you were explicitly writing an Android application. However, in Libgdx, you will want to stay platform-independent as much as possible and access any resource such as assets only through methods provided by Libgdx. You will learn more about accessing resources in the last section of this chapter.

You may wonder how the other platform-specific projects will be able to access the very same assets without having to maintain several copies per project. Needless to say that this would require you to keep all copies manually synchronized each time the assets change.

Luckily, this problem has already been taken care of by the generator as follows:

The **demo-desktop** project uses a linked resource, a feature by Eclipse, to add existing files or folders to other places in a workspace. You can check this out by right-clicking on the **demo-desktop** project then navigating to **Properties | Resource | Linked Resources** and clicking on the **Linked Resources** tab.

The **demo-html** project requires another approach since **Google Web Toolkit (GWT)** has a different build process compared to the other projects. There is a special file GwtDefinition.gwt.xml that allows you to set the asset path by setting the configuration property gdx.assetpath, to the assets folder of the Android project. Notice that it is good practice to use relative paths such as ../demo-android/ assets so that the reference does not get broken in case the workspace is moved from its original location. Take this advice as a precaution to protect you and maybe your fellow developers too from wasting precious time on something that can be easily avoided by using the right setup right from the beginning.

The following is the code listing for GwtDefinition.gwt.xml from **demo-html**:

```
<?xml version="1.0" encoding="UTF-8"?>
<!DOCTYPE module PUBLIC "-//Google Inc.//DTD Google Web Toolkit
  trunk//EN" "http://google-web-toolkit.googlecode.com/svn/trunk/
    distro-source/core/src/gwt-module.dtd">
<module>
<inherits name='com.badlogic.gdx.backends.gdx_backends_gwt' />
<inherits name='MyDemo' />
<entry-point
```

```
    class='com.packtpub.libgdx.demo.client.GwtLauncher' />
    <set-configuration-property name="gdx.assetpath"
      value="../demo-android/assets" />
  </module>
```

Backends

Libgdx makes use of several other libraries to interface the specifics of each platform in order to provide cross-platform support for your applications. Generally, a backend is what enables Libgdx to access the corresponding platform functionalities when one of the abstracted (platform-independent) Libgdx methods is called. For example, drawing an image to the upper-left corner of the screen, playing a sound file at a volume of 80 percent, or reading and writing from/to a file.

Libgdx currently provides the following three backends:

- LWJGL (Lightweight Java Game Library)
- Android
- JavaScript/WebGL

As already mentioned in *Chapter 1, Introduction to Libgdx and Project Setup*, there will also be an iOS backend in the near future.

LWJGL (Lightweight Java Game Library)

LWJGL (Lightweight Java Game Library) is an open source Java library originally started by Caspian Rychlik-Prince to ease game development in terms of accessing the hardware resources on desktop systems. In Libgdx, it is used for the desktop backend to support all the major desktop operating systems, such as Windows, Linux, and Mac OS X.

For more details, check out the official LWJGL website at http://www.lwjgl.org/.

Android

Google frequently releases and updates their official Android SDK. This represents the foundation for Libgdx to support Android in the form of a backend.

There is an API Guide available which explains everything the Android SDK has to offer for Android developers. You can find it at `http://developer.android.com/guide/components/index.html`.

WebGL

WebGL support is one of the latest additions to the Libgdx framework. This backend uses the GWT to translate Java code into JavaScript and **SoundManager2 (SM2)**, among others, to add a combined support for HTML5, WebGL, and audio playback. Note that this backend requires a WebGL-capable web browser to run the application.

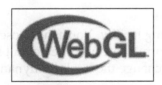

You might want to check out the official website of GWT:
`https://developers.google.com/web-toolkit/`.

You might want to check out the official website of SM2:
`http://www.schillmania.com/projects/soundmanager2/`.

You might want to check out the official website of WebGL:
`http://www.khronos.org/webgl/`.

There is also a list of unresolved issues you might want to check out at `https://github.com/libgdx/libgdx/blob/master/backends/gdx-backends-gwt/issues.txt`.

Modules

Libgdx provides six core modules that allow you to access the various parts of the system your application will run on. What makes these modules so great for you as a developer is that they provide you with a single **Application Programming Interface (API)** to achieve the same effect on more than just one platform. This is extremely powerful because you can now focus on your own application and you do not have to bother with the specialties that each platform inevitably brings, including the nasty little bugs that may require tricky workarounds. This is all going to be transparently handled in a straightforward API which is categorized into logic modules and is globally available anywhere in your code, since every module is accessible as a `static` field in the `Gdx` class.

Naturally, Libgdx does always allow you to create multiple code paths for per-platform decisions. For example, you could conditionally increase the level of detail in a game when run on the desktop platform, since desktops usually have a lot more computing power than mobile devices.

The application module

The application module can be accessed through `Gdx.app`. It gives you access to the logging facility, a method to shutdown gracefully, persist data, query the Android API version, query the platform type, and query the memory usage.

Logging

Libgdx employs its own logging facility. You can choose a log level to filter what should be printed to the platform's console. The default log level is `LOG_INFO`. You can use a settings file and/or change the log level dynamically at runtime using the following code line:

```
Gdx.app.setLogLevel(Application.LOG_DEBUG);
```

The available log levels are:

- `LOG_NONE`: This prints no logs. The logging is completely disabled.
- `LOG_ERROR`: This prints error logs only.
- `LOG_INFO`: This prints error and info logs.
- `LOG_DEBUG`: This prints error, info, and debug logs.

To write an info, debug, or an error log to the console, use the following listings:

```
Gdx.app.log("MyDemoTag", "This is an info log.");
Gdx.app.debug("MyDemoTag", "This is a debug log.");
Gdx.app.error("MyDemoTag", "This is an error log.");
```

Shutting down gracefully

You can tell Libgdx to shutdown the running application. The framework will then stop the execution in the correct order as soon as possible and completely de-allocate any memory that is still in use, freeing both Java and the native heap. Use the following listing to initiate a graceful shutdown of your application:

```
Gdx.app.exit();
```

> You should always do a graceful shutdown when you want to terminate your application. Otherwise, you will risk creating memory leaks, which is a really bad thing. On mobile devices, memory leaks will probably have the biggest negative impact due to their limited resources.

Persisting data

If you want to persist your data, you should use the Preferences class. It is merely a dictionary or a hash map data type which stores multiple key-value pairs in a file. Libgdx will create a new preferences file on the fly if it does not exist yet. You can have several preference files using unique names in order to split up data into categories. To get access to a preference file, you need to request a Preferences instance by its filename as follows:

```
Preferences prefs = Gdx.app.getPreferences("settings.prefs");
```

To write a (new) value, you have to choose a key under which the value should be stored. If this key already exists in a preferences file, it will be overwritten. Do not forget to call flush() afterwards to persist the data, or else all the changes will be lost.

```
prefs.putInteger("sound_volume", 100); // volume @ 100%
prefs.flush();
```

Persisting data needs a lot more time than just modifying values in memory (without flushing). Therefore, it is always better to modify as many values as possible before a final `flush()` method is executed.

To read back a certain value from a preferences file, you need to know the corresponding key. If this key does not exist, it will be set to the default value. You can optionally pass your own default value as the second argument (for example, in the following listing, 50 is for the default sound volume):

```
int soundVolume = prefs.getInteger("sound_volume", 50);
```

Querying the Android API Level

On Android, you can query the Android API Level, which allows you to handle things differently for certain versions of the Android OS. Use the following listing to find out the version:

```
Gdx.app.getVersion();
```

 On platforms other than Android, the version returned is always 0.

Querying the platform type

You may want to write a platform-specific code where it is necessary to know the current platform type. The following example shows how it can be done:

```
switch (Gdx.app.getType()) {
  case Desktop:
  // Code for Desktop application
  break;
  case Android:
  // Code for Android application
  break;
  case WebGL:
  // Code for WebGL application
  break;
  default:
  // Unhandled (new?) platform application
  break;
}
```

Querying memory usage

You can query the system to find out its current memory footprint of your application. This may help you find excessive memory allocations that could lead to application crashes. The following functions return the amount of memory (in bytes) that is in use by the corresponding heap:

```
long memUsageJavaHeap = Gdx.app.getJavaHeap();
long memUsageNativeHeap = Gdx.app.getNativeHeap();
```

Graphics module

The graphics module can be accessed either through Gdx.getGraphics() or by using the shortcut variable Gdx.graphics.

Querying delta time

Query Libgdx for the time span between the current and the last frame in seconds by calling Gdx.graphics.getDeltaTime().

Querying display size

Query the device's display size returned in pixels by calling Gdx.graphics.getWidth() and Gdx.graphics.getHeight().

Querying the FPS (frames per second) counter

Query a built-in frame counter provided by Libgdx to find the average number of frames per second by calling Gdx.graphics.getFramesPerSecond().

Audio module

The audio module can be accessed either through Gdx.getAudio() or by using the shortcut variable Gdx.audio.

Sound playback

To load sounds for playback, call Gdx.audio.newSound().

The supported file formats are WAV, MP3, and OGG.

There is an upper limit of 1 MB for decoded audio data. Consider the sounds to be short effects like bullets or explosions so that the size limitation is not really an issue.

Music streaming

To stream music for playback, call `Gdx.audio.newMusic()`.

The supported file formats are WAV, MP3, and OGG.

Input module

The input module can be accessed either through `Gdx.getInput()` or by using the shortcut variable `Gdx.input`.

In order to receive and handle input properly, you should always implement the `InputProcessor` interface and set it as the global handler for input in Libgdx by calling `Gdx.input.setInputProcessor()`.

Reading the keyboard/touch/mouse input

Query the system for the last x or y coordinate in the screen coordinates where the screen origin is at the top-left corner by calling either `Gdx.input.getX()` or `Gdx.input.getY()`.

- To find out if the screen is touched either by a finger or by mouse, call `Gdx.input.isTouched()`
- To find out if the mouse button is pressed, call `Gdx.input.isButtonPressed()`
- To find out if the keyboard is pressed, call `Gdx.input.isKeyPressed()`

Reading the accelerometer

Query the accelerometer for its value on the x axis by calling `Gdx.input.getAccelerometerX()`. Replace the X in the method's name with Y or Z to query the other two axes. Be aware that there will be no accelerometer present on a desktop, so Libgdx always returns 0.

Starting and canceling vibrator

On Android, you can let the device vibrate by calling `Gdx.input.vibrate()`.

A running vibration can be cancelled by calling `Gdx.input.cancelVibrate()`.

Catching Android soft keys

You might want to catch Android's soft keys to add an extra handling code for them. If you want to catch the back button, call `Gdx.input.setCatchBackKey(true)`. If you want to catch the menu button, call `Gdx.input.setCatchMenuKey(true)`.

On a desktop where you have a mouse pointer, you can tell Libgdx to catch it so that you get a permanent mouse input without having the mouse ever leave the application window. To catch the mouse cursor, call `Gdx.input.setCursorCatched(true)`.

The files module

The files module can be accessed either through `Gdx.getFiles()` or by using the shortcut variable `Gdx.files`.

Getting an internal file handle

You can get a file handle for an internal file by calling `Gdx.files.internal()`.

An internal file is relative to the `assets` folder on the Android and WebGL platforms. On a desktop, it is relative to the `root` folder of the application.

Getting an external file handle

You can get a file handle for an external file by calling `Gdx.files.external()`.

An external file is relative to the SD card on the Android platform. On a desktop, it is relative to the user's home folder. Note that this is not available for WebGL applications.

The network module

The network module can be accessed either through `Gdx.getNet()` or by using the shortcut variable `Gdx.net`.

HTTP GET and HTTP POST

You can make HTTP GET and POST requests by calling either `Gdx.net.httpGet()` or `Gdx.net.httpPost()`.

Client/server sockets

You can create client/server sockets by calling either `Gdx.net.newClientSocket()` or `Gdx.net.newServerSocket()`.

Opening a URI in a web browser

To open a **Uniform Resource Identifier (URI)** in the default web browser, call `Gdx.net.openURI(URI)`.

Libgdx's Application Life-Cycle and Interface

The Application Life-Cycle in Libgdx is a well-defined set of distinct system states. The list of these states is pretty short: create, resize, render, pause, resume, and dispose.

Libgdx defines an `ApplicationListener` interface that contains six methods, one for each system state. The following code listing is a copy that is directly taken from Libgdx's sources. For the sake of readability, all comments have been stripped.

```
public interface ApplicationListener {
  public void create ();
  public void resize (int width, int height);
  public void render ();
  public void pause ();
  public void resume ();
  public void dispose ();
}
```

All you need to do is implement these methods in your main class of the shared game code project. Libgdx will then call each of these methods at the right time.

> **Downloading the example code**
>
> You can download the example code files for all Packt books you have purchased from your account at http://www.packtpub.com. If you purchased this book elsewhere, you can visit http://www.packtpub.com/support and register to have the files e-mailed directly to you.

The following diagram visualizes the Libgdx's Application Life-Cycle:

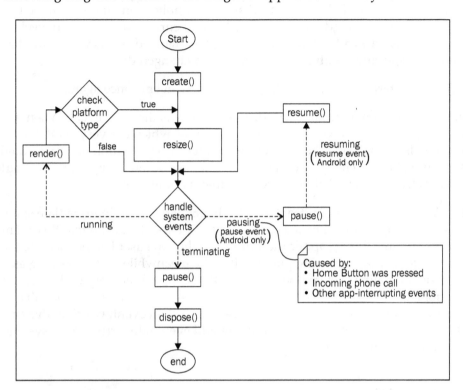

Note that a full and dotted line basically has the same meaning in the preceding figure. They both connect two consecutive states and have a direction of flow indicated by a little arrowhead on one end of the line. A dotted line additionally denotes a system event.

When an application starts, it will always begin with create(). This is where the initialization of the application should happen, such as loading assets into memory and creating an initial state of the game world. Subsequently, the next state that follows is resize(). This is the first opportunity for an application to adjust itself to the available display size (width and height) given in pixels.

Next, Libgdx will handle system events. If no event has occurred in the meanwhile, it is assumed that the application is (still) running. The next state would be render(). This is where a game application will mainly do two things:

- Update the game world model
- Draw the scene on the screen using the updated game world model

Afterwards, a decision is made upon which the platform type is detected by Libgdx. On a desktop or in a web browser, the displaying application window can be resized virtually at any time. Libgdx compares the last and current sizes on every cycle so that `resize()` is only called if the display size has changed. This makes sure that the running application is able to accommodate a changed display size.

Now the cycle starts over by handling (new) system events once again.

Another system event that can occur during runtime is the `exit` event. When it occurs, Libgdx will first change to the `pause()` state, which is a very good place to save any data that would be lost otherwise after the application has terminated. Subsequently, Libgdx changes to the `dispose()` state where an application should do its final clean-up to free all the resources that it is still using.

This is also almost true for Android, except that `pause()` is an intermediate state that is not directly followed by a `dispose()` state at first. Be aware that this event may occur anytime during application runtime while the user has pressed the Home button or if there is an incoming phone call in the meanwhile. In fact, as long as the Android operating system does not need the occupied memory of the paused application, its state will not be changed to `dispose()`. Moreover, it is possible that a paused application might receive a `resume` system event, which in this case would change its state to `resume()`, and it would eventually arrive at the system event handler again.

Starter Classes

A Starter Class defines the entry point (starting point) of a Libgdx application. They are specifically written for a certain platform. Usually, these kinds of classes are very simple and mostly consist of not more than a few lines of code to set certain parameters that apply to the corresponding platform. Think of them as a kind of boot-up sequence for each platform. Once booting has finished, the Libgdx framework hands over control from the Starter Class (for example, the **demo-desktop** project) to your shared application code (for example, the **demo** project) by calling the different methods from the `ApplicationListener` interface that the `MyDemo` class implements. Remember that the `MyDemo` class is where the shared application code begins.

We will now take a look at each of the Starter Classes that were generated during the project setup.

Running the demo application on a desktop

The Starter Class for the desktop application is called `Main.java`.

The following listing is `Main.java` from **demo-desktop**:

```
package com.packtpub.libgdx.demo;

import com.badlogic.gdx.backends.lwjgl.LwjglApplication;
import com.badlogic.gdx.backends.lwjgl.LwjglApplicationConfiguration;

public class Main {
  public static void main(String[] args) {
    LwjglApplicationConfiguration cfg =
      new LwjglApplicationConfiguration();
    cfg.title = "demo";
    cfg.useGL20 = false;
    cfg.width = 480;
    cfg.height = 320;
    new LwjglApplication(new MyDemo(), cfg);
  }
}
```

In the preceding code listing, you see the `Main` class, a plain Java class without the need to implement an interface or inherit from another class. Instead, a new instance of the `LwjglApplication` class is created. This class provides a couple of overloaded constructors to choose from. Here, we pass a new instance of the `MyDemo` class as the first argument to the constructor. Optionally, an instance of the `LwjglApplicationConfiguration` class can be passed as the second argument. The configuration class allows you to set every parameter that is configurable for a Libgdx desktop application. In this case, the window title is set to `demo` and the window's width and height is set to `480` by `320` pixels.

This is all you need to write and configure a Starter Class for a desktop.

Let us try to run the application now. To do this, right-click on the **demo-desktop** project in **Project Explorer** in Eclipse and then navigate to **Run As | Java Application**. Eclipse may ask you to select the Main class when you do this for the first time. Simply select the Main class and also check that the correct package name (**com.packtpub. libgdx.demo**) is displayed next to it.

The desktop application should now be up and running on your computer. If you are working on Windows, you should see a window that looks as follows:

Running the demo application on Android

The Starter Class for the Android application is called `MainActivity.java`.

The following listing is `MainActivity.java` from **demo-android**:

```
package com.packtpub.libgdx.demo;

import android.os.Bundle;
import com.badlogic.gdx.backends.android.AndroidApplication;
import com.badlogic.gdx.backends.android
  .AndroidApplicationConfiguration;

public class MainActivity extends AndroidApplication {
  @Override
  public void onCreate(Bundle savedInstanceState) {
    super.onCreate(savedInstanceState);
    AndroidApplicationConfiguration cfg =
      new AndroidApplicationConfiguration();
    cfg.useGL20 = false;
    initialize(new MyDemo(), cfg);
  }
}
```

In the preceding code listing, you can see the `MainActivity` class that inherits from the `AndroidApplication` class. This is how Libgdx encapsulates tasks such as creating a so-called activity that registers handlers to process touch input, read sensor data, and much more. What is left to do for you is to create an instance of a class that implements the `ApplicationListener` interface. In this case, it is an instance of the `MyDemo` class. The instances of `MyDemo` and `AndroidApplicationConfiguration` are passed as arguments to the `initialize()` method. The configuration is set to not request OpenGL ES 2.0 support on an Android device.

If you are interested in the latest development of Android hardware statistics, be sure to check out **Dashboards** on the official Android Developers website: `http://developer.android.com/about/dashboards/index.html#OpenGL`.

The following screenshot of the OpenGL statistics was taken in February 2013 from the mentioned website:

Open GL Version

This section provides data about the relative number of active devices that support a particular version of OpenGL ES. Note that support for one particular version of OpenGL ES also implies support for any lower version (for example, support for version 2.0 also implies support for 1.1).

To declare which version of OpenGL ES your application requires, you should use the `android:glEsVersion` attribute of the `<uses-feature>` element. You can also use the `<supports-gl-texture>` element to declare the GL compression formats that your application uses.

> **Note:** This data is based on the number of Android devices that have accessed Google Play within a 7-day period ending on the data collection date noted below.

OpenGL ES Version	Distribution
1.1 only	9.2%
2.0 & 1.1	90.8%

GL 2.0 & 1.1

GL 1.1 only

Data collected during a 7-day period ending on October 1, 2012

At the time of writing this book, over 90 percent of today's Android devices support GLES2. So when should GLES2 be used on Android? A better question to ask would be whether you plan to use shaders in your application. If this is the case, opt for GLES2. In any other case, there will be no real benefit except being able to use non-power-of-two textures (also known as NPOT textures); arbitrarily-sized textures that do not equal to widths or heights representable by the formula 2^n, such as 32 x 32, 512 x 512, and 128 x 1024.

NPOT textures are not guaranteed to work on all devices. For example, the Nexus One ignores NPOT textures. Also, they may cause performance penalties on some hardware, so it is best to avoid using this feature at all. In *Chapter 4, Gathering Resources*, you will learn about a technique called **Texture Atlas**. This will allow you to use arbitrarily-sized textures even when not using GLES2.

Additionally, on Android, you will have to take care of a manifest file that defines a huge list of parameters to configure the application. If you are not yet familiar with Android's manifest file, you should take some time to read the official documentation at `http://developer.android.com/guide/topics/manifest/manifest-intro.html`.

The following listing is `AndroidManifest.xml` from **demo-android**:

```xml
<?xml version="1.0" encoding="utf-8"?>
<manifest
  xmlns:android="http://schemas.android.com/apk/res/android"
  package="com.packtpub.libgdx.demo"
  android:versionCode="1"
  android:versionName="1.0" >
  <uses-sdk android:minSdkVersion="5"
            android:targetSdkVersion="17" />
<application
  android:icon="@drawable/ic_launcher"
  android:label="@string/app_name" >
<activity
  android:name=".MainActivity"
  android:label="@string/app_name"
  android:screenOrientation="landscape"
  android:configChanges=
    "keyboard|keyboardHidden|orientation|screenSize">
<intent-filter>
<action android:name="android.intent.action.MAIN" />
<category android:name="android.intent.category.LAUNCHER" />
</intent-filter>
</activity>
</application>
</manifest>
```

The following short (and incomplete) list is meant to give you a quick idea of what could be defined in the manifest file:

- `minSdkVersion`: This is the minimum API Level required for the application to run. Devices running with lower API Levels will not be able to run this application; or if left undeclared, an API Level of 1 is assumed, which may cause your app to crash at runtime when trying to access unavailable APIs.

- `targetSdkVersion`: This is the API Level the application targets. This is used for forward compatibility, where later API Levels may change the behavior of the API that might break old applications. This specification does not prevent the application from running on devices with lower API Levels down to `minSdkVersion`. If left undeclared, its value is set equal to `minSdkVersion`.

- `icon`: This is the application's icon.

- `name`: This is the main class of the application (or the main activity). Note that in terms of Libgdx, this will be the Starter Class for Android.

- `label`: This is the application's name shown next to the application icon and in the title bar.

- `screenOrientation`: This defines the display orientation of the application. The usual values are `portrait` (tall) and `landscape` (wide). See the documentation for more details.

Another crucial part of the manifest file is the correct definition of the permissions that the application should request when a user wants to install it on a device.

 Make sure that you will never request unnecessary permissions and put as much information as required into the description text of your application. Users are extremely suspicious, and justifiably so, when it comes to the list of requested permissions. It is not 100 percent clear for which reason an application needs a certain permission.

For an introduction and much more details on the topic of permissions on Android, check out the official documentation at `http://developer.android.com/guide/topics/security/permissions.html`.

Now, let us try to run the application on a real, physical device. First, make sure that your Android device is connected via a USB cable and is set up for development. To set up your Android device, follow the instructions at `http://developer.android.com/tools/device.html`.

Now, right-click on the **demo-android** project in **Project Explorer** in Eclipse and navigate to **Run As | Android Application**.

The Android application should now be installed as an application icon and should be happily running on your Android device. The following photograph is of the application running on an HTC Desire HD:

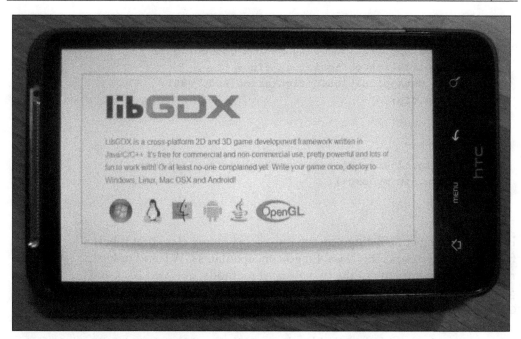

With regards to the Android Emulator that comes with the Android SDK, just a couple of final words, DO NOT USE IT!

At the time of writing this book the emulator appears to have some major issues, such as very slow emulation and unreliable GLES2 support. These issues will hopefully be resolved in future versions. Instead of using the emulator, it is highly recommended to try and test your applications on as many real devices as you can get your hands on.

Running the demo application in a WebGL-capable web browser

The Starter Class for the WebGL application is called GwtLauncher.java.

The following listing is GwtLauncher.java from **demo-html**:

```
package com.packtpub.libgdx.demo.client;

import com.packtpub.libgdx.demo.MyDemo;
import com.badlogic.gdx.ApplicationListener;
import com.badlogic.gdx.backends.gwt.GwtApplication;
import com.badlogic.gdx.backends.gwt.GwtApplicationConfiguration;
```

```
public class GwtLauncher extends GwtApplication {
  @Override
  public GwtApplicationConfiguration getConfig () {
    GwtApplicationConfiguration cfg =
      new GwtApplicationConfiguration(800, 480);
    return cfg;
  }

  @Override
  public ApplicationListener getApplicationListener () {
    return new MyDemo();
  }
}
```

In the preceding code listing you see the `GwtLauncher` class that inherits from the `GwtApplication` class. Libgdx encapsulates GWT and only requires you to implement the two abstract methods, `getConfig()` and `getApplicationListener()`. The `getConfig()` method returns an instance of the `GwtApplicationConfiguration` class. In this case, the window's width and height are directly passed to its constructor. The `getApplicationListener()` method returns an instance of a class that implements the `ApplicationListener` interface, which is the `MyDemo` class in the preceding code.

 Unlike other target platforms, WebGL always uses OpenGL ES 2.0.

Additionally, GWT is organized in so-called modules that bundle together all the configuration settings. In this case, we only have one module called `MyDemo.gwt.xml`. It defines the source path where GWT should look for Java source files, in this case `com/packtpub/libgdx/demo`. These source files will then be cross-compiled by GWT to optimized JavaScript code that is runnable on all major web browsers.

The following listing is `MyDemo.gwt.xml` from **demo**:

```
<?xml version="1.0" encoding="UTF-8"?>
<!DOCTYPE module PUBLIC "-//Google Inc.//DTD Google Web Toolkit
  trunk//EN" "http://google-web-
  toolkit.googlecode.com/svn/trunk/distro-source/core/src/gwt-
  module.dtd">
<module>
  <source path="com/packtpub/libgdx/demo" />
</module>
```

Let us try to run the application now. To do this, right-click on the **demo-html** project in **Project Explorer** in Eclipse and then navigate to **Run As | Web Application**. A new tab titled **Development Mode** should open at the bottom. Simply do what the description preceding the URL says and double-click on it. Your default browser should launch shortly after that. Then try to load the website which is hosted on your local machine right now. Hence, the URL points to 127.0.0.1, the infamous IPv4 loopback address that is just another fancy name for this device or computer.

Keep in mind that using the URL suggested by Eclipse will run your WebGL application in debug mode, which is excruciatingly slow for most games. Just remove everything after the question mark in the URL to run your application in normal mode. The resulting URL should look like this: http://127.0.0.1:8888/index.html.

You might be asked to install the **Google Web Toolkit Developer Plugin** for your web browser to use the **Development Mode**. You need to install it to develop on your local machine.

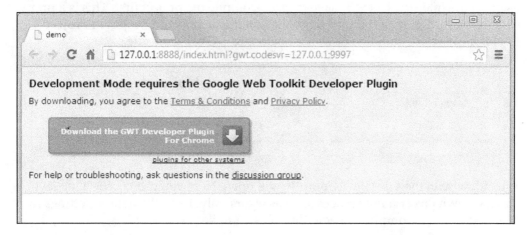

After the plugin has been successfully installed, you should see something like this:

If you want to run this application on a real web server and share it with other users on the Internet, you will have to cross-compile the project first. This is a pretty straightforward process. Simply right-click on the **demo-html** project in **Project Explorer** in Eclipse and then navigate to **Google | GWT Compile**.

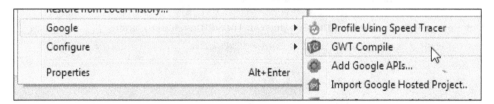

A window with the title **GWT Compile** will open. Here you can choose a log level to narrow down on certain messages such as errors only. Keep the default settings for now and click on **Compile** to begin the cross-compile process.

The compilation process is quite lengthy compared to all the other ones shown in this book. It took over two minutes to finish on an Intel Core i7 (3.4GHz) processor. A good moment to exercise yourself in patience!

Once the compilation has finished, go to the **war** subfolder in the **demo-html** project.

You can now upload everything to your web server that is contained in this folder except the **WEB-INF** folder, which is not needed. Now, you or anyone else can open the URL to your web server and enjoy your Libgdx cross-platform application in a WebGL-capable web browser without having to install any plugin for it to work.

The demo application – time for code

In this section we will take a closer look at the actual code of the **demo** project. Thereafter, we will do some simple modifications to the code and also use the debugger.

Inspecting an example code of the demo application

Let us take a first look at the generated code of MyDemo.java from the **demo** project.

The following code listing shows the class definition:

```
public class MyDemo implements ApplicationListener {
  // ...
}
```

As you can see the MyDemo class implements the ApplicationListener interface. Before we move on to the implementation details of the interface, we will spend some time on the remaining part of this class.

You will find a definition of four member variables, each with a class provided by Libgdx.

```
private OrthographicCamera camera;
private SpriteBatch batch;
private Texture texture;
private Sprite sprite;
```

Here is a brief explanation of the classes from the preceding code listing to give you a basic background knowledge for the code inspection that will follow shortly.

The camera variable is of the class type OrthographicCamera. We will use the orthographic camera for displaying our 2D scenes. The camera is the player's view of the actual scene in the game which is defined by a certain width and height (also called viewport).

For more information about projections, check out the great article *Orthographic vs. Perspective* by *Jeff Lamarche* at http://iphonedevelopment.blogspot.de/2009/04/opengl-es-from-ground-up-part-3.html.

The batch variable is of the class type SpriteBatch. This is where you send all your drawing commands to Libgdx. Beyond the ability of this class to draw images, it is also capable of optimizing the drawing performance under certain circumstances.

The texture variable is of the class type Texture. It holds a reference to the actual image; the texture data that is stored in memory at runtime.

The sprite variable is of the class type Sprite. It is a complex data type that contains lots of attributes to represent a graphical object that has a position in 2D space, width, and height. It can also be rotated and scaled. Internally, it holds a reference to a TextureRegion class that in turn is a means to cut out a certain portion of a texture.

Now that we have a basic knowledge of the involved data types, we can advance to the implementation details of the ApplicationListener interface.

In the MyDemo class, the only methods containing code are create(), render(), and dispose(). The remaining three methods are left empty, which is just fine.

The create() method

This method contains the initialization code to prepare the application on startup:

```
@Override
public void create() {
   float w = Gdx.graphics.getWidth();
   float h = Gdx.graphics.getHeight();

   camera = new OrthographicCamera(1, h / w);
   batch = new SpriteBatch();

   texture = new Texture(Gdx.files.internal("data/libgdx.png"));
   texture.setFilter(TextureFilter.Linear, TextureFilter.Linear);

   TextureRegion region =
     new TextureRegion(texture, 0, 0, 512, 275);

   sprite = new Sprite(region);
   sprite.setSize(0.9f,
     0.9f * sprite.getHeight() / sprite.getWidth());
   sprite.setOrigin(sprite.getWidth() / 2,
     sprite.getHeight() / 2);
   sprite.setPosition(-sprite.getWidth() / 2,
     -sprite.getHeight() / 2);
}
```

At first, the graphics module is queried to return the width and height of the display (for example, a desktop window or the screen of an Android device) and calculate an appropriate width and height for the field of view of the camera. Then a new instance of SpriteBatch is created so that images can be drawn and made visible with the camera. The next step is to load a texture by using the files module to get a file handle to data/libgdx.png.

The loaded texture looks like the following screenshot:

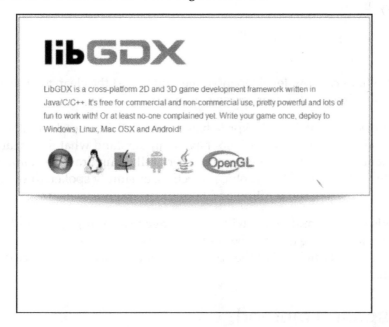

As you can see, there is a lot of empty space in this image. In order to be able to use the filled part of this image only, a new instance of TextureRegion is created. It references the previously loaded texture that contains the full image and has the additional information to cut out all the pixels starting from (0, 0) to (512, 275). These two points describe a rectangle starting at the top-left corner of the image with a width and height of 512 by 275 pixels. Finally, a sprite is created using the information of the previously created texture region. The sprite's size is set to 90 percent of its original size. The sprite's origin is set to half of its width and height to move the origin to its center. Eventually, the position is set to the negative half of the sprite's width and height so that the sprite moves to the center of the scene.

 Libgdx uses a coordinate system which has its origin (0, 0) at the bottom-left corner. This means that the positive x axis points right while the positive y axis points up.

The render() method

This method contains the commands to render a scene on screen:

```
@Override
public void render() {
  Gdx.gl.glClearColor(1, 1, 1, 1);
  Gdx.gl.glClear(GL10.GL_COLOR_BUFFER_BIT);
```

```
    batch.setProjectionMatrix(camera.combined);
    batch.begin();
    sprite.draw(batch);
    batch.end();
}
```

The first two lines call low-level OpenGL methods to set the clear color to a solid white and then execute the clear screen command.

Next, the projection matrix of the sprite batch is set to the camera's combined projection and view matrix. You do not have to understand what this means in detail at the moment. It basically just means that every following drawing command will behave to the rules of an orthographic projection, or simply spoken drawing will be done in 2D space using the position and bounds of the given camera.

The methods `begin()` and `end()` will always have to appear in pairs and must not be nested or there will be errors. The actual drawing of the sprite is accomplished by calling the `draw()` method of the sprite to draw and pass the instance of the sprite batch.

The dispose() method

This is the place where you should clean up and free all resources that are still in use by an application:

```
@Override
public void dispose() {
  batch.dispose();
  texture.dispose();
}
```

There is an interface called `Disposable` that is implemented by every Libgdx class that allocates resources (that is, memory) and can be easily de-allocated by calling the corresponding `dispose()` method. In the preceding code, this is done for the sprite batch and the loaded texture.

The following is a complete listing of the `MyDemo.java` source file from the **demo** project:

```
package com.packtpub.libgdx.demo;

import com.badlogic.gdx.ApplicationListener;
import com.badlogic.gdx.Gdx;
import com.badlogic.gdx.graphics.GL10;
import com.badlogic.gdx.graphics.OrthographicCamera;
import com.badlogic.gdx.graphics.Texture;
```

```
import com.badlogic.gdx.graphics.Texture.TextureFilter;
import com.badlogic.gdx.graphics.g2d.Sprite;
import com.badlogic.gdx.graphics.g2d.SpriteBatch;
import com.badlogic.gdx.graphics.g2d.TextureRegion;

public class MyDemo implements ApplicationListener {
  private OrthographicCamera camera;
  private SpriteBatch batch;
  private Texture texture;
  private Sprite sprite;

  @Override
  public void create() {
    float w = Gdx.graphics.getWidth();
    float h = Gdx.graphics.getHeight();

    camera = new OrthographicCamera(1, h / w);
    batch = new SpriteBatch();

    texture = new Texture(Gdx.files.internal("data/libgdx.png"));
    texture.setFilter(TextureFilter.Linear, TextureFilter.Linear);

    TextureRegion region =
      new TextureRegion(texture, 0, 0, 512, 275);

    sprite = new Sprite(region);
    sprite.setSize(0.9f,
      0.9f * sprite.getHeight() / sprite.getWidth());
    sprite.setOrigin(sprite.getWidth() / 2,
      sprite.getHeight() / 2);
    sprite.setPosition(-sprite.getWidth() / 2,
      -sprite.getHeight() / 2);
  }

  @Override
  public void dispose() {
    batch.dispose();
    texture.dispose();
  }

  @Override
  public void render() {
    Gdx.gl.glClearColor(1, 1, 1, 1);
    Gdx.gl.glClear(GL10.GL_COLOR_BUFFER_BIT);
```

```
        batch.setProjectionMatrix(camera.combined);
        batch.begin();
        sprite.draw(batch);
        batch.end();
    }

    @Override
    public void resize(int width, int height) {
    }

    @Override
    public void pause() {
    }

    @Override
    public void resume() {
    }
}
```

Having fun with the debugger and Code Hot Swapping

In this section we are going to use the debugger to take a look inside the **demo** application at runtime. To do this, we first set a breakpoint where the execution of the application should be halted so that we can easily inspect the current state. Open the `MyDemo.java` source file in Eclipse and set a breakpoint at the line where a new instance of `SpriteBatch` is created.

```
        camera = new OrthographicCamera(1, h/w);
        batch = new SpriteBatch();

        texture = new Texture(Gdx.files.internal("data/libgdx.png"));
        texture.setFilter(TextureFilter.Linear, TextureFilter.Linear);
```

 Double-click on the shaded, empty space at the very left side of the editor window in Eclipse to set or toggle already existing breakpoints, which will put blue dot to signify the breakpoint as shown in the preceding screenshot.

Next, right-click on the **demo-desktop** project in **Project Explorer** in Eclipse and then navigate to **Debug As | Java Application**. The application should be halted almost directly after the application window becomes visible. Eclipse should have automatically changed to the debugging perspective, which shows lots of extra information about an application running in the debug mode.

In the **Variables** tab, you can now inspect every variable that is within the current scope of execution. For example, the two floating-point variables w and h have already been set. You can check this by looking for them in the **Variables** tab. The correct values of the variables are displayed as 480.0 for w and 320.0 for h. To step through, resume, or stop the execution of the application, you can go to the **Run** menu and choose the appropriate menu item. Choose to resume the application for now.

Let us try to do Code Hot Swapping now. Make sure that the **demo** application is currently running and is being executed right now.

The following listing is a modified version of the render() method. The modification is highlighted:

```java
@Override
public void render() {
  Gdx.gl.glClearColor(1, 1, 1, 1);
  Gdx.gl.glClear(GL10.GL_COLOR_BUFFER_BIT);
```

```
    batch.setProjectionMatrix(camera.combined);
    batch.begin();
    sprite.setRotation(45);
    sprite.draw(batch);
    batch.end();
}
```

Add the following line to your code inside the `MyDemo.java` source file right before `sprite.draw()` is called:

```
    sprite.setRotation(45);
```

It will make the sprite rotate by 45 degrees in a counter-clockwise direction. The next step is to save your changes to the source file. What you should see now is that the change you have just made to the code is immediately reflected in the still running application!

 For Code Hot Swapping to work, it is required that the automatic (re)build feature is enabled. You can quickly check this by going to the **Project** menu and making sure that the menu item **Build Automatically** is checked.

You might already sense the possibilities that this great feature enables a developer to do. Just think of a somewhat more complex scene where you are trying to find the best-looking positions for your objects, or you just want to see how it would look with a couple of different settings. It is a piece of cake with a tool like Code Hot Swapping at your disposal.

Let us take the preceding example a bit further and make the image rotate continuously.

We will need a variable to store the current rotation value. This value is going to be increased over time by adding lots of small deltas of time to it. To avoid a possible overflow in `rot`, we calculate the remainder of the new rotation value divided by 360 degrees. This can be done in an easy way by using the modulo operator (`%`) to wrap around a certain value.

The rotation is calculated in degrees per second. Afterwards, we set the new rotation value of the sprite and draw it while the rotation value is advanced step-by-step.

The following listing is the modified code for the rotating image:

```
private float rot;

@Override
public void render() {
   Gdx.gl.glClearColor(1, 1, 1, 1);
   Gdx.gl.glClear(GL10.GL_COLOR_BUFFER_BIT);

   batch.setProjectionMatrix(camera.combined);
   batch.begin();
   final float degressPerSecond = 10.0f;
   rot = (rot + Gdx.graphics.getDeltaTime() *
     degressPerSecond) % 360;
   sprite.setRotation(rot);
   sprite.draw(batch);
   batch.end();
}
```

Now that we have a changing value for the rotation, let us have some more fun with it and turn the continuous rotation effect into a shake effect.

Since the Sine (or Cosine) function has an oscillating behavior, we can make perfect use of it to make the image shake by a certain amount to the left and right. The amount (amplitude) can be increased and decreased by multiplying it with the answer of the Sine function.

The following listing is the modified code for the shaking image:

```
@Override
public void render() {
   Gdx.gl.glClearColor(1, 1, 1, 1);
   Gdx.gl.glClear(GL10.GL_COLOR_BUFFER_BIT);
```

```
batch.setProjectionMatrix(camera.combined);
batch.begin();
float degressPerSecond = 10.0f;
rot = (rot + Gdx.graphics.getDeltaTime() *
  degressPerSecond) % 360;
final float shakeAmplitudeInDegrees = 5.0f;
float shake = MathUtils.sin(rot) * shakeAmplitudeInDegrees;
sprite.setRotation(shake);
sprite.draw(batch);
batch.end();
}
```

The following diagram visualizes the effect of both the rotation and the shake:

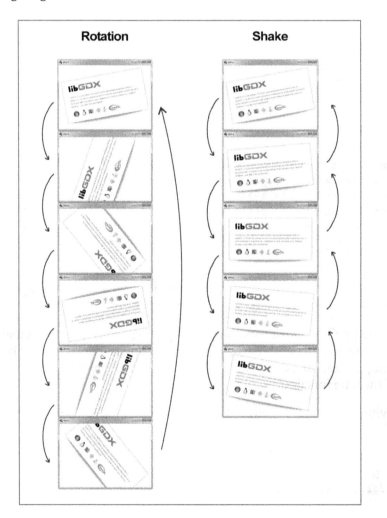

Summary

We learned a lot in this chapter about Libgdx and how all the projects of an application work together. We covered Libgdx's backends, modules, and Starter Classes. Additionally, we covered what the Application Life-Cycle and corresponding interface are and how they are meant to work. The debugger has been used to inspect the **demo** application at runtime, and furthermore we made use of the JVM Code Hot Swapping feature.

We now know the basics of the Libgdx applications, so now we are ready to start developing a real game. We will start at the very beginning of the development cycle step-by-step. Since Libgdx is a framework but not a game engine, we first have to build our own engine. So, we will learn how to create an appropriate program architecture that is suitable to handle our game in the next chapter.

3
Configuring the Game

In this chapter you will begin to build the game called **Canyon Bunny** that has been discussed earlier in *Chapter 1*, *Introduction to Libgdx and Project Setup*. As with any new application, the first step is to create the appropriate project setup. After that, you will learn about the game's architecture that has been chosen for this book.

A **UML class diagram** will give you the necessary overview of all the new classes that need to be implemented. UML is going to be explained later in this chapter. When looking from a software engineer's perspective, the architecture and the shown implementation code in this book does not always follow the best design decisions on purpose to keep the discussed examples simple and easy to understand where possible. Keep in mind that the primary objective of this book is to teach you how to work with and manage the vast complexity that creating games involve by using Libgdx. The following parts are going to be very code oriented, so be sure to make use of the class diagram as a point of orientation to not get lost in all these code listings and their corresponding explanations.

In the end, you will have created and tested the base code that serves as the foundation for all the subsequent chapters in which more game features will be added successively.

Setting up the Canyon Bunny project

Run the `gdx-setup-ui` tool from Libgdx and use the following settings:

- **Name:** `CanyonBunny`
- **Package:** `com.packtpub.libgdx.canyonbunny`
- **Game class:** `CanyonBunnyMain`
- **Destination:** `C:\libgdx`
- **Generate the desktop project:** select the checkbox
- **Generate the html project:** select the checkbox

The following is a screenshot of the described configuration:

Next, click on **Open the generation screen** followed by another click on **Launch!** to generate all the projects. Now there should be four projects in C:\libgdx with the names: CanyonBunny, CanyonBunny-desktop, CanyonBunny-android, and CanyonBunny-html.

Now, run Eclipse and import these projects into your workspace.

 Refer to section *Creating a new application* in *Chapter 1, Introduction to Libgdx and Project Setup* for more details.

Next, go to the **Project Explorer** window in Eclipse and open the file strings.xml under CanyonBunny-android/res/strings.xml. There is a name variable that is used for the application's name that users will see on their smartphones. The **Project Explorer** window can be opened through the menu at **Window | Show View | Project Explorer**.

Currently, the line of code should look like this:

```
<string name="app_name">My LibGDX Game</string>
```

Change the name to something more appropriate such as Canyon Bunny:

```
<string name="app_name">Canyon Bunny</string>
```

Save and close the `strings.xml` file. Also, in the **Project Explorer** window, remove the following two files and a directory that comes with the generated projects:

- `CanyonBunny/src/com/packtpub/libgdx/canyonbunny/CanyonBunnyMain.java`
- `CanyonBunny-android/assets/data/libgdx.png`
- `CanyonBunny-android/assets/data/`

Then, open `CanyonBunny-desktop/com/packtpub/libgdx/canyonbunny/Main.java` and change the resolution parameters for width and height to 800 x 480 pixels like this:

```
cfg.width = 800;
cfg.height = 480;
```

Save and close the file to continue.

All done! You have finished the project setup for Canyon Bunny.

Using a class diagram for Canyon Bunny

We will now take a closer look at the architecture of Canyon Bunny. A so-called class diagram is used to help us visualizing and explaining the architecture in a standardized and structured form. The class diagram is illustrated as follows:

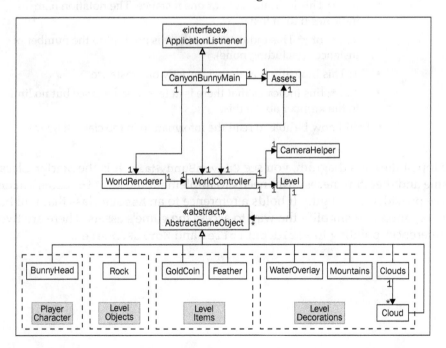

In this class diagram, you will find a lot of classes that will be used in this game. It also shows important information about the kind of classes and how they are interconnected. Firstly, before we continue, please do not become scared of all these boxes, lines, and arrows pointing in every direction. In case you are not familiar with reading class diagrams or UML (Unified Modeling Language) in general, take a look at the information box for a quick explanation of what you should know to be able to read it. Otherwise, simply skip to the next paragraph to continue.

Each class is represented in a rectangle. If it is a special kind of class (stereotype in UML), it is indicated in double angle quotation marks above its name like **«abstract»** for an abstract class or **«interface»** for an interface. Lines are used to show the relationship between the two classes.

A line without arrows designates a bidirectional relationship between two classes, meaning that they depend on each other in order to work correctly. If there is a line with a filled arrowhead at one end, it means that the class that points to the other class needs it to work properly but not vice versa. Otherwise, if there is a line with an unfilled arrowhead at one end, it always points from an implementing class (specialization in UML) to its super class (generalization in UML) which can either be an interface or an abstract class.

Lastly, there are numbers to describe the multiplicity or, in other words, how many instances of an object will exist from one class in another. The syntax for this is:

- `0..1`: This indicates zero or one instance. The notation n..m indicates n to m instances.
- `0..*` or `*`: This indicates that there is no limit to the number of instances (including none).
- `1`: This indicates that there is exactly one instance.
- `1..*`: this indicates that there is at least one instance but no limit to the number above this.

You should now be able to read the information in the class diagram.

At the top of the class diagram, you see `CanyonBunnyMain`. It is the **Starter Class** of the game and therefore necessarily needs to implement the `ApplicationListener` interface provided by Libgdx. It holds a reference to an `Assets` class that will be used to organize and simplify the way to access the game's assets. There are two more references pointing to `WorldController` and `WorldRenderer`.

The `WorldController` class contains all the game logic to initialize and modify the game world. It also needs access to `CameraHelper`, a helper class for the camera that, for example, enables it to target and follow any game object; `Level` that holds the level data; and a list of `AbstractGameObject` instances representing any game object that exists in the game world.

The rendering takes place in `WorldRenderer` that apparently also requires it to have access to the list of `AbstractGameObject` instances. Since the game objects need to be created before the process of modification and rendering, `Level` needs access to the list of `AbstractGameObject` instances as well when a level is loaded from a level file at the beginning of the game.

What is still left is the bottom row of classes in the diagram all of which point to the abstract class, `AbstractGameObject`. They all implement a specialized type of this class, and thus share a common functionality of being a general game object that can be rendered in the game world. Furthermore, these classes have been grouped in this diagram to indicate their purpose in this game. You might want to peek at the end of *Chapter 1, Introduction to Libgdx and Project Setup* again and take a quick look at the sketch that shows all the relevant game objects in one picture. Here is a brief description of the grouped classes:

- Player Character
    - `BunnyHead`: It represents the character that is controlled by the player.

- Level Objects
    - `Rock`: It represents a platform that has an edge to the left and the right side, and a middle part that can be set to an arbitrary length. It is the ground in a level where the player will move on.

- Level Items
    - `GoldCoin`: It represents an item that will increase the player's score when picked up.
    - `Feather`: It represents a power-up that will grant the ability to fly to the player's character when picked up.

- Level Decorations
    - `WaterOverlay`: It represents an image that is attached to the camera's horizontal position and thus is always visible regardless of wherever the camera is moving on its x axis.
    - `Mountains`: It represents two mountain images moving at different speeds to simulate a parallax optical illusion.
    - `Cloud`: It represents one cloud moving slowly to the left in the sky.

These classes will be covered in much more detail in *Chapter 4, Gathering Resources* to *Chapter 6, Adding the Actors*.

Laying foundations

Let us now move on from theory to practice and get down to the actual implementation details. We will begin with implementing the first basic version of `CanyonBunnyMain`, `WorldController`, and `WorldRenderer`. Additionally, we will use a utility class for storing constant values in a new class called `Constants`. It is true that this class does not appear in the class diagram, as it is just there for our convenience to avoid scattering or, even worse, duplicating certain constants all over the source code files. Also, since the stored values in `Constants` are meant to be used in virtually any other class, it would only clutter up the class diagram by drawing one additional line for each class to `Constants`.

 For simplicity, we will use the `Constants` class for storing our constant values. Alternatively, game constants could be made data driven via a settings file. This would avoid the need to recompile your code when a constant is changed.

Implementing Constants

Here is a listing of the code for `Constants`:

```
package com.packtpub.libgdx.canyonbunny.util;

public class Constants {
   // Visible game world is 5 meters wide
   public static final float VIEWPORT_WIDTH = 5.0f;

   // Visible game world is 5 meters tall
   public static final float VIEWPORT_HEIGHT = 5.0f;
}
```

First, we need to define the visible world size that can be seen at once when not moving around in the game world. In this case, we have chosen a visible world size of five meters in terms of width and height.

Next, we will create the other three mentioned classes but only add the so-called method stubs (empty methods). This way we can focus on the layout first and gradually implement the code and other new features later when needed. Hopefully, this approach will give you the best insight into the whole development process from start to finish.

Implementing CanyonBunnyMain

The following listing shows the first implementation of `CanyonBunnyMain`:

```
package com.packtpub.libgdx.canyonbunny;

import com.badlogic.gdx.ApplicationListener;
import com.packtpub.libgdx.canyonbunny.game.WorldController;
import com.packtpub.libgdx.canyonbunny.game.WorldRenderer;

public class CanyonBunnyMain implements ApplicationListener {
  private static final String TAG =
    CanyonBunnyMain.class.getName();

  private WorldController worldController;
  private WorldRenderer worldRenderer;

  @Override public void create () { }
  @Override public void render () { }
  @Override public void resize (int width, int height) { }
  @Override public void pause () { }
  @Override public void resume () { }
  @Override public void dispose () { }
}
```

This class implements `ApplicationListener` to become one of Libgdx's starter classes.

A reference each to `WorldController` and `WorldRenderer` enables this class to update and control the game's flow and also to render the game's current state to the screen.

There is a `TAG` variable that holds a unique label derived from the class's name. It will be used for any logging purposes. Libgdx's built-in logging facility requires you to pass in a so-called tag name for every message to be logged. So, to stay consistent in our code, we will simply add a tag variable to each class.

Implementing WorldController

The following listing shows the first implementation of `WorldController`:

```
package com.packtpub.libgdx.canyonbunny.game;

public class WorldController {
  private static final String TAG =
    WorldController.class.getName();
```

```
    public WorldController () { }

    private void init () { }

    public void update (float deltaTime) { }
}
```

This class has an internal method `init()` that initializes it. Naturally, all the initialization code could also be put into the constructor. However, it appears to be very helpful in many ways when an initialization code is available in a separate method. Whenever we need to reset an object in the game, we do not always want or have to completely rebuild it and thereby save a lot of performance. Also, this approach can greatly reduce the interruptions by the **Garbage Collector (GC)**. Instead, we try to actively re-use existing objects, which is always a recommended design goal to maximize performance and minimize memory usage. This is especially true for smartphones such as Android with limited resources.

The `update()` method will contain the game logic and will be called several hundred times per second. It requires a delta time so that it can apply updates to the game world according to the fraction of time that has passed since the last rendered frame.

 The configurations of our starter classes use **vertical synchronization** (**vsync**), which is enabled by default. Using vsync will cap your frame rate and likewise the calls to `update()` at a maximum of 60 frames per second.

Implementing WorldRenderer

The following listing shows the first implementation of `WorldRenderer`:

```
package com.packtpub.libgdx.canyonbunny.game;

import com.badlogic.gdx.graphics.OrthographicCamera;
import com.badlogic.gdx.graphics.g2d.SpriteBatch;
import com.badlogic.gdx.utils.Disposable;
import com.packtpub.libgdx.canyonbunny.util.Constants;

public class WorldRenderer implements Disposable {
    private OrthographicCamera camera;
    private SpriteBatch batch;
    private WorldController worldController;

    public WorldRenderer (WorldController worldController) { }
```

```
    private void init () { }

    public void render () { }
    public void resize (int width, int height) { }

    @Override public void dispose () { }
}
```

This class also has an internal `init()` method for its initialization. Furthermore, it contains a `render()` method that will contain the logic to define in which order game objects are drawn over others. Whenever the screen size is changed, including the event at the start of the program, `resize()` will spring into action and initiate the required steps to accommodate the new situation.

The rendering is accomplished by using an orthographic camera that is suitable for two-dimensional projections. Fortunately, Libgdx comes with a ready-to-use `OrthographicCamera` class to simplify our 2D rendering tasks. The `SpriteBatch` class is the actual workhorse that draws all our objects with respect to the camera's current settings (for example, position, zoom, and so on) to the screen. Since `SpriteBatch` implements Libgdx's `Disposable` interface, it is advisable to always call its `dispose()` method to free the allocated memory when it is no longer needed. We will do this in `WorldRenderer` by also implementing the `Disposable` interface. This allows us to easily cascade the disposal process when `dispose()` in `CanyonBunnyMain` is called by Libgdx. In this case, we will simply call the `WorldRenderer`'s class' `dispose()` method which in turn will call the `SpriteBatch` class' `dispose()` method.

Notice that this class requires a reference to an instance of `WorldController` in its constructor so that it will be accessible later on to render all the game world objects that are managed by the controller.

Putting it all together

We will now begin to fill the stub methods with some life. The game loop is a good starting point as it is our driving engine that keeps the game world updating and rendering in a continuous way. After that, we will add some sprites and verify that the updating and rendering mechanism is working fine. In order to manipulate the world and game objects, controls are added to receive and react upon user input. Finally, the `CameraHelper` class will be implemented to allow us to move around freely in the game world and to select a game object of our choice that the camera is supposed to follow.

Additions and modifications in code listings will be highlighted.

Building the game loop

The game loop will reside in the CanyonBunnyMain class' render() method. Before we can add the new code, we have to import the following packages to gain access to some classes that we are going to use:

```
import com.badlogic.gdx.Application;
import com.badlogic.gdx.Gdx;
import com.badlogic.gdx.graphics.GL10;
```

After that, add the following code to create():

```
@Override
public void create () {
    // Set Libgdx log level to DEBUG
    Gdx.app.setLogLevel(Application.LOG_DEBUG);
    // Initialize controller and renderer
    worldController = new WorldController();
    worldRenderer = new WorldRenderer(worldController);
}
```

First, we set the log level of Libgdx's built-in logger to debug the mode in order to print out everything to the console that might be logged during runtime.

 Do not forget to change the log level to something more appropriate such as LOG_NONE or LOG_INFO before publishing your game.

After that we simply create a new instance of WorldController and WorldRenderer and save them in their respective member variables.

To continuously update and render the game world to the screen, add the following code to render():

```
@Override
public void render () {
    // Update game world by the time that has passed
    // since last rendered frame.
    worldController.update(Gdx.graphics.getDeltaTime());
    // Sets the clear screen color to: Cornflower Blue
```

```
Gdx.gl.glClearColor(0x64/255.0f, 0x95/255.0f, 0xed/255.0f,
  0xff/255.0f);
// Clears the screen
Gdx.gl.glClear(GL10.GL_COLOR_BUFFER_BIT);
// Render game world to screen
worldRenderer.render();
}
```

The game world is incrementally updated using delta times. Luckily, Libgdx already does the math and housekeeping behind this for us, so all we need to do is to query the value by calling getDeltaTime() from the Gdx.graphics module and pass it to update() of WorldController. After that, Libgdx is instructed to execute two direct OpenGL calls using the Gdx.gl module. The first call glClearColor() sets the color white to a light blue color using RGBA (red, green, blue, and alpha) values written in hexadecimal notation. Each color component needs to be expressed as a floating-point value ranging between 0 and 1 with a resolution of 8 bits. This is the reason why we are also dividing each color component by the value of 255.0f (8 bit = 2^8 = 256 = 0..255 distinct levels per color component).

Some prefer hexadecimal notation while others prefer decimal notation. Here is an example of setting the same color in decimal notation if you prefer to do so.

```
Gdx.gl.glClearColor(
    100/255.0f, 149/255.0f, 237/255.0f, 255/255.0f);
```

The second call glClear() uses the color white we set before to fill the screen and therefore erase all of the screen's previous contents. The last step renders the new frame of the updated game world to the screen.

You should never reverse the order of code execution as shown in the preceding listing. For example, you could first try to render and then update the game world. Now, in this case, the displayed game world will always lag one frame behind of its actual state. The change is very subtle and may even go unnoticed. This, of course, depends on many factors. If it is an action game that requires fast reactions, it will probably be much more noticeable as compared to a slow-paced cardboard game with enough pauses to bridge the time gap until the screen eventually shows the true game world state.

Next, add the following code to `resize()`:

```
@Override
public void resize (int width, int height) {
  worldRenderer.resize(width, height);
}
```

Whenever a resize event occurs, the `resize()` method of the `ApplicationListener` interface will be called. Since this event is related to rendering, we want it to be handled in `WorldRenderer` and therefore simply hand over the incoming values to its own `resize()` method.

The same is almost true for the code to be added in `dispose()`:

```
@Override
public void dispose() {
  worldRenderer.dispose();
}
```

Whenever a `dispose` event occurs, it is passed on to the renderer.

There is one more tiny addition to improve the code for execution on Android devices. As we have learned in *Chapter 2, Cross Platform Development – Build Once Deploy Anywhere*, there are system events on Android for pausing and resuming its applications. In case of an incoming pause or resume event, we also want the game to either stop or continue updating our game world accordingly. To make this work, we need a new member variable called `paused`. Add the following line of code to the class:

```
private boolean paused;
```

Then modify the methods `create()` and `render()` as shown in the following code snippet:

```
@Override
public void create () {
  // Set Libgdx log level to DEBUG
  Gdx.app.setLogLevel(Application.LOG_DEBUG);
  // Initialize controller and renderer
  worldController = new WorldController();
  worldRenderer = new WorldRenderer(worldController);
```

```java
    // Game world is active on start
    paused = false;
}


@Override
public void render () {
  // Do not update game world when paused.
  if (!paused) {
    // Update game world by the time that has passed
    // since last rendered frame.
    worldController.update(Gdx.graphics.getDeltaTime());
  }
  // Sets the clear screen color to: Cornflower Blue
  Gdx.gl.glClearColor(0x64/255.0f, 0x95/255.0f, 0xed/255.0f,
    0xff/255.0f);
  // Clears the screen
  Gdx.gl.glClear(GL10.GL_COLOR_BUFFER_BIT);
  // Render game world to screen
  worldRenderer.render();
}
```

Lastly, add the following code to pause() and resume() to let the game respond to these events by setting paused to the correct state:

```java
@Override
public void pause () {
  paused = true;
}


@Override
public void resume () {
  paused = false;
}
```

We now have reached a stage in our development process where it is well worth to take a quick look if everything works as expected. Run the game on a platform of your choice to test it. The following is a picture of the game running on Windows:

You should see a window entirely filled with the blue color. Seriously, the result is not very exciting yet nor does it resemble anything like a game. However, all the work we have done so far gives us a foundation onto which we can continue to build our next extensions for the game.

Adding test sprites

Let us now add some test code to try out the mechanism we built for updating and rendering. We will do this by adding some simple test sprites that are procedurally generated at runtime.

First, add some more imports to WorldController:

```
import com.badlogic.gdx.graphics.Pixmap;
import com.badlogic.gdx.graphics.Pixmap.Format;
import com.badlogic.gdx.graphics.Texture;
import com.badlogic.gdx.graphics.g2d.Sprite;
import com.badlogic.gdx.math.MathUtils;
```

After that, add the following code:

```
public Sprite[] testSprites;
public int selectedSprite;

public WorldController () {
  init();
}

private void init () {
  initTestObjects();
}

private void initTestObjects() {
  // Create new array for 5 sprites
  testSprites = new Sprite[5];
  // Create empty POT-sized Pixmap with 8 bit RGBA pixel data
  int width = 32;
  int height = 32;
  Pixmap pixmap = createProceduralPixmap(width, height);
  // Create a new texture from pixmap data
  Texture texture = new Texture(pixmap);
  // Create new sprites using the just created texture
  for (int i = 0; i < testSprites.length; i++) {
    Sprite spr = new Sprite(texture);
    // Define sprite size to be 1m x 1m in game world
    spr.setSize(1, 1);
    // Set origin to sprite's center
    spr.setOrigin(spr.getWidth() / 2.0f, spr.getHeight() / 2.0f);
    // Calculate random position for sprite
    float randomX = MathUtils.random(-2.0f, 2.0f);
    float randomY = MathUtils.random(-2.0f, 2.0f);
    spr.setPosition(randomX, randomY);
    // Put new sprite into array
    testSprites[i] = spr;
  }
  // Set first sprite as selected one
  selectedSprite = 0;
}

private Pixmap createProceduralPixmap (int width, int height) {
  Pixmap pixmap = new Pixmap(width, height, Format.RGBA8888);
  // Fill square with red color at 50% opacity
  pixmap.setColor(1, 0, 0, 0.5f);
  pixmap.fill();
  // Draw a yellow-colored X shape on square
  pixmap.setColor(1, 1, 0, 1);
```

```
    pixmap.drawLine(0, 0, width, height);
    pixmap.drawLine(width, 0, 0, height);
    // Draw a cyan-colored border around square
    pixmap.setColor(0, 1, 1, 1);
    pixmap.drawRectangle(0, 0, width, height);
    return pixmap;
}

public void update (float deltaTime) {
    updateTestObjects(deltaTime);
}

private void updateTestObjects(float deltaTime) {
    // Get current rotation from selected sprite
    float rotation = testSprites[selectedSprite].getRotation();
    // Rotate sprite by 90 degrees per second
    rotation += 90 * deltaTime;
    // Wrap around at 360 degrees
    rotation %= 360;
    // Set new rotation value to selected sprite
    testSprites[selectedSprite].setRotation(rotation);
}
}
```

The new code adds two new member variables testSprites and selectedSprite. The first one holds instances of the Sprite objects. We chose to add five sprites for our test. The second variable holds the index of the currently selected sprite that is stored in the array. The Sprite class can be used to display textures. Since we do not have any textures added to our project yet, we are generating one for our test on the fly using the Pixmap class. Pixmap holds the actual pixel data (in a map of bytes) to represent any image. Its class provides some basic drawing methods that we are using in this code to draw a 32 x 32 pixel-sized transparent red box with a yellow "X" crossing it diagonally and a cyan border. The final pixel data is then put in a new Texture object. This object is eventually attached to each new Sprite we create so that it will show our hand-crafted image when rendered. Here is an image of the procedurally generated test sprite.

Each sprite's size is set to 1 x 1 meter. Remember that we have defined our visible world size to be 5 x 5 meters at the beginning of this chapter. So, these sprites will exactly be one-fifth in size in our game world. This fact is very important to understand because it is not the dimension of pixels in your image that defines the size of your game objects. Everything needs to be defined in virtual meters that relates to the visible game world. The origin of the sprite is set to its center point. This allows us to rotate the sprites around itself without an added translation effect. The position is set randomly between two meters in negative and positive directions. Additionally, we set the index to 0 (the first element in the array) for the initially selected sprite. In `updateTestObjects()`, we refer to the selected sprite to rotate it on each update cycle. This allows us to easily see which of the shown sprites is currently the selected one.

All that we have achieved so far is to add the logic to create and modify the game world with its objects, but none of them are rendered to the screen yet. This is what we will change next.

First, add one new line to also import the `Sprite` class in `WorldRenderer`:

```
import com.badlogic.gdx.graphics.g2d.Sprite;
```

After that, add the following code to `WorldRenderer`:

```
public WorldRenderer (WorldController worldController) {
   this.worldController = worldController;
   init();
}

private void init () {
   batch = new SpriteBatch();
   camera = new OrthographicCamera(Constants.VIEWPORT_WIDTH,
     Constants.VIEWPORT_HEIGHT);
   camera.position.set(0, 0, 0);
   camera.update();
}

public void render () {
   renderTestObjects();
}

private void renderTestObjects() {
   batch.setProjectionMatrix(camera.combined);
   batch.begin();
   for(Sprite sprite : worldController.testSprites) {
     sprite.draw(batch);
   }
   batch.end();
```

```
        }

        public void resize (int width, int height) {
          camera.viewportWidth = (Constants.VIEWPORT_HEIGHT / height) *
            width;
          camera.update();
        }

        @Override
        public void dispose () {
          batch.dispose();
        }
```

The first action in `WorldRenderer` is to store the reference to `WorldController` when it is instantiated. This is necessary for the renderer to access the game objects that are managed by the controller. In `init()`, a new `SpriteBatch` object is created which will be used for all our rendering tasks. Before we can start to render objects, we need to create a camera and define its viewport properly. The camera's viewport defines the size of the captured game world it is looking at. It works basically the same as a real camera. Obviously, when looking through a camera, you cannot see anything else except the area it is currently pointed at. For example, if you want to see what is to the left of it, you would have to move your camera to the left, which holds true for both real and virtual cameras. We are using the width and height defined in `Constants` to set the viewport. In the event of a resized displaying area, `resize()` will be called by Libgdx. This is our chance to adapt to the new display dimensions and redefine how the game world should be rendered in that case. The code we added in `resize()` calculates the aspect ratio between our desired visible world height and the currently available display height. The answer is then multiplied with the available display width to find the new viewport width for the camera. The resulting effect of this calculation is that the world's visible height will always be kept to its full extent, while the world's width will scale accordingly to the calculated aspect ratio. It is very important to not forget to call `camera.update()` whenever changes are made to the camera to let them take effect.

The rendering of the game world takes place in the `render()` method. The `SpriteBatch` class offers two methods called `begin()` and `end()`. These methods are used to start and end a new batch of drawing commands. Before any drawing command can be executed, it is mandatory to call `begin()`. In `renderTestObjects()`, we loop through all the sprites by accessing the previously stored reference to `WorldController` and calling the `Sprite` class' `draw()` method to draw it. After all drawing commands have been executed, we end the batch with the corresponding call to `end()`, which is just as mandatory as `begin()`.

All done! You can now run the game to try it out. One of the sprites should be constantly rotating around its center point that tells us that this must be the currently selected sprite.

Here is a screenshot of the game with the rendered test sprites running on Windows:

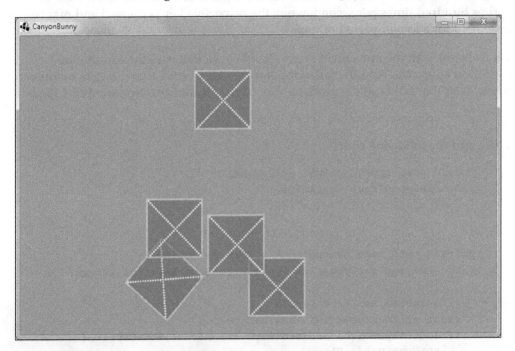

Adding game world's debug controls

During development, it can be a very powerful feature to have debug controls built into an application to be able to directly manipulate certain behaviors. Debug controls are what gamers usually call game cheats; although, this is a very elastic term. What is certain is that it will make your life as a developer a lot easier and more fun too. Just be sure to remove or disable all debug controls before publishing your game as long as you do not intend them to be available to the user.

There are two ways to handle input events. We will make use of both of them shortly to demonstrate when and how to use them. The debug controls we are going to implement will allow us to do the following:

- Move a selected sprite into any of the four directions (left, right, up, or down)
- Reset the game world to its initial state
- Cycle through the list of sprites to select the other ones

The first of the three requirements is quite different to the other two in respect of continuity. For example, when holding down a key for a "move" action, you would expect this action to be repeatedly executed while the key is still being pressed. In contrast, the other two actions are characterized by being nonrecurring events. This is because you usually do not want to reset the game or cycle through the list of sprites hundred times per second, when the respective key is pressed and maybe even held for a longer period of time.

Let us begin with the movement of a selected sprite that uses the continuous execution approach. Add the following line of code to `WorldController` to import a new class that holds all the available key constants that are supported by Libgdx:

```
import com.badlogic.gdx.Input.Keys;
```

Then, add the following code:

```
public void update (float deltaTime) {
    handleDebugInput(deltaTime);
    updateTestObjects(deltaTime);
}

private void handleDebugInput (float deltaTime) {
    if (Gdx.app.getType() != ApplicationType.Desktop) return;

    // Selected Sprite Controls
    float sprMoveSpeed = 5 * deltaTime;
    if (Gdx.input.isKeyPressed(Keys.A)) moveSelectedSprite(
      -sprMoveSpeed, 0);
    if (Gdx.input.isKeyPressed(Keys.D))
      moveSelectedSprite(sprMoveSpeed, 0);
    if (Gdx.input.isKeyPressed(Keys.W)) moveSelectedSprite(0,
      sprMoveSpeed);
    if (Gdx.input.isKeyPressed(Keys.S)) moveSelectedSprite(0,
      -sprMoveSpeed);
}

private void moveSelectedSprite (float x, float y) {
    testSprites[selectedSprite].translate(x, y);
}
```

The new code adds two new methods: `handleDebugInput()` and `moveSelectedSprite()` to the class. The `handleDebugInput()` method is added as the topmost call to ensure that the available user inputs are handled first before other update logic is executed. Otherwise, similar to the order of updating and rendering in the game loop, it might introduce some sort of lagging behind the user input and response to such an event. This method also takes the delta time as an argument.

It is used for the same purpose as it is used in `updateTestObjects()` — to apply incremental updates in relation to the time that has passed since the last frame was rendered. As a measure of precaution, the handling of our debug controls is skipped if the game is not run on a system that is identified as "desktop" by Libgdx. In this way, if we were to only target Android for our game, we could leave all the code for the debug controls in the game, without having to worry about it any time later.

The `Gdx.input` module provides an `isKeyPressed()` method that can be used to find out whether a key is (still) pressed. You have to use Libgdx's `Keys` class for valid constants to receive the correct results. So what we basically did here is ask whether any possible combination of the keys *A*, *D*, *W* and *S* is currently pressed. If a condition returns true, meaning that the key is really pressed, `moveSelectedSprite()` is called. The method requires two values that indicate the direction and magnitude of the desired motion that is to be applied to the selected sprite. The magnitude here is `sprMoveSpeed` with a constant value of 5 meters multiplied by the delta time, which means that our sprite will effectively be able to move at a speed of 5 meters per second.

You can now start the game at the desktop and try it out. Press any of the keys (*A*, *D*, *W*, or *S*) to move around the selected sprite in the game world.

The next controls to implement are the keys to reset the game world and to select the next sprite. Once again, add another line of code to `WorldController` to import a new class:

```
import com.badlogic.gdx.InputAdapter;
```

The `InputAdapter` class is a default implementation of the `InputListener` interface that provides various methods for handling input events. We want to use the adapter variant instead of the listener. This is because it is a convenient way of not being forced to implement all the interface methods when you know that you are not going to implement most of them anyway. It would be perfectly valid, of course, to still use the `InputListener` interface since it is just a matter of taste. Derive `WorldController` from `InputAdapter` by changing the existing class like this:

```
public class WorldController extends InputAdapter {
  // ...
}
```

Then, add the following code:

```
private void init () {
  Gdx.input.setInputProcessor(this);
  initTestObjects();
}
```

The `WorldController` class serves a second purpose from now on by also being an instance of the `InputListener` interface that can receive input events. Libgdx needs to be told about where it should send the received input events. This is done by calling `setInputProcessor()` from the `Gdx.Input` module. Since `WorldController` is also our `InputListener`, we can simply pass it into this method.

Now that Libgdx will send all the input events to our listener, we need to actually implement an event handler for each event we are interested in. In our case, this will only be the event where a key was released. Those events are handled in `keyUp()`. Override the adapter's default implementation of this method with the following code:

```
@Override
public boolean keyUp (int keycode) {
  // Reset game world
  if (keycode == Keys.R) {
    init();
    Gdx.app.debug(TAG, "Game world resetted");
  }
  // Select next sprite
  else if (keycode == Keys.SPACE) {
    selectedSprite = (selectedSprite + 1) % testSprites.length;
    Gdx.app.debug(TAG, "Sprite #" + selectedSprite + " selected");
  }
  return false;
}
```

The code will check whether `keycode` contains the code for either *R* or Space bar. If it is *R*, the initialization method `init()` of `WorldController` is called. This results in an internal restart of the game as if the whole game was restarted. If Space bar was pressed, the index stored in `selectedSprite` is incremented by one. The modulo operator (`%`) that is followed by the size of the array is used to wrap around the incremented value in case it exceeds the maximum value allowed.

This handler method is called only when there is an event. This is the huge difference as compared to the previous way we were handling user input. Both ways are correct, as it only depends on your situation and how you need the input in question to be handled.

You can now start the game and try it out on your desktop. You should be able to reset the game world with the *R* key. The test sprites should be shuffling around on every executed reset action. Selecting another sprite using the Space bar should make the previously selected one stop rotating and in turn let the newly selected sprite start rotating. You can also use the keys *A*, *D*, *W*, and *S* that will only move the currently selected sprite one at a time.

Adding CameraHelper

We now want to implement a helper class called `CameraHelper` that will assist us to manage and manipulate certain parameters of the camera we use to render the game world.

Here is the implementation of `CameraHelper`:

```
package com.packtpub.libgdx.canyonbunny.util;

import com.badlogic.gdx.graphics.OrthographicCamera;
import com.badlogic.gdx.graphics.g2d.Sprite;
import com.badlogic.gdx.math.MathUtils;
import com.badlogic.gdx.math.Vector2;

public class CameraHelper {
  private static final String TAG = CameraHelper.class.getName();

  private final float MAX_ZOOM_IN = 0.25f;
  private final float MAX_ZOOM_OUT = 10.0f;

  private Vector2 position;
  private float zoom;
  private Sprite target;

  public CameraHelper () {
    position = new Vector2();
    zoom = 1.0f;
  }

  public void update (float deltaTime) {
    if (!hasTarget()) return;

    position.x = target.getX() + target.getOriginX();
    position.y = target.getY() + target.getOriginY();
  }
```

```
public void setPosition (float x, float y) {
  this.position.set(x, y);
}
public Vector2 getPosition () { return position; }

public void addZoom (float amount) { setZoom(zoom + amount); }
public void setZoom (float zoom) {
  this.zoom = MathUtils.clamp(zoom, MAX_ZOOM_IN, MAX_ZOOM_OUT);
}
public float getZoom () { return zoom; }

public void setTarget (Sprite target) { this.target = target; }
public Sprite getTarget () { return target; }
public boolean hasTarget () { return target != null; }
public boolean hasTarget (Sprite target) {
  return hasTarget() && this.target.equals(target);
}

public void applyTo (OrthographicCamera camera) {
  camera.position.x = position.x;
  camera.position.y = position.y;
  camera.zoom = zoom;
  camera.update();
}
}
```

The helper class stores the current `position` and `zoom` value for the camera. Furthermore, it can follow one game object at a time when set as a target by calling `setTarget()`. The target can also be set to `null` to make the camera stop following at all. To find out what the last set target is, you can call `getTarget()`. Usually, you will want to do this for `null` checks or to find out whether the set target is a certain sprite. These checks are wrapped into the `hasTarget()` method and can be used either with or without a sprite argument to find out whether a certain target has been set if any. The `update()` method should be called on every update cycle to let it update the camera position whenever needed. The `applyTo()` method should always be called at the beginning of the rendering of a new frame as it takes care of updating the camera's attributes.

Adding camera debug controls using CameraHelper

The last step in this chapter will be to add the camera debug controls using the `CameraHelper` helper class. This will greatly improve your debugging abilities just because you can freely move around the game world, zoom in and out to/from game objects, and follow any game object.

Before we can use `CameraHelper`, we have to import it in `WorldController`:

```
import com.packtpub.libgdx.canyonbunny.util.CameraHelper;
```

After that, add the following code to `WorldController`:

```
public CameraHelper cameraHelper;

private void init () {
  Gdx.input.setInputProcessor(this);
  cameraHelper = new CameraHelper();
  initTestObjects();
}

public void update (float deltaTime) {
  handleDebugInput(deltaTime);
  updateTestObjects(deltaTime);
  cameraHelper.update(deltaTime);
}

@Override
public boolean keyUp (int keycode) {
  // Reset game world
  if (keycode == Keys.R) {
    init();
    Gdx.app.debug(TAG, "Game world resetted");
  }
  // Select next sprite
  else if (keycode == Keys.SPACE) {
    selectedSprite = (selectedSprite + 1) % testSprites.length;
    // Update camera's target to follow the currently
    // selected sprite
    if (cameraHelper.hasTarget()) {
      cameraHelper.setTarget(testSprites[selectedSprite]);
    }
    Gdx.app.debug(TAG, "Sprite #" + selectedSprite + "
      selected");
```

```
        }
        // Toggle camera follow
        else if (keycode == Keys.ENTER) {
            cameraHelper.setTarget(cameraHelper.hasTarget() ? null :
                testSprites[selectedSprite]);
            Gdx.app.debug(TAG, "Camera follow enabled: " +
                cameraHelper.hasTarget());
        }
        return false;
    }
```

The `WorldController` class now has an instance of `CameraHelper` that is initialized in `init()` and appended at the end of `update()`. Remember to continuously call `update()` of `CameraHelper` on every update cycle to ensure that its internal calculations are also performed. In the `keyUp()` method, we add two new functionalities. The first one is that the target of the camera helper is updated accordingly to a newly selected sprite. Secondly, when the *Enter* key is pressed, the target is toggled on and off.

Additionally, add the following code to `WorldRenderer`:

```
    public void renderTestObjects () {
        worldController.cameraHelper.applyTo(camera);
        batch.setProjectionMatrix(camera.combined);
        batch.begin();
        for(Sprite sprite : worldController.testSprites) {
            sprite.draw(batch);
        }
        batch.end();
    }
```

The `applyTo()` method should be called on each frame right at the beginning in the `renderTestObjects()` method of `WorldRenderer`. It will take care of correctly setting up the camera object that is passed.

You can now start the game on your desktop and try it out. To enable the camera follow feature, simply press the *Enter* key to toggle the state. A message is also logged to the console that informs you about the current state it is in. When camera follow is enabled, use the keys *A, D, W,* and *S* to move the selected sprite. However, the difference now is that the camera is following you to every location until camera follow is disabled again.

The last change to the code deals with adding a lot of new keys to control the camera in various ways.

Add the following code to `WorldController`:

```
private void handleDebugInput (float deltaTime) {
  if (Gdx.app.getType() != ApplicationType.Desktop) return;

  // Selected Sprite Controls
  float sprMoveSpeed = 5 * deltaTime;
  if (Gdx.input.isKeyPressed(Keys.A)) moveSelectedSprite(
    -sprMoveSpeed, 0);
  if (Gdx.input.isKeyPressed(Keys.D))
    moveSelectedSprite(sprMoveSpeed, 0);
  if (Gdx.input.isKeyPressed(Keys.W)) moveSelectedSprite(0,
    sprMoveSpeed);
  if (Gdx.input.isKeyPressed(Keys.S)) moveSelectedSprite(0,
    -sprMoveSpeed);

  // Camera Controls (move)
  float camMoveSpeed = 5 * deltaTime;
  float camMoveSpeedAccelerationFactor = 5;
  if (Gdx.input.isKeyPressed(Keys.SHIFT_LEFT)) camMoveSpeed *=
    camMoveSpeedAccelerationFactor;
  if (Gdx.input.isKeyPressed(Keys.LEFT)) moveCamera(-camMoveSpeed,
    0);
  if (Gdx.input.isKeyPressed(Keys.RIGHT)) moveCamera(camMoveSpeed,
    0);
  if (Gdx.input.isKeyPressed(Keys.UP)) moveCamera(0, camMoveSpeed);
  if (Gdx.input.isKeyPressed(Keys.DOWN)) moveCamera(0,
    -camMoveSpeed);
  if (Gdx.input.isKeyPressed(Keys.BACKSPACE))
    cameraHelper.setPosition(0, 0);

  // Camera Controls (zoom)
  float camZoomSpeed = 1 * deltaTime;
  float camZoomSpeedAccelerationFactor = 5;
  if (Gdx.input.isKeyPressed(Keys.SHIFT_LEFT)) camZoomSpeed *=
    camZoomSpeedAccelerationFactor;
  if (Gdx.input.isKeyPressed(Keys.COMMA))
    cameraHelper.addZoom(camZoomSpeed);
  if (Gdx.input.isKeyPressed(Keys.PERIOD)) cameraHelper.addZoom(
    -camZoomSpeed);
  if (Gdx.input.isKeyPressed(Keys.SLASH)) cameraHelper.setZoom(1);
}

private void moveCamera (float x, float y) {
  x += cameraHelper.getPosition().x;
  y += cameraHelper.getPosition().y;
  cameraHelper.setPosition(x, y);
}
```

There are two new code blocks to control the moving and zooming features of the camera in `handleDebugInput()`. They look and also work similar to the block above them that deals with the controls for the selected sprite. Keys are checked for their state and if pressed, the respective action is taken.

Camera controls (move):

- The arrow keys left, right, up, and down control the movement of the camera.
- The magnitude of motion is set to 500 percent while the *Shift* key is pressed.
- Pressing the *Backspace* key resets the camera position to the origin (0, 0) of the game world.

Camera controls (zoom):

- The comma (,) and period (.) keys control the zoom level of the camera.
- The magnitude of motion is set to 500 percent while the *Shift* key is pressed.
- The slash (/) key resets the zoom level to 100 percent (the original position).

The `moveCamera()` method is used for executing relative movements of the camera similar to what `moveSelectedSprite()` is doing by calling sprite's `translate()` method.

Summary

In this chapter, we learned how to set up the Canyon Bunny project. We used an UML class diagram to structure the game into manageable and logical pieces. The first classes have been implemented to lay the foundation for later extensions to the game. The discussion about the implementation details took place at a gradual and steady pace so that we could learn from the development process as a whole instead of only talking about accomplished facts.

In the next chapter, we will gather all the resources (assets) needed for Canyon Bunny, including graphics, audio files, and level data. We will also learn how to prepare data for use in our game.

4
Gathering Resources

In this chapter we are going to gather and prepare the resources for Canyon Bunny to spice up the visual appearance of the game. We will do this using a collection of image files that have been created beforehand. You will learn how to replace the Android default launcher icon that comes with every new Android project. Additionally, you will be introduced to the technique of texture atlases and also learn how to create and use them in conjunction with Libgdx.

You will learn why it is important to keep track of your assets at runtime and how to make it an almost hassle-free task by delegating most of it to Libgdx. Hassle-free means that you will not have to worry about keeping track when unloading or reloading your assets become necessary. Instead, Libgdx only needs to know what assets should be loaded to manage them transparently for you in the background.

Organizing the access to loaded assets is another important topic. You will learn how to create your own Assets class that allows convenient and structured access from anywhere in the game code.

After this, you will put everything together. To verify that the images of the game objects are loaded and work just fine, you will replace the test sprite texture from *Chapter 3, Configuring the Game*, with a random selection of some of the loaded images.

Finally, you will learn how to handle level data. This will enable you to create your own game world and populate it with game objects to your liking.

 All assets shown and discussed in this book, including any other project files, can be downloaded from Packt's website at http://www.packtpub.com/learning-libgdx-game-development/book.

Setting a custom Android application icon

First we want to replace the default launcher icon that came with the generated Canyon Bunny Android project. There is a special directory called `res` that resides in the Android `CanyonBunny-android` project. It contains resource files that are exclusively available to the Android application.

You should see the following three folders starting with "drawable" in names:

- `drawable-ldpi` (low density screen)
- `drawable-mdpi` (medium density screen)
- `drawable-hdpi` (high density screen)

These folders are used by Android to support different screen sizes and resolutions resulting in different screen densities. For the sake of simplicity, we will ignore the whole topic of screen support and create a special common folder called `drawable`. Android will use the contents of this folder regardless of the screen density detected.

The following screenshot shows the default launcher icon called `ic_launcher.png` that our application is currently using:

Now, delete all three files of the default launcher icon from `drawable-ldpi`, `drawable-mdpi`, and `drawable-hdpi`.

The following screenshot is the image we want to use for the application icon of Canyon Bunny:

Copy the new `ic_launcher.png` icon to the common `drawable` folder. Since we have not changed the icon's name, it will work without any additional changes. Also, do not forget to change the icon's reference in the `AndroidManifest.xml` file if you want to rename it. The corresponding line should look like the following listing:

```
<application
    android:icon="@drawable/ic_launcher"
    ... />
```

The application icon is now replaced with our very own Canyon Bunny application icon.

The following screenshot shows the installed application on Google Nexus 4:

The support of different screens and resource sizes is a complex topic of its own, which is beyond the scope of this book. For more information, check out the official Android Developer websites at `http://developer.android.com/guide/practices/screens_support.html` and `http://developer.android.com/design/style/iconography.html`.

Creating texture atlases

Before we start creating a texture atlas, let us first find out what this technique is actually good for. A texture atlas (also known as a sprite sheet) is just an ordinary image file that can be rendered to the screen like any other image. So what makes it so special? It is used as a container image that holds several smaller subimages arranged in such a way that they do not overlap each other and still fit into the size of the texture atlas. This way, we can greatly reduce the amount of textures that are sent to the graphics processor, which will significantly improve the overall render performance. The texture atlases are especially useful for games where a lot of small and different images are rendered at once. The reason for this is that switching between different textures is a very costly process. Each time you change textures while rendering, new data needs to be sent into video memory. If you use the same texture for everything, this can be avoided.

The texture atlases will not only increase the frame rate of the game significantly but will also allow us to use subimages as **Non-Power-Of-Two** (**NPOT**) textures. However, the texture atlas' size should always be a power-of-two in each dimension to avoid issues on hardware that may not support NPOT textures. The reason why our subimages can be of arbitrary size is that the power-of-two rule only applies to textures that are loaded into video memory. Therefore, when we actually render a subimage, we are still using the texture atlas, which is a power-of-two texture as our pixel source; however, we will only use a certain part of it as our final texture to draw something.

Take a look at the following screenshot that shows all the images of our game objects in separate image files:

You might wonder why the **cloud** and **mountain** images in the preceding screenshot are filled with plain white color. This is because they contain only white and transparent pixels, so it is indeed hard or rather impossible to make out the actual image information on a white background, as it usually is in print media. Therefore, all the following images of our game objects will be shown with an added gray background to rectify this small display issue. However, the actual image files still remain unchanged as shown in the preceding screenshot.

Libgdx has a built-in texture packer that we will use to automate the process of creating and refreshing the texture atlas for Canyon Bunny. We will put all the game's object images shown in the preceding screenshot into the atlas to get the following result:

The images have been nicely arranged on the atlas without any overlapping. The purple border around each image is a debugging feature of Libgdx's texture packer that can be toggled on and off. It can be used to visualize the true size of your subimages which otherwise can be difficult to see if the subimages use transparency. Good examples of this are the **cloud** and **mountain** images in our texture atlas. Also when padding is enabled, which is the default by using two pixels for each direction, you would barely see the difference without the enabled debugging lines.

Padding your images inside a texture atlas helps you avoid an issue that is known as texture bleeding (also known as pixel bleeding) while texture filtering and/or mip-mapping is enabled.

The texture filter mode can be set to smooth pixels of a texture. This is basically done by looking for the pixel information which is next to the current pixel that is to be smoothened. The problem here is that if there is a pixel of a neighboring subimage, its pixels may also be taken into account, which results in the unwanted effect of pixels bleeding from one subimage into another.

For the texture packer, some preparations need to be done beforehand since it is a so-called extension to Libgdx that is not a part of the core functionality. Go to `C:\libgdx\` and extract `extensions/gdx-tools.jar` from the `libgdx-0.9.7.zip` file you downloaded earlier in *Chapter 1, Introduction to Libgdx and Project Setup*. Put the `gdx-tools.jar` file in the `CanyonBunny-desktop/libs` subfolder. Next, the extension has to be added to **Build Path** in Eclipse. In Eclipse, right-click on the **CanyonBunny-desktop** project and navigate to **Build Path | Configure Build Path ... | Libraries**. Then, click on the **Add JARs ...** button, which will open a new window titled **JAR selection** that shows a list of projects. In this list, search for the **CanyonBunny-desktop** project and expand it until you reach the `libs` subfolder. Finally, select the newly added `gdx-tools.jar` extension and confirm each opened window by clicking on their **OK** buttons.

We will now add the code to automate the generation process of the texture atlas. Create a new folder called `assets-raw` under `CanyonBunny-desktop`. Also, add a subfolder named `assets-raw/images`. This is where we put our image files to be included in the texture atlas.

Next, add the following two lines of code to import the `TexturePacker2` and its `Settings` class:

```
import com.badlogic.gdx.tools.imagepacker.TexturePacker2;
import com.badlogic.gdx.tools.imagepacker.TexturePacker2.Settings;
```

Then, apply the following changes to `Main` in `CanyonBunny-desktop`:

```
public class Main {
  private static boolean rebuildAtlas = true;
  private static boolean drawDebugOutline = true;

  public static void main (String[] args) {
    if (rebuildAtlas) {
      Settings settings = new Settings();
```

```
        settings.maxWidth = 1024;
        settings.maxHeight = 1024;
        settings.debug = drawDebugOutline;
        TexturePacker2.process(settings, "assets-raw/images",
            "../CanyonBunny-android/assets/images",
            "canyonbunny.pack");
    }

    LwjglApplicationConfiguration cfg =
    new LwjglApplicationConfiguration();
    cfg.title = "CanyonBunny";
    cfg.useGL20 = false;
    cfg.width = 800;
    cfg.height = 480;
    new LwjglApplication(new CanyonBunnyMain(), cfg);
    }
}
```

The added code provides a convenient way to rebuild the texture atlas every time the game is run on the desktop. The rebuildAtlas variable controls whether the atlas is rebuilt on startup or not by setting it to true or false. Using the TexturePacker2 class to create the texture atlas is pretty straightforward. It contains a static method called process() that takes an optional Settings object to configure the way the texture atlas will be generated as well as three parameters that are mandatory. The first mandatory parameter is the source folder that contains our image files. The second one is the destination folder where the generated texture atlas should be created. And finally, the third parameter is the name of the description file that is needed to load and use the texture atlas.

The source folder (in our example, assets-raw/images) is specified relative to the desktop project since the texture packer code is executed from there. The destination folder (in our example, ../CanyonBunny-android/assets/images) is also specified relative to the desktop project. However, the resulting texture atlas has to be put into the assets folder of the Android project so that it becomes available to all platform-specific projects. The description file (in our example, canyonbunny.pack) will be created by TexturePacker2 and will contain all the information about all the subimages, such as their location in the texture atlas, their size, and offsets.

The `maxWidth` and `maxHeight` variables of the `Settings` instance define the maximum dimensions (in pixels) for the texture atlas. Always make sure that a single subimage does not exceed the maximum size of the atlas either in width or height or both dimensions. Padding the subimages in the atlas will reduce the available size a little bit more, so make sure to take this factor into account also. The `debug` variable controls whether the debug lines should be added to the atlas or not. We use the `drawDebugOutline` variable to set the value for debugging. The static variables `rebuildAtlas` and `drawDebugOutline` are there just for our convenience to make these two behavior controls stand out a bit more, because we usually change these variables every now and then while debugging our game.

If the texture packer cannot fit all subimages into a single texture, it will automatically split them up into several texture atlases. However, there is a chance that subimages are distributed in an unfavorable way between those atlases, which in turn could have an impact on render performance.

Libgdx's texture packer has a very smart feature to tackle this type of problem. All you need to do is group the subimages in their own subfolder in `assets-raw`. This way the texture packer will create one image file per subfolder that belongs to the texture atlas. You have to use the full path to the subimage if you want to use this functionality; for example, a subimage `assets-raw/items/gold_coin.png` would be referenced as `items/gold_coin`.

Now you know how to create texture atlases in code. This approach mostly works very well, but it is not very user friendly in terms of seeing the outcome directly when a setting or an image is changed in the atlas. Fortunately, there is already a nice tool called **TexturePacker-GUI** that has been developed by Aurélien Ribon. This tool is directly designed for Libgdx to work with its texture packer.

Check out the official project website
at `https://code.google.com/p/libgdx-texturepacker-gui/`.

The following is a screenshot taken from the project's website which shows the tool
in action:

There is also a popular commercial tool called **TexturePacker** for creating texture
atlases. This tool has been developed by Andreas Löw and is available for all
three major platforms. For more information, check out the official website at
`http://www.codeandweb.com/texturepacker`.

Loading and tracking assets

The next step after making assets, such as making our texture atlas available to the
game, is to load and use them. Loading an asset such as a texture can be as simple as
the following line of code:

```
Texture texture = new
    Texture(Gdx.files.internal("texture.png"));
```

In the preceding example, we ask Libgdx to get an internal file handle to the `texture.png` file. Invoking an internal file means that Libgdx has to resolve the file's path by scanning the `assets` folder of the game. Then, the handle is passed over as an argument to the constructor of the `Texture` class to instantiate a new object of this type. This texture instance can now be directly rendered to the screen with another line of code, as shown in the following listing:

```
batch.draw(texture, x, y);
```

Obviously, working with assets is basically very easy. However, this matter becomes a lot more complicated when we want to use several assets. It gets even worse if want to run the game on Android. As we have learned in earlier chapters, there are pause and resume events that may involve a so-called context loss. When a context loss occurs on Android, it means that the operating system has decided to forcefully free the memory that was occupied with your loaded assets. Therefore, directly accessing your assets after a context loss would immediately crash the resumed game. To prevent these crashes, you need to reload your assets before accessing them again. Furthermore, you should always free the memory when your game is no longer using a certain asset by calling its `dispose()` method as shown in the following listing:

```
texture.dispose();
```

You probably already guessed that this is not going to be much fun since you have to worry about all the housekeeping for loading, reloading, and unloading while using lots of assets; especially since these actions will add up very quickly with each new asset that will be used. This is one of the reasons why Libgdx provides a manager class for this task, which is called `AssetManager`. It allows you to delegate the work of keeping a list of the loaded assets to the manager. The manager is also able to asynchronously load new assets, which simply means that loading is done in the background and therefore does not stop the updating and rendering to the screen. This is a very useful functionality; for example, it allows for rendering and updating a progress bar showing the current loading status. Nonetheless, the actual loading of our assets still has to be done ourselves. For this reason, we are going to create our own `Assets` class, which will also help us to structure our loaded assets in logical units and make them accessible from everywhere in the game code.

Organizing assets

We will now create our own `Assets` class to organize and structure our assets. First, add a new constant to the `Constants` class that points to the description file of the texture atlas:

```
public class Constants {
  // Visible game world is 5 meters wide
  public static final float VIEWPORT_WIDTH = 5.0f;
  // Visible game world is 5 meters tall
  public static final float VIEWPORT_HEIGHT = 5.0f;
  // Location of description file for texture atlas
  public static final String TEXTURE_ATLAS_OBJECTS =
    "images/canyonbunny.pack";
}
```

Next, create a new file for the `Assets` class and add the following code:

```
package com.packtpub.libgdx.canyonbunny.game;

import com.badlogic.gdx.Gdx;
import com.badlogic.gdx.assets.AssetErrorListener;
import com.badlogic.gdx.assets.AssetManager;
import com.badlogic.gdx.graphics.g2d.TextureAtlas;
import com.badlogic.gdx.utils.Disposable;
import com.packtpub.libgdx.canyonbunny.util.Constants;

public class Assets implements Disposable, AssetErrorListener {
  public static final String TAG = Assets.class.getName();
  public static final Assets instance = new Assets();
  private AssetManager assetManager;

  // singleton: prevent instantiation from other classes
  private Assets () {}

  public void init (AssetManager assetManager) {
    this.assetManager = assetManager;
    // set asset manager error handler
    assetManager.setErrorListener(this);
    // load texture atlas
    assetManager.load(Constants.TEXTURE_ATLAS_OBJECTS,
      TextureAtlas.class);
    // start loading assets and wait until finished
    assetManager.finishLoading();
```

```
      Gdx.app.debug(TAG, "# of assets loaded: "
        + assetManager.getAssetNames().size);
      for (String a : assetManager.getAssetNames())
        Gdx.app.debug(TAG, "asset: " + a);
    }

    @Override
    public void dispose () {
      assetManager.dispose();
    }

    @Override
    public void error (String filename, Class type,
      Throwable throwable) {
      Gdx.app.error(TAG, "Couldn't load asset '"
        + filename + "'", (Exception)throwable);
    }
  }
```

There is quite a lot going on in the preceding code, so let us break it down. First, notice that this class is using a design pattern called **singleton**. Simply put, a singleton class ensures that only a single instance of it will exist; hence the name singleton. This makes sense here because there is no reason to have multiple instances that point to the same resources. A singleton is implemented by defining a private constructor that prevents other classes from instantiating it. The `instance` variable holds the actual instance of the class and uses the `public static final` modifiers which allow read-only access, and now also poses the one-and-only way to access this class at all. The static-ness of this class allows us to access it from virtually anywhere in the game code without having to pass over its reference to every method where we will be using it.

A **singleton** can be implemented to do either lazy or eager initialization. Using lazy initialization means that the instance is created only when it is requested for the very first time. Any subsequent requests will always yield the exact same instance. In contrast, eager initialization means that the instance is directly created on startup.

For more information, refer to the book *Design Patterns: Elements of Reusable Object-Oriented Software* by *Erich Gamma, Richard Helm, Ralph Johnson,* and *John Vlissides* (Gang of Four).

The `init()` method will be called at the very beginning when the game starts. It will initialize the asset manager, which in turn will load all assets. Loading assets using the asset manager is simply done by calling its `load()` method. The method takes the path and filename as the first argument and the corresponding class to instantiate as the second argument. The loading process is started by calling `finishLoading()`. This is a blocking method that waits until all assets have been fully loaded. After that, we always print the number of loaded assets and their names to the console to easily check if it is working the way we expect it to work.

The `Assets` class implements the `Disposable` and `AssetErrorListener` interfaces. Since we know that assets should always be unloaded when they are no longer needed, we have implemented the `dispose()` method to delegate these requests to the asset manager. The `error()` method will be called whenever an error has occurred in the asset manager. However, before the asset manager will call our implementation of the interface, it needs to be told about the class that implements the `AssetErrorListener` interface by calling the asset manager's `setErrorListener()` method. We are using the `error()` method to print error logs only to the console. You could add additional code here to handle errors and therefore avoid the game from crashing in this case.

The next step is to retrieve our subimages from the loaded texture atlas. In general, this is done by calling the atlas's `findRegion()` method, which takes the asset's name as an argument. The method returns an object of the `AtlasRegion` class that contains information about the subimage found and also some additional information about how it is stored in the atlas.

Now, for example, if we wanted to find a subimage that is stored in `assets/my_image.png`, we would have to write the following code:

```
atlas.findRegion("my_image");
```

Note that the prefix `assets/` is always omitted just like any file extension, such as `.png`. However, the subfolder needs to be specified. The method will silently return `null` if the lookup fails. Therefore, be sure to double-check your spelling of the filename in this case. One very important fact to know about this method is that the lookup of a subimage is an expensive function call. Consequently, caching the results after their initial lookup is highly recommended to avoid severe performance issues.

Add the following line of code to `Assets` to import the `AtlasRegion` class:

```
import com.badlogic.gdx.graphics.g2d.TextureAtlas.AtlasRegion;
```

The following is a step-by-step implementation of several smaller inner classes of the `Assets` class. These classes allow us to structure (or group) the subimages in logical units and also to permanently store (that is, cache) the looked up references.

We will begin with the player character and we will call its class `AssetBunny`. It contains a member variable called `head` that holds the reference to the texture atlas subimage that originates from the `bunny_head.png` file. The lookup is done inside the constructor of the inner class. The constructor takes a reference of the corresponding atlas in which it will find the atlas region it wants.

Add the following inner class to the `Assets` class:

```
public class AssetBunny {
  public final AtlasRegion head;
  public AssetBunny (TextureAtlas atlas) {
    head = atlas.findRegion("bunny_head");
  }
}
```

Next is the rock game object, which represents the platform in our game world. It consists of two image files: `rock_edge.png` and `rock_middle.png`. Both images get their own variable in the inner class called `AssetRock`.

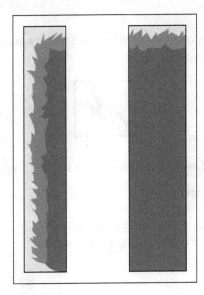

Add the following inner class to the `Assets` class:

```
public class AssetRock {
  public final AtlasRegion edge;
  public final AtlasRegion middle;
  public AssetRock (TextureAtlas atlas) {
    edge = atlas.findRegion("rock_edge");
    middle = atlas.findRegion("rock_middle");
  }
}
```

Next is the gold coin. Its original filename is `item_gold_coin.png` and the inner class is named `AssetGoldCoin`.

Add the following inner class to the `Assets` class:

```
public class AssetGoldCoin {
  public final AtlasRegion goldCoin;
  public AssetGoldCoin (TextureAtlas atlas) {
    goldCoin = atlas.findRegion("item_gold_coin");
  }
}
```

Next is the feather item. Its original filename is `item_feather.png` and the inner class is named `AssetFeather`.

Add the following inner class to the `Assets` class:

```
public class AssetFeather {
  public final AtlasRegion feather;
  public AssetFeather (TextureAtlas atlas) {
    feather = atlas.findRegion("item_feather");
  }
}
```

Next is the last inner class called `AssetLevelDecoration`. It contains all the decorative images that only add to the look and feel of the level. This collection of assets consists of three differently shaped clouds (`cloud01.png`, `cloud02.png`, and `cloud03.png`), a very wide mountain that spans across two image halves (`mountain_left.png` and `mountain_right.png`), and an overlay (`water_overlay.png`) that will be stretched along the x axis to give the illusion of water existing everywhere in the game world.

The overlay image for the water could have been shrunk down to a total width of one pixel because the content repeats on the x axis along which we plan to stretch it anyway. Furthermore, it makes no difference to the render performance how far an image is stretched. However, it is easier to show you an image in a printed book that is wider than one pixel.

Add the following inner class to the `Assets` class:

```
public class AssetLevelDecoration {
  public final AtlasRegion cloud01;
  public final AtlasRegion cloud02;
  public final AtlasRegion cloud03;
  public final AtlasRegion mountainLeft;
  public final AtlasRegion mountainRight;
  public final AtlasRegion waterOverlay;

  public AssetLevelDecoration (TextureAtlas atlas) {
    cloud01 = atlas.findRegion("cloud01");
    cloud02 = atlas.findRegion("cloud02");
    cloud03 = atlas.findRegion("cloud03");
    mountainLeft = atlas.findRegion("mountain_left");
    mountainRight = atlas.findRegion("mountain_right");
    waterOverlay = atlas.findRegion("water_overlay");
  }
}
```

So far, we have established a way to group our assets in logic units which also cache their references after their initial look up. What is still missing is the code that uses our new inner classes.

Add the following two imports to the `Assets` class:

```
import com.badlogic.gdx.graphics.Texture;
import com.badlogic.gdx.graphics.Texture.TextureFilter;
```

Then, add the following new code to the same class:

```
public AssetBunny bunny;
public AssetRock rock;
public AssetGoldCoin goldCoin;
public AssetFeather feather;
public AssetLevelDecoration levelDecoration;

public void init (AssetManager assetManager) {
  this.assetManager = assetManager;
  // set asset manager error handler
  assetManager.setErrorListener(this);
  // load texture atlas
  assetManager.load(Constants.TEXTURE_ATLAS_OBJECTS,
    TextureAtlas.class);
  // start loading assets and wait until finished
  assetManager.finishLoading();

  Gdx.app.debug(TAG, "# of assets loaded: "
    + assetManager.getAssetNames().size);
  for (String a : assetManager.getAssetNames())
    Gdx.app.debug(TAG, "asset: " + a);

  TextureAtlas atlas =
    assetManager.get(Constants.TEXTURE_ATLAS_OBJECTS);

  // enable texture filtering for pixel smoothing
  for (Texture t : atlas.getTextures())
    t.setFilter(TextureFilter.Linear, TextureFilter.Linear);

  // create game resource objects
  bunny = new AssetBunny(atlas);
  rock = new AssetRock(atlas);
  goldCoin = new AssetGoldCoin(atlas);
  feather = new AssetFeather(atlas);
  levelDecoration = new AssetLevelDecoration(atlas);
}
```

Now the Assets class has one member variable for each instance of our inner classes. In the init() method, we first retrieve the reference to the loaded texture atlas by calling the get() method of the asset manager. Next, we iterate through all textures of the atlas (which currently is just one) and set the texture filter mode to TextureFilter.Linear. This will enable smoothing of the pixels when the texture is rendered. The reason why we pass this constant value twice to the method is because the mode has to be set for both cases, minification and magnification, where a rendered texture is either scaled down or up from its original size. The default texture filter mode is set to TextureFilter.Nearest for both cases.

The following screenshot is an example to compare the difference between both modes:

Finally, we create each instance of our inner classes and pass them the reference to the texture atlas.

Testing assets

We are now ready to test our `Assets` class with the rest of the already built game code.

Add the following two imports to `CanyonBunnyMain`:

```
import com.badlogic.gdx.assets.AssetManager;
import com.packtpub.libgdx.canyonbunny.game.Assets;
```

After that, we add the calls to load, reload, and unload our assets with the following changes to the code:

```
@Override
public void create () {
  // Set Libgdx log level to DEBUG
  Gdx.app.setLogLevel(Application.LOG_DEBUG);
  // Load assets
  Assets.instance.init(new AssetManager());
  // Initialize controller and renderer
  worldController = new WorldController();
  worldRenderer = new WorldRenderer(worldController);
}

@Override
public void resume () {
  Assets.instance.init(new AssetManager());
  paused = false;
```

```
  }

  @Override
  public void dispose () {
    worldRenderer.dispose();
    Assets.instance.dispose();
  }
```

In `create()`, we instantiate a new `AssetManager` object and pass it to the `init()` method of our `Assets` class. Note that we initialized `AssetManager` before `WorldController` is created so that our assets are loaded and ready to be accessed. Remember, an instance of our class does already exist and can be directly accessed through the instance variable. In `resume()`, we actually do the exact same as we did in `create()`; as for Android, the context loss requires all assets to be reloaded when resumed. Finally in `dispose()`, we call the `dipose()` method of our Assets class, which in turn delegates this request to its internally stored instance of the asset manager.

The final change will be to replace our test sprites with the ones from the texture atlas. Add the following two imports to `WorldController`:

```
import com.badlogic.gdx.graphics.g2d.TextureRegion;
import com.badlogic.gdx.utils.Array;
```

After that, apply the modifications shown in the following code:

```
private void initTestObjects () {
  // Create new array for 5 sprites
  testSprites = new Sprite[5];
  // Create a list of texture regions
  Array<TextureRegion> regions = new Array<TextureRegion>();
  regions.add(Assets.instance.bunny.head);
  regions.add(Assets.instance.feather.feather);
  regions.add(Assets.instance.goldCoin.goldCoin);
  // Create new sprites using a random texture region
  for (int i = 0; i < testSprites.length; i++) {
    Sprite spr = new Sprite(regions.random());
    // Define sprite size to be 1m x 1m in game world
    spr.setSize(1, 1);
    // Set origin to sprite's center
    spr.setOrigin(spr.getWidth() / 2.0f,
      spr.getHeight() / 2.0f);
    // Calculate random position for sprite
    float randomX = MathUtils.random(-2.0f, 2.0f);
    float randomY = MathUtils.random(-2.0f, 2.0f);
    spr.setPosition(randomX, randomY);
```

```
    // Put new sprite into array
    testSprites[i] = spr;
}
// Set first sprite as selected one
selectedSprite = 0;
}
```

We are still creating five sprites in `initTestObjects()` as before. The difference is that we are now using the bunny head, feather, and gold coin texture regions. To make our test a little bit more interesting, we create a dynamic array called `regions` that holds all the texture regions we want to use. Then, inside the set up loop we create a `Sprite` instance with a randomly picked texture region from the dynamic array. This results in a random number of similar looking objects in the test scene.

You can now run the game to test it out. The following is a screenshot that shows a possible outcome due to the randomness we built in:

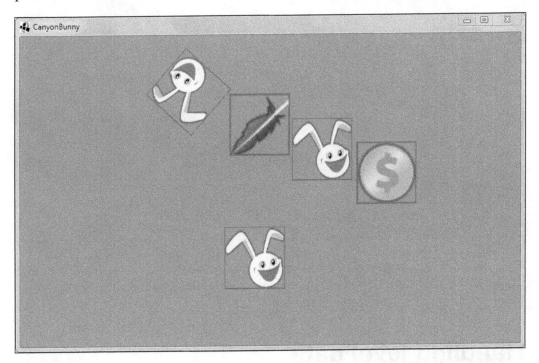

As you can see, we left the debug outlines enabled. You can easily disable them by just flipping the `drawDebugOutlines` variable from `true` to `false` in the `Main` class of the `desktop` project. Do not forget to set `rebuildAtlas` to `true` for at least one run of the `desktop` project to refresh the texture atlas.

Sometimes your changes to the texture atlas might appear to have no effect at all. If this is the case, Eclipse may not have detected a change to the texture atlas file and therefore did not rebuild the project binaries. A second restart of the game does help from time to time. Alternatively, you can always force Eclipse to rebuild the project by navigating to **Project | Clean...** to clean the project from all compiled files.

The resulting scene should now look similar to the following screenshot:

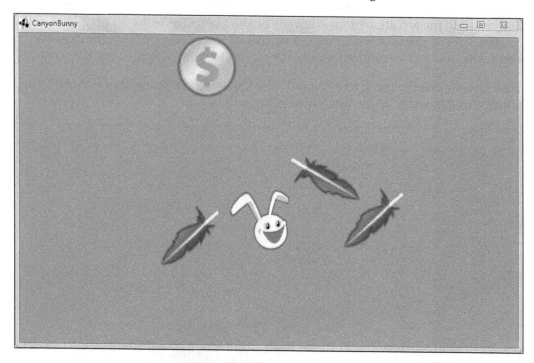

Great! We now have super cool graphics in our game and we can still do all the other things we built earlier, such as moving the camera, selecting an object and moving it, following an object, or zooming in and out.

Handling level data

It is now time to think about how we can handle level data to lay out our levels, put objects into them at certain positions, define a starting position, and so on. This usually implies a lot of work before visible results will appear because creating levels requires some kind of a tool to create, modify, save, and load their level data. Furthermore, before we can even load or save levels, we will have to define an appropriate file format to describe the data of a level.

Luckily, there is an easy route as long as we keep our requirements simple enough. We will not have to build our own level editor. Instead, we will use a drawing program such as **GNU Image Manipulation Program** (**GIMP**) (http://www.gimp.org/) or Paint.NET (http://www.getpaint.net/) to draw an image where each pixel's color represents some object that is still to be defined. The position of a pixel in this image will also represent the position in our game world. Job done! We just defined our level format in a somewhat creative way by reusing an already existing format and overlaying it with our way of interpreting the content.

The following is a level diagram to give you a better idea of how this works:

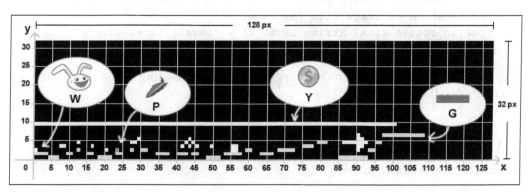

Since we are dealing here with an image that is not going to be rendered to the screen, we will also not add it to the texture atlas. Therefore, we are bound to the power-of-two rule once again, so be sure to keep that in mind. In the preceding diagram, the dimension of the level is 128 pixels times 32 pixels in width and height. The diagram has been overlaid with a Cartesian coordinate system for better visibility of the position of a pixel (or object in terms of our future interpretation of this information) inside the level.

The following is a list that defines the mapping between pixel colors and game objects:

- **W**: This stands for white and is the starting position of the player (Spawn Point)
- **P**: This stands for purple and represents the feather
- **Y**: This stands for yellow and represents the gold coin
- **G**: This stands for green and represents the rock

The black background represents empty spaces in the game world.

Create a subfolder in the `assets` folder named `levels` and copy the `level-01.png` level file into it. After that, add a new constant to the `Constants` class:

```
public class Constants {
  // Visible game world is 5 meters wide
  public static final float VIEWPORT_WIDTH = 5.0f;
  // Visible game world is 5 meters tall
  public static final float VIEWPORT_HEIGHT = 5.0f;
  // Location of description file for texture atlas
  public static final String TEXTURE_ATLAS_OBJECTS =
    "images/canyonbunny.pack";
  // Location of image file for level 01
  public static final String LEVEL_01 = "levels/level-01.png";
}
```

This concludes our preparations for the game level. The loading of the level data will be covered in the next chapter.

Summary

In this chapter, we have learned:

- How to set a custom Android app icon for our game
- How to use texture atlases and why they are useful
- How to load, track, and organize assets

We have combined our new `Assets` class with the existing game code and verified that we can now use textured objects while the remaining functionalities still work.

A brief introduction about handling level data has been given. We have defined our editing tool to be any drawing program and declared certain color values for pixels to represent a specific game object in the game world.

In the next chapter, we will discuss how to create a scene in order to visualize the actual game world. This includes writing a level loader that reads, interprets, and acts on the image data according to the rules we have just defined.

5
Making a Scene

In this chapter we will make a scene that shows the actual game world of Canyon Bunny. The game world will be composed of several game objects that all share common attributes and functionalities. However, the way these objects are rendered to the scene varies from simply drawing its assigned texture to compound rendering using two or more textures.

All the game objects are represented in pixel colors in an image file whose format has been defined in the last chapter. The next step will be to implement a level loader that is able to parse the level information stored in our level image file level-01.png.

After implementing the game objects and the mentioned level loader, we will put the new code into action by adding it to our world controller and renderer respectively.

The following screenshot illustrates an example scene of what the game will look like at this point:

As a last addition, we will add a **Graphical User Interface (GUI)** to the scene that overlays the game world. Sometimes this is also called a **Head-Up Display (HUD)**, but we will use the term GUI here. The GUI will show the player's score, the number of extra lives left, and an **FPS** counter to measure the performance of the game.

Creating game objects

Before we start implementing each individual game object, we will create an abstract class called `AbstractGameObject`. It will hold all the common attributes and functionalities that each of our game objects will inherit from.

 You might want to check the Canyon Bunny class diagram in *Chapter 3, Configuring the Game,* again to get an overview of the class hierarchy of the game objects.

Create a new file for the `AbstractGameObject` class and add the following code:

```
package com.packtpub.libgdx.canyonbunny.game.objects;
import com.badlogic.gdx.graphics.g2d.SpriteBatch;
import com.badlogic.gdx.math.Vector2;

public abstract class AbstractGameObject {
  public Vector2 position;
  public Vector2 dimension;
  public Vector2 origin;
  public Vector2 scale;
  public float rotation;
  public AbstractGameObject () {
    position = new Vector2();
    dimension = new Vector2(1, 1);
    origin = new Vector2();
    scale = new Vector2(1, 1);
    rotation = 0;
  }

  public void update (float deltaTime) {}

  public abstract void render (SpriteBatch batch);
}
```

This class is able to store the position, dimension, origin, scale factor, and angle of rotation of a game object. Its methods `update()` and `render()` will be called inside our world controller and renderer accordingly. The default implementation for updating a game object is currently empty. So the game objects inheriting from `AbstractGameObject` will do nothing when updated. For rendering, a specific implementation has to be provided for each game object because we defined the `render()` method to be `abstract`.

The rock object

The rock game object basically consists of three distinct parts: a left edge, a middle part, and a right edge. There is one specialty about the middle part, as it must be repeatable to be able to create different rocks with arbitrary lengths. Furthermore, the image for the right edge can be easily created by mirroring the image of the left edge. This means that we will need only two textures from our texture atlas to draw a complete rock of any size.

Create a new file for the `Rock` class and add the following code:

```
package com.packtpub.libgdx.canyonbunny.game.objects;

import com.badlogic.gdx.graphics.g2d.SpriteBatch;
import com.badlogic.gdx.graphics.g2d.TextureRegion;
import com.packtpub.libgdx.canyonbunny.game.Assets;

public class Rock extends AbstractGameObject {
  private TextureRegion regEdge;
```

```
      private TextureRegion regMiddle;
      private int length;

      public Rock () {
         init();
      }

      private void init () {
         dimension.set(1, 1.5f);
         regEdge = Assets.instance.rock.edge;
         regMiddle = Assets.instance.rock.middle;
         // Start length of this rock
         setLength(1);
      }

      public void setLength (int length) {
         this.length = length;
      }

      public void increaseLength (int amount) {
         setLength(length + amount);
      }
   }
```

The Rock class has the two variables regEdge and regMiddle to store the
corresponding texture regions for the edge and the middle part of a rock.
Additionally, there is a length variable that describes the number of middle parts
to use for a rock, or in other words, the resulting length of the rock. In the init()
method, we set the dimension, the width, and the height of the rock. Remember
that these values are given in meters which relate to our game world. So, in this
case, a rock is 1 meter wide and 1.5 meters tall. Next, the texture regions are stored
in local variables. Obviously, this is not a necessary step and is really just for our
convenience to allow quick and easy changes to the texture regions the code will use
to render a specific part. Finally, setLength() is called to set the start length of the
rock. The increaseLength() method allows to increase the length of the rock by
a given amount. It will come in handy later when our yet-to-be-implemented level
loader eventually creates these rocks.

Since Rock inherits from AbstractGameObject, it is mandatory to also implement its
render() method. Add the following code to the Rock class:

```
      @Override
      public void render (SpriteBatch batch) {
         TextureRegion reg = null;
```

```
float relX = 0;
float relY = 0;

// Draw left edge
reg = regEdge;
relX -= dimension.x / 4;
batch.draw(reg.getTexture(),
           position.x + relX, position.y + relY,
           origin.x, origin.y,
           dimension.x / 4, dimension.y,
           scale.x, scale.y,
           rotation,
           reg.getRegionX(), reg.getRegionY(),
           reg.getRegionWidth(), reg.getRegionHeight(),
           false, false);

// Draw middle
relX = 0;
reg = regMiddle;
for (int i = 0; i < length; i++) {
  batch.draw(reg.getTexture(),
             position.x + relX, position.y + relY,
             origin.x, origin.y,
             dimension.x, dimension.y,
             scale.x, scale.y,
             rotation,
             reg.getRegionX(), reg.getRegionY(),
             reg.getRegionWidth(), reg.getRegionHeight(),
             false, false);
  relX += dimension.x;
}

// Draw right edge
reg = regEdge;
batch.draw(reg.getTexture(),
           position.x + relX, position.y + relY,
           origin.x + dimension.x / 8, origin.y,
           dimension.x / 4, dimension.y,
           scale.x, scale.y,
           rotation,
           reg.getRegionX(), reg.getRegionY(),
           reg.getRegionWidth(), reg.getRegionHeight(),
           true, false);
}
```

Before we continue, let us take a look at the signature of draw() from SpriteBatch to clear up the more or less convoluted lines of source code that are used to draw the texture regions.

```
public void draw (Texture texture,
                     float x, float y,
                     float originX, float originY,
                     float width, float height,
                     float scaleX, float scaleY,
                     float rotation,
                     int srcX, int srcY,
                     int srcWidth, int srcHeight,
                     boolean flipX, boolean flipY);
```

This method cuts out a rectangle (defined by srcX, srcY, srcWidth, and srcHeight) from texture (here: our texture atlas) and draws it to a given position (x, y). The origin (originX, originY) defines a relative position to where the rectangle is shifted. An origin at (0, 0) denotes the bottom-left corner. The width and height define the dimension of the image to be displayed. The scaling factor (scaleX, scaleY) defines the scale of the rectangle around the origin. The angle of rotation defines the rotation of the rectangle around the origin. The flipping of one or both the axes (flipX, flipY) means to mirror the corresponding axis of that image.

The rendering of the rock is split up in the following three drawing steps:

1. Draw the left edge at current position of the rock. A relative x- and y-value, relX and relY, is also added to the position. This is used to align the left edge to the left side of the object's local y axis. The result of doing this is that the following middle parts will now start at 0 on the x axis. This makes it much easier to handle the positioning of rocks since each middle part represents one pixel in a level image while the edges are just cosmetic details.

2. Draw all middle parts according to the set length of the rock. The drawing starts at 0, which is directly next to where the left edge ends. Each subsequent middle part is drawn next to the last middle part. This is achieved by adding the middle part's width to the relative position relX for each iteration inside the loop.

3. Finally, the mirrored left edge is drawn next to where the last middle part ends. The mirroring is achieved by setting the flipX parameter to true.

The variable reg is used to store the currently selected texture region for each step.

The mountains object

The mountains game object consists of three mountains that are put in their own layer. A tinting color and positional offset can be specified for each layer. A single mountain consists of a left and a right image. The ends of both image parts have been carefully crafted so that they can be seamlessly tiled. The following screenshot illustrates this:

The white color for the mountain images has been chosen on purpose to allow tinting.

Create a new file for the `Mountains` class and add the following code:

```
package com.packtpub.libgdx.canyonbunny.game.objects;

import com.badlogic.gdx.graphics.g2d.SpriteBatch;
import com.badlogic.gdx.graphics.g2d.TextureRegion;
import com.badlogic.gdx.math.MathUtils;
import com.packtpub.libgdx.canyonbunny.game.Assets;

public class Mountains extends AbstractGameObject {
   private TextureRegion regMountainLeft;
   private TextureRegion regMountainRight;
   private int length;

   public Mountains (int length) {
      this.length = length;
      init();
   }

   private void init () {
      dimension.set(10, 2);

      regMountainLeft =
          Assets.instance.levelDecoration.mountainLeft;
      regMountainRight =
          Assets.instance.levelDecoration.mountainRight;

      // shift mountain and extend length
      origin.x = -dimension.x * 2;
```

```
          length += dimension.x * 2;
  }

  private void drawMountain (SpriteBatch batch, float offsetX,
                            float offsetY, float tintColor) {
    TextureRegion reg = null;
    batch.setColor(tintColor, tintColor, tintColor, 1);
    float xRel = dimension.x * offsetX;
    float yRel = dimension.y * offsetY;

    // mountains span the whole level
    int mountainLength = 0;
    mountainLength += MathUtils.ceil(length / (2 * dimension.x));
    mountainLength += MathUtils.ceil(0.5f + offsetX);
    for (int i = 0; i < mountainLength; i++) {
      // mountain left
      reg = regMountainLeft;
      batch.draw(reg.getTexture(),
                 origin.x + xRel, position.y + origin.y + yRel,
                 origin.x, origin.y,
                 dimension.x, dimension.y,
                 scale.x, scale.y,
                 rotation,
                 reg.getRegionX(), reg.getRegionY(),
                 reg.getRegionWidth(), reg.getRegionHeight(),
                 false, false);
      xRel += dimension.x;

      // mountain right
      reg = regMountainRight;
      batch.draw(reg.getTexture(),
                 origin.x + xRel, position.y + origin.y + yRel,
                 origin.x, origin.y,
                 dimension.x, dimension.y,
                 scale.x, scale.y,
                 rotation,
                 reg.getRegionX(), reg.getRegionY(),
                 reg.getRegionWidth(), reg.getRegionHeight(),
                 false, false);
      xRel += dimension.x;
    }
    // reset color to white
    batch.setColor(1, 1, 1, 1);
  }
```

```
@Override
public void render (SpriteBatch batch) {
  // distant mountains (dark gray)
  drawMountain(batch, 0.5f, 0.5f, 0.5f);
  // distant mountains (gray)
  drawMountain(batch, 0.25f, 0.25f, 0.7f);
  // distant mountains (light gray)
  drawMountain(batch, 0.0f, 0.0f, 0.9f);
  }
}
```

The construction of the `Mountains` class is quite similar to the `Rock`. It inherits from `AbstractGameObject` and uses a `length` variable to store the number of times the image needs to be repeated.

The method `drawMountain()` is used to encapsulate the drawing code of a mountain layer so that the task to draw the three layers is greatly simplified. The tinting is achieved by setting the drawing color of the `SpriteBatch` to the desired color value using the `setColor()` method. All subsequent draw calls will now produce tinted images. Afterwards, the drawing color is reset to a neutral white color, which simply means that the texture colors will be no longer manipulated. This might cause future calls to the `SpriteBatch` to tint whatever is drawn next.

The water overlay object

The water overlay game object is very simple compared to the previous game objects. It consists of only one image. This image needs to overlay the ground of the whole level. There are several ways to achieve this. One would be to span the image from side to side of the camera's viewport and move the overlay together with the camera whenever the camera is moved. This is a good way to create an illusion of water being everywhere in the level. Unfortunately, special care needs to be taken if the camera is also moved in a vertical direction. Another way to implement the showing of water everywhere in the level is to just draw a single, horizontally stretched water overlay image from start to end. This is exactly what the following code will do.

Create a new file for the WaterOverlay class and add the following code:

```
package com.packtpub.libgdx.canyonbunny.game.objects;

import com.badlogic.gdx.graphics.g2d.SpriteBatch;
import com.badlogic.gdx.graphics.g2d.TextureRegion;
import com.packtpub.libgdx.canyonbunny.game.Assets;

public class WaterOverlay extends AbstractGameObject {
  private TextureRegion regWaterOverlay;
  private float length;

  public WaterOverlay (float length) {
    this.length = length;
    init();
  }

  private void init () {
    dimension.set(length * 10, 3);
    regWaterOverlay =
        Assets.instance.levelDecoration.waterOverlay;
    origin.x = -dimension.x / 2;
  }

  @Override
  public void render (SpriteBatch batch) {
    TextureRegion reg = null;
    reg = regWaterOverlay;
    batch.draw(reg.getTexture(),
               position.x + origin.x, position.y + origin.y,
               origin.x, origin.y,
               dimension.x, dimension.y,
               scale.x, scale.y,
               rotation,
               reg.getRegionX(), reg.getRegionY(),
               reg.getRegionWidth(), reg.getRegionHeight(),
               false, false);
  }
}
```

The WaterOverlay class is constructed similar to the previous game objects.

The clouds object

The clouds game object consists of a number of clouds. A cloud will use one of the three available cloud images from the texture atlas. The number of clouds depends on the given length which is divided by a constant factor to determine the final distribution of the clouds. The following screenshot illustrates this:

Create a new file for the Clouds class and add the following code:

```
package com.packtpub.libgdx.canyonbunny.game.objects;

import com.badlogic.gdx.graphics.g2d.SpriteBatch;
import com.badlogic.gdx.graphics.g2d.TextureRegion;
import com.badlogic.gdx.math.MathUtils;
import com.badlogic.gdx.math.Vector2;
import com.badlogic.gdx.utils.Array;
import com.packtpub.libgdx.canyonbunny.game.Assets;

public class Clouds extends AbstractGameObject {
  private float length;
  private Array<TextureRegion> regClouds;
  private Array<Cloud> clouds;

  private class Cloud extends AbstractGameObject {
    private TextureRegion regCloud;

    public Cloud () {}

    public void setRegion (TextureRegion region) {
      regCloud = region;
    }

    @Override
    public void render (SpriteBatch batch) {
      TextureRegion reg = regCloud;
      batch.draw(reg.getTexture(),
                 position.x + origin.x, position.y + origin.y,
                 origin.x, origin.y,
                 dimension.x, dimension.y,
```

```
                scale.x, scale.y,
                rotation,
                reg.getRegionX(), reg.getRegionY(),
                reg.getRegionWidth(), reg.getRegionHeight(),
                false, false);
    }
  }

  public Clouds (float length) {
    this.length = length;
    init();
  }

  private void init () {
    dimension.set(3.0f, 1.5f);
    regClouds = new Array<TextureRegion>();
    regClouds.add(Assets.instance.levelDecoration.cloud01);
    regClouds.add(Assets.instance.levelDecoration.cloud02);
    regClouds.add(Assets.instance.levelDecoration.cloud03);
    int distFac = 5;
    int numClouds = (int)(length / distFac);
    clouds = new Array<Cloud>(2 * numClouds);
    for (int i = 0; i < numClouds; i++) {
      Cloud cloud = spawnCloud();
      cloud.position.x = i * distFac;
      clouds.add(cloud);
    }
  }

  private Cloud spawnCloud () {
    Cloud cloud = new Cloud();
    cloud.dimension.set(dimension);
    // select random cloud image
    cloud.setRegion(regClouds.random());
    // position
    Vector2 pos = new Vector2();
    pos.x = length + 10; // position after end of level
    pos.y += 1.75; // base position
    // random additional position
    pos.y += MathUtils.random(0.0f, 0.2f)
          * (MathUtils.randomBoolean() ? 1 : -1);
    cloud.position.set(pos);
    return cloud;
  }
```

```
    @Override
    public void render (SpriteBatch batch) {
      for (Cloud cloud : clouds)
        cloud.render(batch);
    }
  }
```

The `Clouds` class is also constructed like the previous game objects. The distribution of the clouds over the level is determined by the given `length` value and the constant factor `distFact`, which is 5 in this code, meaning that there will be a cloud every five meters.

A single cloud is defined by the `Clouds` inner class `Cloud` which also inherits from `AbstractGameObject`. So a `Cloud` object is the actual cloud object while `Clouds` is the container that maintains a list of all the currently created clouds. A new cloud can be created by simply calling the `spawnCloud()` method of `Clouds`. This will create a new `Cloud` object, assign a random cloud image to it, move it to the end of the level, and randomly shift it up or down a bit. The newly created cloud is also added to the list and returned to the calling method.

Implementing the level loader

We will now implement the level loader that will be able to read and interpret the image data.

 You might want to check the handling of level data in *Chapter 3, Configuring the Game*, where we defined and discussed the level format.

Create a new file for the `Level` class and add the following code:

```
package com.packtpub.libgdx.canyonbunny.game;

import com.badlogic.gdx.Gdx;
import com.badlogic.gdx.graphics.Pixmap;
import com.badlogic.gdx.graphics.g2d.SpriteBatch;
import com.badlogic.gdx.utils.Array;
import
   com.packtpub.libgdx.canyonbunny.game.objects.AbstractGameObject;
import com.packtpub.libgdx.canyonbunny.game.objects.Clouds;
import com.packtpub.libgdx.canyonbunny.game.objects.Mountains;
import com.packtpub.libgdx.canyonbunny.game.objects.Rock;
import com.packtpub.libgdx.canyonbunny.game.objects.WaterOverlay;

public class Level {
```

```
      public static final String TAG = Level.class.getName();

      public enum BLOCK_TYPE {
        EMPTY(0, 0, 0),                      // black
        ROCK(0, 255, 0),                     // green
        PLAYER_SPAWNPOINT(255, 255, 255),    // white
        ITEM_FEATHER(255, 0, 255),           // purple
        ITEM_GOLD_COIN(255, 255, 0);         // yellow

        private int color;

        private BLOCK_TYPE (int r, int g, int b) {
          color = r << 24 | g << 16 | b << 8 | 0xff;
        }

        public boolean sameColor (int color) {
          return this.color == color;
        }

        public int getColor () {
          return color;
        }
      }

      // objects
      public Array<Rock> rocks;

      // decoration
      public Clouds clouds;
      public Mountains mountains;
      public WaterOverlay waterOverlay;

      public Level (String filename) {
        init(filename);
      }

      private void init (String filename) {}
      public void render (SpriteBatch batch) {}
    }
```

The Level class contains an enum data type that we will use to represent all our game world objects. These objects have a unique **RGBA** color value that is used to identify them. We will not use the alpha channel and always expect full opacity for our game object color values. Since each color component is represented as an 8-bit value, the sum of an RGBA color is 32 bits or 4 bytes. The int data type of Java is also defined as a 32 bit value which makes it the appropriate place to store RGBA color codes in a compact way.

> The compact color value is stored in an RGBA format. Also, in the following code, we are going to use bit shift operations. For more information, check out the blog article at: http://sierakowski.
> eu/list-of-tips/37-bit-shifting-and-masking-bitwise-
> operators-in-as-3-getting-alpha-channel-out-of-the-
> color.html

The method sameColor() will allow us to easily find out if two colors are exactly the same by comparing only one value instead of four.

The Level holds a list of Rock instances called rocks. There is also a variable to hold an instance of Clouds, Mountains, and WaterOverlay. All these variables are filled during the level loading process that takes places in the init() method.

Add the following code to the still empty init() method:

```
private void init (String filename) {
  // objects
  rocks = new Array<Rock>();

  // load image file that represents the level data
  Pixmap pixmap = new Pixmap(Gdx.files.internal(filename));
  // scan pixels from top-left to bottom-right
  int lastPixel = -1;
  for (int pixelY = 0; pixelY < pixmap.getHeight(); pixelY++) {
    for (int pixelX = 0; pixelX < pixmap.getWidth(); pixelX++) {
      AbstractGameObject obj = null;
      float offsetHeight = 0;
      // height grows from bottom to top
      float baseHeight = pixmap.getHeight() - pixelY;
      // get color of current pixel as 32-bit RGBA value
      int currentPixel = pixmap.getPixel(pixelX, pixelY);
      // find matching color value to identify block type at (x,y)
      // point and create the corresponding game object if there is
      // a match
```

```
                // empty space
                if (BLOCK_TYPE.EMPTY.sameColor(currentPixel)) {
                  // do nothing
                }
                // rock
                else if (BLOCK_TYPE.ROCK.sameColor(currentPixel)) {
                  if (lastPixel != currentPixel) {
                    obj = new Rock();
                    float heightIncreaseFactor = 0.25f;
                    offsetHeight = -2.5f;
                    obj.position.set(pixelX,
                                     baseHeight * obj.dimension.y
                                           * heightIncreaseFactor
                                           + offsetHeight);
                    rocks.add((Rock)obj);
                  } else {
                    rocks.get(rocks.size - 1).increaseLength(1);
                  }
                }
                // player spawn point
                else if
                    (BLOCK_TYPE.PLAYER_SPAWNPOINT.sameColor(currentPixel)) {
                }
                // feather
                else if (BLOCK_TYPE.ITEM_FEATHER.sameColor(currentPixel)) {
                }
                // gold coin
                else if (BLOCK_TYPE.ITEM_GOLD_COIN.sameColor(currentPixel)) {
                }
                // unknown object/pixel color
                else {
                  int r = 0xff & (currentPixel >>> 24); //red color channel
                  int g = 0xff & (currentPixel >>> 16); //green color channel
                  int b = 0xff & (currentPixel >>> 8);  //blue color channel
                  int a = 0xff & currentPixel;          //alpha channel
                  Gdx.app.error(TAG, "Unknown object at x<" + pixelX
                                          + "> y<" + pixelY
                                          + ">: r<" + r
                                          + "> g<" + g
                                          + "> b<" + b
                                          + "> a<" + a + ">");
                }
                lastPixel = currentPixel;
            }
```

```
    }

    // decoration
    clouds = new Clouds(pixmap.getWidth());
    clouds.position.set(0, 2);
    mountains = new Mountains(pixmap.getWidth());
    mountains.position.set(-1, -1);
    waterOverlay = new WaterOverlay(pixmap.getWidth());
    waterOverlay.position.set(0, -3.75f);

    // free memory
    pixmap.dispose();
    Gdx.app.debug(TAG, "level '" + filename + "' loaded");
}
```

This method starts with creating a new and empty list for the rocks. Then it uses `Gdx.files.internal()` to get a file handle, which in turn is used to create a new `Pixmap` object. It contains the pixel data of the level image that is to be scanned and interpreted.

The scanning is done by looping through each pixel starting from the top-left corner of the image to the bottom-right. The `baseHeight` variable is set to the maximum level height minus the current height of the currently scanned pixel resulting in a flipped vertical pixel position. What this basically means is that the game objects will appear at their correct height in the game world, although scanning is done from top to bottom and the game objects grow from the bottom up. The `offsetHeight` variable is used to individually offset an object to correctly fit into the game world. The `currentPixel` variable stores the color value of the currently scanned pixel. Next, this value is compared to each defined color code of a game object until a match has been found. If no color code matches, there will be an error message logged to the console to indicate an implementation error in our game. The error can either mean a use of an undefined color code or that the identification method does not handle this color code. The error message will contain the decoded RGBA values to make troubleshooting a bit less painful.

After the scanning process, there are still some game objects left that need to be initialized. These are the decoration game objects `Clouds`, `Mountains`, and `WaterOverlay`. They are passed over the width of the `Pixmap`, which is the actual length of the level they need to know to work correctly.

Lastly, the `Pixmap` is disposed to properly free the occupied memory.

The code part we left out up until now is to look at what happens if there is a matching color code. The current implementation already handles the color code of every game object we want to use, but except for rock game objects, there is no defined action for them yet. A new rock will be created and added to the list of `rocks` if the corresponding color code is matching. There is also a `lastPixel` variable that stores the last value of `currentPixel` after each iteration inside the loop. This value is used to detect adjacent rock pixels that will increase the length of the last created rock by one in this case instead of creating a new one.

Add the following code to the still empty `render()` method:

```
public void render (SpriteBatch batch) {
  // Draw Mountains
  mountains.render(batch);
  // Draw Rocks
  for (Rock rock : rocks)
    rock.render(batch);
  // Draw Water Overlay
  waterOverlay.render(batch);
  // Draw Clouds
  clouds.render(batch);
}
```

This will finally draw all the elements of a loaded level to create the scene for the game world. The order of the draw calls is important because every subsequent draw call is drawing on top of the scene. The drawing order can be imagined as layers although there is no real depth or z axis like in 3D space.

Nevertheless, if one would try to look at the example scene that is shown at the beginning of this chapter from a 45 degree angled view, it might look like this:

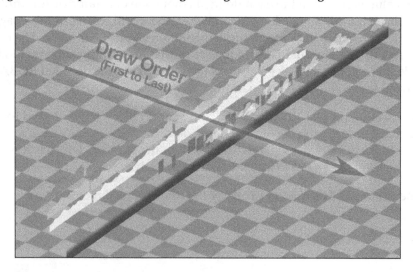

All objects that are drawn first will appear further in the background. Thus, the mountains are further away than the rocks or the stretched water overlay.

Assembling the game world

We will now remove some of the old code that was used to draw test sprites. Additionally, we will add three new constants to define the amount of start, extra lives, and the viewport dimension of the GUI camera.

Change the code of Constants class as follows:

```
public class Constants {
    // Visible game world is 5 meters wide
    public static final float VIEWPORT_WIDTH = 5.0f;
    // Visible game world is 5 meters tall
    public static final float VIEWPORT_HEIGHT = 5.0f;
    // GUI Width
    public static final float VIEWPORT_GUI_WIDTH = 800.0f;
    // GUI Height
    public static final float VIEWPORT_GUI_HEIGHT = 480.0f;
    // Location of description file for texture atlas
    public static final String TEXTURE_ATLAS_OBJECTS =
        "images/canyonbunny.pack";
    // Location of image file for level 01
    public static final String LEVEL_01 = "levels/level-01.png";
    // Amount of extra lives at level start
    public static final int LIVES_START = 3;
}
```

Now, remove these two lines of code in WorldController:

```
public Sprite[] testSprites;
public int selectedSprite;
```

Additionally, remove the following methods in WorldController:

- initTestObjects()
- updateTestObjects()
- moveSelectedSprite()

Remove the following code in the `handleDebugInput()` method of `WorldController`:

```
// Selected Sprite Controls
float sprMoveSpeed = 5 * deltaTime;
if (Gdx.input.isKeyPressed(Keys.A))
    moveSelectedSprite(-sprMoveSpeed, 0);
if (Gdx.input.isKeyPressed(Keys.D))
    moveSelectedSprite(sprMoveSpeed, 0);
if (Gdx.input.isKeyPressed(Keys.W))
    moveSelectedSprite(0, sprMoveSpeed);
if (Gdx.input.isKeyPressed(Keys.S))
    moveSelectedSprite(0, -sprMoveSpeed);
```

Next, remove the code below the two comments "Select next sprite" and "Toggle camera follow" in the `keyUp()` method of `WorldController` so that the resulting method looks like this:

```
@Override
public boolean keyUp (int keycode) {
  // Reset game world
  if (keycode == Keys.R) {
    init();
    Gdx.app.debug(TAG, "Game world resetted");
  }
  return false;
}
```

Add the following two imports to `WorldController`:

```
import com.packtpub.libgdx.canyonbunny.game.objects.Rock;
import com.packtpub.libgdx.canyonbunny.util.Constants;
```

Next, add the following code to `WorldController`:

```
public Level level;
public int lives;
public int score;

private void initLevel () {
  score = 0;
  level = new Level(Constants.LEVEL_01);
}
```

Change the code in the `init()` method of `WorldController` as follows:

```
private void init () {
  Gdx.input.setInputProcessor(this);
  cameraHelper = new CameraHelper();
  lives = Constants.LIVES_START;
  initLevel();
}
```

Finally, remove the call to the deleted `updateTestObjects()` method in `update()`.

We have now removed all of the old code and added level loading to the controller. There are also two variables `score` and `lives` that count the player's score and the player's extra lives.

We have to make some minor changes to the `CameraHelper` class to make the switch from using `Sprite` objects to `AbstractGameObject` objects.

Remove the following import line in `CameraHelper`:

```
import com.badlogic.gdx.graphics.g2d.Sprite;
```

Next, add this import line in `CameraHelper`:

```
import com.packtpub.libgdx.canyonbunny.game.objects.
  AbstractGameObject;
```

Now, change the code in `CameraHelper` as follows:

```
private AbstractGameObject target;

public void update (float deltaTime) {
  if (!hasTarget()) return;

  position.x = target.position.x + target.origin.x;
  position.y = target.position.y + target.origin.y;
}

public void setTarget (AbstractGameObject target) {
  this.target = target;
}

public AbstractGameObject getTarget () {
  return target;
}
```

```
public boolean hasTarget (AbstractGameObject target) {
    return hasTarget() && this.target.equals(target);
}
```

Next, add the following code in `WorldRenderer`:

```
private void renderWorld (SpriteBatch batch) {
    worldController.cameraHelper.applyTo(camera);
    batch.setProjectionMatrix(camera.combined);
    batch.begin();
    worldController.level.render(batch);
    batch.end();
}
```

Then remove the `renderTestObjects()` method in `WorldRenderer`.

Lastly, replace the call to the deleted `renderTestObjects()` method with the newly added `renderWorld()` method in `render()`:

```
public void render () {
    renderWorld(batch);
}
```

Now, the world renderer will call the `renderWorld()` method, which in turn calls the `render()` method of `Level` to draw all the game objects of the loaded level.

Implementing the game GUI

In this last part of the chapter, we are going to implement the game's GUI and add it to the scene. The GUI will display the achieved score, extra lives, and an FPS counter.

We will need to load a bitmap font before we are able to write any text output to the screen. Fortunately, Libgdx provides a default font (Arial 15pt) that we can use. Copy the two files `arial-15.fnt` and `arial-15.png` to `CanyonBunny-android/assets/images/`.

 The Libgdx font files can be downloaded on Packt's website at: `http://www.packtpub.com/learning-libgdx-game-development/book`

This is how Libgdx's default bitmap font looks:

Add the following import line to `Assets`:

```
import com.badlogic.gdx.graphics.g2d.BitmapFont;
```

Add the following lines of code to `Assets` as follows:

```
public AssetFonts fonts;

public class AssetFonts {
  public final BitmapFont defaultSmall;
  public final BitmapFont defaultNormal;
  public final BitmapFont defaultBig;

  public AssetFonts () {
    // create three fonts using Libgdx's 15px bitmap font
    defaultSmall = new BitmapFont(
        Gdx.files.internal("images/arial-15.fnt"), true);
    defaultNormal = new BitmapFont(
        Gdx.files.internal("images/arial-15.fnt"), true);
    defaultBig = new BitmapFont(
        Gdx.files.internal("images/arial-15.fnt"), true);
    // set font sizes
    defaultSmall.setScale(0.75f);
    defaultNormal.setScale(1.0f);
    defaultBig.setScale(2.0f);
    // enable linear texture filtering for smooth fonts
    defaultSmall.getRegion().getTexture().setFilter(
        TextureFilter.Linear, TextureFilter.Linear);
    defaultNormal.getRegion().getTexture().setFilter(
        TextureFilter.Linear, TextureFilter.Linear);
    defaultBig.getRegion().getTexture().setFilter(
        TextureFilter.Linear, TextureFilter.Linear);
  }
}
```

```
    public void init (AssetManager assetManager) {
      this.assetManager = assetManager;
      // set asset manager error handler
      assetManager.setErrorListener(this);
      // load texture atlas
      assetManager.load(Constants.TEXTURE_ATLAS_OBJECTS,
                        TextureAtlas.class);
      // start loading assets and wait until finished
      assetManager.finishLoading();

      Gdx.app.debug(TAG, "# of assets loaded: "
                         + assetManager.getAssetNames().size);
      for (String a : assetManager.getAssetNames())
        Gdx.app.debug(TAG, "asset: " + a);

      TextureAtlas atlas =
          assetManager.get(Constants.TEXTURE_ATLAS_OBJECTS);

      // enable texture filtering for pixel smoothing
      for (Texture t : atlas.getTextures())
        t.setFilter(TextureFilter.Linear, TextureFilter.Linear);

      // create game resource objects
      fonts = new AssetFonts();
      bunny = new AssetBunny(atlas);
      rock = new AssetRock(atlas);
      goldCoin = new AssetGoldCoin(atlas);
      feather = new AssetFeather(atlas);
      levelDecoration = new AssetLevelDecoration(atlas);
    }

    @Override
    public void dispose () {
      assetManager.dispose();
      fonts.defaultSmall.dispose();
      fonts.defaultNormal.dispose();
      fonts.defaultBig.dispose();
    }
```

The added code includes a new inner class AssetFonts that holds the default
bitmap font in three differently configured sizes. The size is configured by scaling
the font either up or down. Bitmap fonts must be disposed manually so that the
corresponding calls are added to the dispose() method.

We are now ready to begin with the implementation of the game's GUI. It is always good to have an idea of what should be implemented so that we have a picture of what we are aiming for.

In the top-left corner, you see an image of the gold coin and the player's current score as text. In the top-right corner, you see three bunny heads that represent the number of extra lives the player has left. Lastly, in the bottom-right corner is a small FPS counter that shows how good or bad the performance of the running game is. The color of the FPS counter will depend on the achieved frames per second.

Add the following import line in `WorldRenderer`:

```
import com.badlogic.gdx.graphics.g2d.BitmapFont;
```

Next, add the following code in `WorldRenderer`:

```
private OrthographicCamera cameraGUI;

private void init () {
  batch = new SpriteBatch();
  camera = new OrthographicCamera(Constants.VIEWPORT_WIDTH,
                                  Constants.VIEWPORT_HEIGHT);
  camera.position.set(0, 0, 0);
  camera.update();
```

```
        cameraGUI = new OrthographicCamera(Constants.VIEWPORT_GUI_WIDTH,
                              Constants.VIEWPORT_GUI_HEIGHT);
        cameraGUI.position.set(0, 0, 0);
        cameraGUI.setToOrtho(true); // flip y-axis
        cameraGUI.update();
    }

    public void resize (int width, int height) {
        camera.viewportWidth = (Constants.VIEWPORT_HEIGHT
                        / (float)height) * (float)width;
        camera.update();
        cameraGUI.viewportHeight = Constants.VIEWPORT_GUI_HEIGHT;
        cameraGUI.viewportWidth = (Constants.VIEWPORT_GUI_HEIGHT
                        / (float)height) * (float)width;
        cameraGUI.position.set(cameraGUI.viewportWidth / 2,
                        cameraGUI.viewportHeight / 2, 0);
        cameraGUI.update();
    }
```

The added code creates a second camera that is specifically set up just for rendering the game's GUI. The viewport of the GUI camera is defined using a different set of constants that uses much higher values. We have to do this to correctly render the bitmap font that is 15 pixels high. If we would use the 5 meters times 5 meters viewport, only one third of the font's glyph would be visible at any time. The rest of the added code does the same as the game camera. Also, this allows us to move the world camera (camera) independently from the GUI (cameraGUI).

The following describes the implementation of the methods for each GUI element.

The GUI score

Here is a screenshot of the GUI element showing the current player's score:

Add the following code in WorldRenderer:

```
    private void renderGuiScore (SpriteBatch batch) {
        float x = -15;
        float y = -15;
        batch.draw(Assets.instance.goldCoin.goldCoin,
```

```
    x, y, 50, 50, 100, 100, 0.35f, -0.35f, 0);
  Assets.instance.fonts.defaultBig.draw(batch,
    "" + worldController.score,
    x + 75, y + 37);
}
```

The gold coin image is drawn at the top-left corner of the screen. Next to it, the player's current score is displayed using the big default font.

The GUI extra lives

Here is a screenshot of the GUI element showing the player's remaining extra lives:

Add the following code in `WorldRenderer`:

```
private void renderGuiExtraLive (SpriteBatch batch) {
  float x = cameraGUI.viewportWidth - 50
Constants.LIVES_START * 50;
  float y = -15;
  for (int i = 0; i < Constants.LIVES_START; i++) {
    if (worldController.lives <= i)
      batch.setColor(0.5f, 0.5f, 0.5f, 0.5f);
    batch.draw(Assets.instance.bunny.head,
      x + i * 50, y, 50, 50, 120, 100, 0.35f, -0.35f, 0);
    batch.setColor(1, 1, 1, 1);
  }
}
```

Three bunny head images that will represent the extra lives of the player are drawn at the top-right corner of the screen. The method starts to draw from left to right. Before a new bunny head is drawn, there is an additional check to find out whether this extra life is used up already. If this is the case, the bunny head is darkened and gets a slightly transparent look by setting the tint color of the sprite batch.

The GUI FPS counter

Here is a screenshot of the GUI element showing the actual frames per second:

Add the following code in `WorldRenderer`:

```
private void renderGuiFpsCounter (SpriteBatch batch) {
  float x = cameraGUI.viewportWidth - 55;
  float y = cameraGUI.viewportHeight - 15;
  int fps = Gdx.graphics.getFramesPerSecond();
  BitmapFont fpsFont = Assets.instance.fonts.defaultNormal;
  if (fps >= 45) {
    // 45 or more FPS show up in green
    fpsFont.setColor(0, 1, 0, 1);
  } else if (fps >= 30) {
    // 30 or more FPS show up in yellow
    fpsFont.setColor(1, 1, 0, 1);
  } else {
    // less than 30 FPS show up in red
    fpsFont.setColor(1, 0, 0, 1);
  }
  fpsFont.draw(batch, "FPS: " + fps, x, y);
  fpsFont.setColor(1, 1, 1, 1); // white
}
```

An FPS counter showing the text **FPS:** followed by the current number of frames per second is drawn at the bottom-right corner of the screen. The color of the text depends on the achieved frame rate. If the FPS is 45 or higher, the text will show up in green, indicating a good rendering performance. Otherwise, if there still are 30 or more FPS, then the text will show up in yellow indicating an average rendering performance. Anything below 30 FPS will show up in red indicating a really poor rendering performance.

Rendering the GUI

Add the following code in `WorldRenderer`:

```
private void renderGui (SpriteBatch batch) {
  batch.setProjectionMatrix(cameraGUI.combined);
  batch.begin();
```

```
    // draw collected gold coins icon + text
    // (anchored to top left edge)
    renderGuiScore(batch);
    // draw extra lives icon + text (anchored to top right edge)
    renderGuiExtraLive(batch);
    // draw FPS text (anchored to bottom right edge)
    renderGuiFpsCounter(batch);
    batch.end();
}
```

Furthermore, change `render()` in `WorldRenderer` as following:

```
public void render () {
  renderWorld(batch);
  renderGui(batch);
}
```

The implementation of the game's GUI is now finished.

Summary

In this chapter, we learned how to implement our game objects. We also learned how to create compound game objects using several textures. Additionally, the implementation of the level loader has been discussed. Afterwards, we assembled the game world using the level loader, which in turn will create all our game objects from now on. We learned how to use bitmap fonts and used Libgdx's built-in font for the game's GUI texts. In addition, GUI elements have been added to display the game's status, such as the player's current score and extra lives.

Remember, we are still using our camera helper class that allows us to easily move around inside our scene. You can also still zoom in and out.

The next chapter will continue to implement the rest of the basic game elements, such as the player character, items, player movement, basic collision detection, and so on.

6
Adding the Actors

In this chapter we will implement the remaining game objects which represent our actors in the game world. These are the player character bunny head and both the collectible items; the gold coin and the feather power-up. We will complete the level loader by adding support for the actor game objects so that they are handled properly when a level is loaded.

The game will be extended to feature a simple physics simulation that allows any game object to be moved using physical properties, such as velocity, acceleration, and friction. In addition, the game logic will also need to be able to detect collisions of the game objects to trigger certain events. For example, we want the player character to be able to jump, stand, and walk on a rock (platform), collect items by walking over them, and lose a life when it falls into the water. The game logic will also include a check to find out if the game over condition is met so that the game immediately ends and a **Game Over** text message is displayed.

The GUI will be extended to display a little feather icon whenever the feather power-up has been collected. There will be a small number next to this icon that indicates the time that is left before the power-up effect vanishes.

Implementing the actor game objects

First, let us make some preparations by extending the `AbstractGameObject` class with some additional attributes and general functionalities for our upcoming physics and collision detection code.

Add the following import to `AbstractGameObject`:

```
import com.badlogic.gdx.math.Rectangle;
```

Then, add the following member variables and initialization code to the same class:

```
public Vector2 velocity;
public Vector2 terminalVelocity;
public Vector2 friction;
public Vector2 acceleration;
public Rectangle bounds;

public AbstractGameObject () {
  position = new Vector2();
  dimension = new Vector2(1, 1);
  origin = new Vector2();
  scale = new Vector2(1, 1);
  rotation = 0;
  velocity = new Vector2();
  terminalVelocity = new Vector2(1, 1);
  friction = new Vector2();
  acceleration = new Vector2();
  bounds = new Rectangle();
}
```

The following list contains a brief description of the purpose of each variable:

- `velocity`: This is the object's current speed in m/s.
- `terminalVelocity`: This is the object's positive and negative maximum speed in m/s.
- `friction`: This is an opposing force that slows down the object until its velocity equals zero. This value is given as a coefficient which is dimensionless. A value of zero means no friction, and thus the object's velocity will not decrease.
- `acceleration`: This is the object's constant acceleration in m/s^2.
- `bounds`: The object's bounding box describes the physical body that will be used for collision detection with other objects. The bounding box can be set to any size and is completely independent of the actual dimension of the object in the game world.

We will now add a simple physics simulation code that makes use of the new physics attributes, namely `velocity`, `terminalVelocity`, `friction`, and `acceleration`.

Add the following import to `AbstractGameObject`:

```
import com.badlogic.gdx.math.MathUtils;
```

Furthermore, add the following code to the same class:

```
protected void updateMotionX (float deltaTime) {
  if (velocity.x != 0) {
    // Apply friction
    if (velocity.x > 0) {
      velocity.x =
          Math.max(velocity.x - friction.x * deltaTime, 0);
    } else {
      velocity.x =
          Math.min(velocity.x + friction.x * deltaTime, 0);
    }
  }
  // Apply acceleration
  velocity.x += acceleration.x * deltaTime;
  // Make sure the object's velocity does not exceed the
  // positive or negative terminal velocity
  velocity.x = MathUtils.clamp(velocity.x,
      -terminalVelocity.x, terminalVelocity.x);
}

protected void updateMotionY (float deltaTime) {
  if (velocity.y != 0) {
    // Apply friction
    if (velocity.y > 0) {
      velocity.y =
          Math.max(velocity.y - friction.y * deltaTime, 0);
    } else {
      velocity.y =
          Math.min(velocity.y + friction.y * deltaTime, 0);
    }
  }
  // Apply acceleration
  velocity.y += acceleration.y * deltaTime;
  // Make sure the object's velocity does not exceed the
  // positive or negative terminal velocity
  velocity.y = MathUtils.clamp(velocity.y,
      -terminalVelocity.y, terminalVelocity.y);
}
```

Finally, make the following change to the already existing `update()` method:

```
public void update (float deltaTime) {
   updateMotionX(deltaTime);
   updateMotionY(deltaTime);
   // Move to new position
   position.x += velocity.x * deltaTime;
   position.y += velocity.y * deltaTime;
}
```

The two new methods `updateMotionX()` and `updateMotionY()` are called on every update cycle to calculate the next x and y components of the object's velocity in terms of the given delta time. The calculation is done in three steps:

1. If the object's velocity is not equal to zero, the object must be in motion. Therefore, friction needs to be applied on the velocity to slow it down. Since the property of friction is meant to decrease velocity, the friction coefficient needs to be either subtracted from positive or only added to negative velocity values. The velocity is directly set to zero as soon as the algebraic sign changes to fully stop the ongoing motion using the `Math.max` and `Math.min` functions.

2. Next, an acceleration is applied to the current velocity.

3. Finally, it is made sure that the new velocity value will always be inside the range of the positive and negative terminal velocity.

After both velocity components have been updated, the displacement that simulates the actual motion of an object is done by simply adding the new velocity vector to the position vector that holds the last position.

Creating the gold coin object

The gold coin game object consists of only one image. It is a collectible item, which means it can be collected by the player character by simply walking over it. As a result of the gold coin being collected, the object will turn invisible for the rest of the game.

Create a new file for the GoldCoin class and add the following code:

```
package com.packtpub.libgdx.canyonbunny.game.objects;

import com.badlogic.gdx.graphics.g2d.SpriteBatch;
import com.badlogic.gdx.graphics.g2d.TextureRegion;
import com.packtpub.libgdx.canyonbunny.game.Assets;

public class GoldCoin extends AbstractGameObject {
  private TextureRegion regGoldCoin;
  public boolean collected;

  public GoldCoin () {
    init();
  }

  private void init () {
    dimension.set(0.5f, 0.5f);
    regGoldCoin = Assets.instance.goldCoin.goldCoin;
    // Set bounding box for collision detection
    bounds.set(0, 0, dimension.x, dimension.y);
    collected = false;
  }

  public void render (SpriteBatch batch) {
    if (collected) return;

    TextureRegion reg = null;
    reg = regGoldCoin;
    batch.draw(reg.getTexture(),
                position.x, position.y,
                origin.x, origin.y,
                dimension.x, dimension.y,
                scale.x, scale.y,
                rotation,
                reg.getRegionX(), reg.getRegionY(),
                reg.getRegionWidth(), reg.getRegionHeight(),
                false, false);
  }

  public int getScore() {
    return 100;
  }
}
```

The gold coin uses the collected variable to store its current state of visibility. The `render()` method will always check the collected state to decide whether the object should be rendered or not. The `getScore()` method returns the item's score that the player will receive for collecting it. The bounding box `bounds` is set to the exact same size as its dimension inside the game world.

Creating the feather object

The feather game object is very similar to the gold coin. It consists of only one image and is a collectible item that will turn invisible when it is collected by the player character.

Create a new file for the `Feather` class and add the following code:

```
package com.packtpub.libgdx.canyonbunny.game.objects;

import com.badlogic.gdx.graphics.g2d.SpriteBatch;
import com.badlogic.gdx.graphics.g2d.TextureRegion;
import com.packtpub.libgdx.canyonbunny.game.Assets;

public class Feather extends AbstractGameObject {
  private TextureRegion regFeather;
  public boolean collected;

  public Feather () {
    init();
  }

  private void init () {
    dimension.set(0.5f, 0.5f);
    regFeather = Assets.instance.feather.feather;
    // Set bounding box for collision detection
    bounds.set(0, 0, dimension.x, dimension.y);
    collected = false;
  }

  public void render (SpriteBatch batch) {
    if (collected) return;
```

```
      TextureRegion reg = null;
      reg = regFeather;
      batch.draw(reg.getTexture(),
                  position.x, position.y,
                  origin.x, origin.y,
                  dimension.x, dimension.y,
                  scale.x, scale.y,
                  rotation,
                  reg.getRegionX(), reg.getRegionY(),
                  reg.getRegionWidth(), reg.getRegionHeight(),
                  false, false);
    }

    public int getScore() {
      return 250;
    }
  }
```

Obviously, this code is nearly the same when compared to the code of the gold coin. The only difference between them is the image used and that the `getScore()` method returns a slightly higher score.

Creating the bunny head object

The bunny head or player character is the most complex game object that we will create in this project. It consists of only one image, but involves quite a lot of code to enable jumping and falling as well as handling the feather power-up effect.

Create a new file for the `BunnyHead` class and add the following code:

```
package com.packtpub.libgdx.canyonbunny.game.objects;

import com.badlogic.gdx.Gdx;
import com.badlogic.gdx.graphics.g2d.SpriteBatch;
import com.badlogic.gdx.graphics.g2d.TextureRegion;
import com.packtpub.libgdx.canyonbunny.game.Assets;
```

```
import com.packtpub.libgdx.canyonbunny.util.Constants;

public class BunnyHead extends AbstractGameObject {
  public static final String TAG = BunnyHead.class.getName();

  private final float JUMP_TIME_MAX = 0.3f;
  private final float JUMP_TIME_MIN = 0.1f;
  private final float JUMP_TIME_OFFSET_FLYING =
      JUMP_TIME_MAX - 0.018f;

  public enum VIEW_DIRECTION { LEFT, RIGHT }
  public enum JUMP_STATE {
    GROUNDED, FALLING, JUMP_RISING, JUMP_FALLING
  }

  private TextureRegion regHead;
  public VIEW_DIRECTION viewDirection;
  public float timeJumping;
  public JUMP_STATE jumpState;
  public boolean hasFeatherPowerup;
  public float timeLeftFeatherPowerup;

  public BunnyHead () {
    init();
  }

  public void init () {};
  public void setJumping (boolean jumpKeyPressed) {};
  public void setFeatherPowerup (boolean pickedUp) {};
  public boolean hasFeatherPowerup () {};
}
```

Now that we have defined the viewing direction, a state for jumping, and another state for the feather power-up, we can go on and fill in the specific implementation details of the still empty methods.

Now, add the following code to the init() method:

```
public void init () {
  dimension.set(1, 1);
  regHead = Assets.instance.bunny.head;
  // Center image on game object
  origin.set(dimension.x / 2, dimension.y / 2);
  // Bounding box for collision detection
```

```
    bounds.set(0, 0, dimension.x, dimension.y);
    // Set physics values
    terminalVelocity.set(3.0f, 4.0f);
    friction.set(12.0f, 0.0f);
    acceleration.set(0.0f, -25.0f);
    // View direction
    viewDirection = VIEW_DIRECTION.RIGHT;
    // Jump state
    jumpState = JUMP_STATE.FALLING;
    timeJumping = 0;
    // Power-ups
    hasFeatherPowerup = false;
    timeLeftFeatherPowerup = 0;
}
```

The preceding code initializes the bunny head game object by setting its physics values, a starting view direction, and jump state, and it also deactivates the feather power-up effect.

Next, add the following code to the setJumping() method:

```
public void setJumping (boolean jumpKeyPressed) {
  switch (jumpState) {
    case GROUNDED: // Character is standing on a platform
      if (jumpKeyPressed) {
        // Start counting jump time from the beginning
        timeJumping = 0;
        jumpState = JUMP_STATE.JUMP_RISING;
      }
      break;
    case JUMP_RISING: // Rising in the air
      if (!jumpKeyPressed)
      jumpState = JUMP_STATE.JUMP_FALLING;
      break;
    case FALLING:// Falling down
    case JUMP_FALLING: // Falling down after jump
      if (jumpKeyPressed && hasFeatherPowerup) {
        timeJumping = JUMP_TIME_OFFSET_FLYING;
        jumpState = JUMP_STATE.JUMP_RISING;
      }
      break;
  }
}
```

The preceding code allows us to make the bunny jump. The state handling in the code will decide whether jumping is currently possible and whether it is a single or a multi jump.

Next, add the following code to the `setFeatherPowerup()` method:

```
public void setFeatherPowerup (boolean pickedUp) {
  hasFeatherPowerup = pickedUp;
  if (pickedUp) {
    timeLeftFeatherPowerup =
        Constants.ITEM_FEATHER_POWERUP_DURATION;
  }
}

public boolean hasFeatherPowerup () {
  return hasFeatherPowerup && timeLeftFeatherPowerup > 0;
}
```

The preceding code allows us to toggle the feather power-up effect via the `setFeatherPowerup()` method. The `hasFeatherPowerup()` method can be used to find out whether the power-up is still active.

Next, add the following code to override the `update()` method:

```
@Override
public void update (float deltaTime) {
  super.update(deltaTime);
  if (velocity.x != 0) {
    viewDirection = velocity.x < 0 ? VIEW_DIRECTION.LEFT
                                   : VIEW_DIRECTION.RIGHT;
  }
  if (timeLeftFeatherPowerup > 0) {
    timeLeftFeatherPowerup -= deltaTime;
    if (timeLeftFeatherPowerup < 0) {
      // disable power-up
      timeLeftFeatherPowerup = 0;
      setFeatherPowerup(false);
    }
  }
}
```

The preceding code handles the switching of the viewing direction according to the current move direction. Also, the time remaining of the power-up effect is checked. If the time is up, the feather power-up effect is disabled.

Next, add the following code to override the `updateMotionY()` method:

```
@Override
protected void updateMotionY (float deltaTime) {
  switch (jumpState) {
    case GROUNDED:
      jumpState = JUMP_STATE.FALLING;
      break;
    case JUMP_RISING:
      // Keep track of jump time
      timeJumping += deltaTime;
      // Jump time left?
      if (timeJumping <= JUMP_TIME_MAX) {
        // Still jumping
        velocity.y = terminalVelocity.y;
      }
      break;
    case FALLING:
      break;
    case JUMP_FALLING:
      // Add delta times to track jump time
      timeJumping += deltaTime;
      // Jump to minimal height if jump key was pressed too short
      if (timeJumping > 0 && timeJumping <= JUMP_TIME_MIN) {
        // Still jumping
        velocity.y = terminalVelocity.y;
      }
  }
  if (jumpState != JUMP_STATE.GROUNDED)
  super.updateMotionY(deltaTime);
}
```

The preceding code handles the calculations and switching of states that needed to enable jumping and falling.

Next, add the following code to override the `render()` method:

```
@Override
public void render (SpriteBatch batch) {
  TextureRegion reg = null;

  // Set special color when game object has a feather power-up
  if (hasFeatherPowerup)
  batch.setColor(1.0f, 0.8f, 0.0f, 1.0f);
```

```
    // Draw image
    reg = regHead;
    batch.draw(reg.getTexture(),
                position.x, position.y,
                origin.x, origin.y,
                dimension.x, dimension.y,
                scale.x, scale.y,
                rotation,
                reg.getRegionX(), reg.getRegionY(),
                reg.getRegionWidth(), reg.getRegionHeight(),
                viewDirection == VIEW_DIRECTION.LEFT, false);

    // Reset color to white
    batch.setColor(1, 1, 1, 1);
}
```

The preceding code handles the drawing of the image for the bunny head game object. The image will be tinted orange if the feather power-up effect is active.

Furthermore, add the following code to `Constants`:

```
// Duration of feather power-up in seconds
public static final float ITEM_FEATHER_POWERUP_DURATION = 9;
```

The viewing direction `viewDirection` will change according to the object's velocity as long as it is unequal to zero. It will be set to `VIEW_DIRECTION.LEFT` when the horizontal velocity is negative, otherwise it will be set to `VIEW_DIRECTION.RIGHT`. This simply means that the player character will always look in the direction it is moving.

There are four different states for jumping:

- `GROUNDED`: In this state, the player is standing on a platform.
- `FALLING`: In this state, the player is falling down.
- `JUMP_RISING`: In this state, the player has initiated a jump and is still rising. The maximum jump height has not been reached.
- `JUMP_FALLING`: In this state, the player is falling down after a previously initiated jump. This state is reached either by jumping as long as possible or by releasing the jump key earlier than that.

The state for jumping is stored in `jumpState`. There is a minimum and maximum jump time defined by the constants `JUMP_TIME_MIN` and `JUMP_TIME_MAX`. These time limits and the jump power affect the resulting possible minimum and maximum jump heights. A minimum jump is enforced on the player whenever the jump key is released before the time defined in `JUMP_TIME_MIN`.

The currently elapsed jump time is accumulated in `timeJumping` and is reset on every new jump. There is a third constant `JUMP_TIME_OFFSET_FLYING` that is used to let the elapsed jump time start at a certain time, which effectively shortens the overall height of such jumps. This is used for the multi jump power-up effect of the feather item. It allows the bunny head to fly by rapidly jumping repeatedly. A multi jump can only be executed while the bunny head is in midair. A shorter jump time for multi jumps makes it more difficult for the player to handle them, which adds a neat detail to the gameplay feeling.

This is all done inside the overridden `updateMotionY()` method. Notice that the original method of `updateMotionY()` from `AbstractGameObject` is also called whenever an actual motion needs to happen, which is always the case when the player is not in the `GROUNDED` jump state.

The following diagram visualizes the flow of the preceding method:

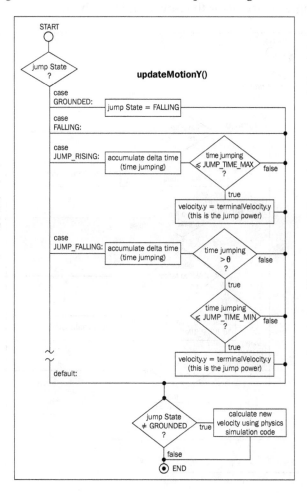

As you can see, the jump state will always change to FALLING whenever it is set to GROUNDED. The reason for this is that we want grounded objects like the player character to be able to fall down from platforms where they end. There must be a trigger that tests this event so that the jump state will be in fact permanently changed from GROUNDED to FALLING as long as there is a collision detected that resets the jump state back to GROUNDED. Otherwise, the player character will start to fall down as intended.

A new jump is triggered by calling the setJumping() method. A value of true can be passed as the argument to denote a press of the jump key. So this method checks the current jump state of the bunny and also tests whether the jump key is currently pressed by the player to perform the appropriate actions. Those actions can be to start a new jump, cancel an ongoing jump, or allow multi jumps with the help of the feather power-up.

The following diagram visualizes the flow of this method:

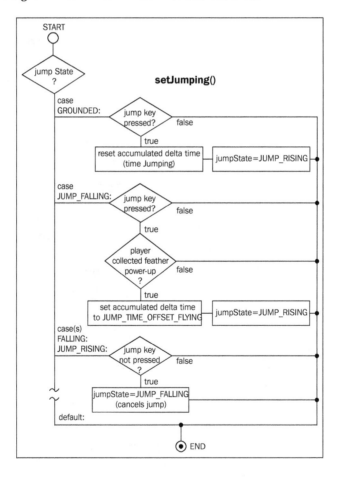

The variables `hasFeatherPowerup` and `timeLeftFeatherPowerup` describe whether the player has collected the feather power-up or not and how much time the effect will last. The power-up effect can be enabled and disabled by calling `setFeatherPowerup()`. The method `hasFeatherPowerup()` is used as a combined test to find out if the power-up has been collected and if the effect is still lasting.

The `render()` method will tint the image of the player character orange if the feather power-up has been collected. The viewing direction `viewDirection` is used to decide whether the image needs to be flipped on the x axis.

Updating the rock object

Last but not least, change the `setLength()` method of `Rock` to the following listings:

```
public void setLength (int length) {
  this.length = length;
  // Update bounding box for collision detection
  bounds.set(0, 0, dimension.x * length, dimension.y);
}
```

This will make sure that the size of the bounding box is adjusted whenever the length of a rock is changed.

Completing the level loader

Now that we have implemented all the game objects of Canyon Bunny, we can complete the level loader.

First, add the following import lines to `Level`:

```
import com.packtpub.libgdx.canyonbunny.game.objects.BunnyHead;
import com.packtpub.libgdx.canyonbunny.game.objects.Feather;
import com.packtpub.libgdx.canyonbunny.game.objects.GoldCoin;
```

Additionally, add these three member variables to the same class:

```
public BunnyHead bunnyHead;
public Array<GoldCoin> goldcoins;
public Array<Feather> feathers;
```

After that, modify the two methods `init()` and `render()` as follows:

```java
private void init (String filename) {
  // player character
  bunnyHead = null;
  // objects
  rocks = new Array<Rock>();
  goldcoins = new Array<GoldCoin>();
  feathers = new Array<Feather>();
  // load image file that represents the level data
  Pixmap pixmap = new Pixmap(Gdx.files.internal(filename));
  // scan pixels from top-left to bottom-right
  int lastPixel = -1;
  for (int pixelY = 0; pixelY < pixmap.getHeight(); pixelY++) {
    for (int pixelX = 0; pixelX < pixmap.getWidth(); pixelX++) {
      ...
      // rock
      else if (BLOCK_TYPE.ROCK.sameColor(currentPixel)) {
        ...
      }
      // player spawn point
      else if
      (BLOCK_TYPE.PLAYER_SPAWNPOINT.sameColor(currentPixel)) {
        obj = new BunnyHead();
        offsetHeight = -3.0f;
        obj.position.set(pixelX,baseHeight * obj.dimension.y
          + offsetHeight);
        bunnyHead = (BunnyHead)obj;
      }
      // feather
      else if(BLOCK_TYPE.ITEM_FEATHER.sameColor(currentPixel)) {
        obj = new Feather();
        offsetHeight = -1.5f;
        obj.position.set(pixelX,baseHeight * obj.dimension.y
          + offsetHeight);
        feathers.add((Feather)obj);
      }
      // gold coin
      else if
      (BLOCK_TYPE.ITEM_GOLD_COIN.sameColor(currentPixel)) {
        obj = new GoldCoin();
        offsetHeight = -1.5f;
        obj.position.set(pixelX,baseHeight * obj.dimension.y
          + offsetHeight);
        goldcoins.add((GoldCoin)obj);
```

```
      }
      // unknown object/pixel color
      else {
        ...
      }
      lastPixel = currentPixel;
    }
  }
  ...
}
```

This code adds the actors to the level loading process in the init() method.

Next, make the following changes to the render() method:

```
public void render (SpriteBatch batch) {
  // Draw Mountains
  mountains.render(batch);
  // Draw Rocks
  for (Rock rock : rocks)
    rock.render(batch);
  // Draw Gold Coins
  for (GoldCoin goldCoin : goldcoins)
    goldCoin.render(batch);
  // Draw Feathers
  for (Feather feather : feathers)
    feather.render(batch);
  // Draw Player Character
  bunnyHead.render(batch);
  // Draw Water Overlay
  waterOverlay.render(batch);
  // Draw Clouds
  clouds.render(batch);
}
```

Then, add the following lines to Level:

```
public void update (float deltaTime) {
  bunnyHead.update(deltaTime);
  for(Rock rock : rocks)
    rock.update(deltaTime);
  for(GoldCoin goldCoin : goldcoins)
    goldCoin.update(deltaTime);
  for(Feather feather : feathers)
    feather.update(deltaTime);
  clouds.update(deltaTime);
}
```

We added the new actors to the `render()` method and created a new `update()` method so that we can collectively update all the game world objects in a level in one call.

Finally, modify the `update()` method of `WorldController` as the following listings:

```
public void update (float deltaTime) {
  handleDebugInput(deltaTime);
  level.update(deltaTime);
  cameraHelper.update(deltaTime);
}
```

This change makes sure that all the game objects contained within the level will be updated when the `update()` method of `WorldController` is called.

Adding the game logic

The next step would be to add the game logic that constitutes the rules of our game world. However, the game logic will need to be able to detect the so-called collisions between two game objects before it can handle all of our events, such as walking over an item to collect it. So, we will implement a very basic collision detection method that tests two overlapping rectangles. If an overlap is detected, it means that there is also a collision between those two tested objects. So, we can bind a certain action to this event in the game logic to handle collisions as required.

Adding collision detection

First, add the following import lines to `WorldController`:

```
import com.badlogic.gdx.math.Rectangle;
import com.packtpub.libgdx.canyonbunny.game.objects.BunnyHead;
import com.packtpub.libgdx.canyonbunny.game.objects.BunnyHead
    .JUMP_STATE;
import com.packtpub.libgdx.canyonbunny.game.objects.Feather;
import com.packtpub.libgdx.canyonbunny.game.objects.GoldCoin;
import com.packtpub.libgdx.canyonbunny.game.objects.Rock;
```

After that, add the following code to the same class:

```
// Rectangles for collision detection
private Rectangle r1 = new Rectangle();
private Rectangle r2 = new Rectangle();

private void onCollisionBunnyHeadWithRock(Rock rock) {};
private void onCollisionBunnyWithGoldCoin(GoldCoin goldcoin) {};
```

```
private void onCollisionBunnyWithFeather(Feather feather) {};

private void testCollisions () {
  r1.set(level.bunnyHead.position.x,
         level.bunnyHead.position.y,
         level.bunnyHead.bounds.width,
         level.bunnyHead.bounds.height);

  // Test collision: Bunny Head <-> Rocks
  for (Rock rock : level.rocks) {
    r2.set(rock.position.x, rock.position.y,
           rock.bounds.width, rock.bounds.height);
    if (!r1.overlaps(r2)) continue;
    onCollisionBunnyHeadWithRock(rock);
    // IMPORTANT: must do all collisions for valid
    // edge testing on rocks.
  }

  // Test collision: Bunny Head <-> Gold Coins
  for (GoldCoin goldcoin : level.goldcoins) {
    if (goldcoin.collected) continue;
    r2.set(goldcoin.position.x, goldcoin.position.y,
           goldcoin.bounds.width, goldcoin.bounds.height);
    if (!r1.overlaps(r2)) continue;
    onCollisionBunnyWithGoldCoin(goldcoin);
    break;
  }

  // Test collision: Bunny Head <-> Feathers
  for (Feather feather : level.feathers) {
    if (feather.collected) continue;
    r2.set(feather.position.x, feather.position.y,
           feather.bounds.width, feather.bounds.height);
    if (!r1.overlaps(r2)) continue;
    onCollisionBunnyWithFeather(feather);
    break;
  }
}
```

This code adds a new method called `testCollisions()` that iterates through all the game objects and tests whether there is a collision between the bunny head and another game object. This particular test is subdivided into three separate methods called `onCollisionBunnyHeadWithRock()`, `onCollisionBunnyWithGoldCoin()`, and `onCollisionBunnyWithFeather()`, which are still empty.

Next, fill the `onCollisionBunnyHeadWithRock()` method with the following code:

```java
private void onCollisionBunnyHeadWithRock (Rock rock) {
  BunnyHead bunnyHead = level.bunnyHead;
  float heightDifference = Math.abs(bunnyHead.position.y
                          - (   rock.position.y
                            + rock.bounds.height));
  if (heightDifference > 0.25f) {
    boolean hitLeftEdge = bunnyHead.position.x
                        > (   rock.position.x
                          + rock.bounds.width / 2.0f);
    if (hitLeftEdge) {
      bunnyHead.position.x = rock.position.x
                            + rock.bounds.width;
    } else {
      bunnyHead.position.x = rock.position.x
                            - bunnyHead.bounds.width;
    }
    return;
  }

  switch (bunnyHead.jumpState) {
    case GROUNDED:
      break;
    case FALLING:
    case JUMP_FALLING:
      bunnyHead.position.y = rock.position.y
                            + bunnyHead.bounds.height
                            + bunnyHead.origin.y;
      bunnyHead.jumpState = JUMP_STATE.GROUNDED;
      break;
    case JUMP_RISING:
      bunnyHead.position.y = rock.position.y
                            + bunnyHead.bounds.height
                            + bunnyHead.origin.y;
      break;
  }
}
```

This code handles collisions between the bunny head game object and a rock game object and is called when a collision is detected. Then, the bunny head game object is moved accordingly to prevent it from falling through our platforms—the rock game objects.

Next, fill the `onCollisionBunnyWithGoldCoin()` method with the following code:

```
private void onCollisionBunnyWithGoldCoin (GoldCoin goldcoin) {
   goldcoin.collected = true;
   score += goldcoin.getScore();
   Gdx.app.log(TAG, "Gold coin collected");
}
```

This code handles collisions between the bunny head game object and a gold coin game object. It simply flags the gold coin as being collected so that it will disappear. Furthermore, the player's score increases by the value the gold coin game object returns from its `getScore()` method.

Finally, fill the `onCollisionBunnyWithFeather()` method with the following code:

```
private void onCollisionBunnyWithFeather (Feather feather) {
   feather.collected = true;
   score += feather.getScore();
   level.bunnyHead.setFeatherPowerup(true);
   Gdx.app.log(TAG, "Feather collected");
}
```

This code handles collisions between the bunny head game object and a feather game object. The handling of this collision is similar to the `onCollisionBunnyWithGoldCoin()` method, but it also activates or refreshes the power-up effect for the bunny head.

Now let us make one more modification to the `update()` method of `WorldController`:

```
public void update (float deltaTime) {
   handleDebugInput(deltaTime);
   level.update(deltaTime);
   testCollisions();
   cameraHelper.update(deltaTime);
}
```

You can now run the game to check whether the level loading and collision detection works. Within a very short time span, you should see that the player character falls down a bit and then stops on top of the rock underneath it. The following is a screenshot of this scene:

You can still use all the keys (left/right/up/down arrows, comma, dot, and so on) for controlling the camera, so now is a good opportunity to just fly around a bit in the game world to verify that all the game objects appear at their correct locations.

The following is a screenshot where the camera has been zoomed out a bit to view all the new game objects at once:

Next, we will add a toggle key to choose whether the arrow keys should control the player character or the camera. The camera should follow the player character while being in the player control mode. Otherwise, the camera can be freely moved around. We will also add another key to let the player character jump.

Let us begin with the camera that is set to follow the player character at the start of the level. Add the highlighted line of code to the `initLevel()` method of `WorldController`:

```
private void initLevel () {
  score = 0;
  level = new Level(Constants.LEVEL_01);
  cameraHelper.setTarget(level.bunnyHead);
}
```

Next, change the methods `handleDebugInput()` and `keyUp()` of `WorldController`:

```
private void handleDebugInput (float deltaTime) {
  if (Gdx.app.getType() != ApplicationType.Desktop) return;

  if (!cameraHelper.hasTarget(level.bunnyHead)) {
    // Camera Controls (move)
    float camMoveSpeed = 5 * deltaTime;
    float camMoveSpeedAccelerationFactor = 5;
    if (Gdx.input.isKeyPressed(Keys.SHIFT_LEFT))
      camMoveSpeed *= camMoveSpeedAccelerationFactor;
    if (Gdx.input.isKeyPressed(Keys.LEFT))
      moveCamera(-camMoveSpeed, 0);
    if (Gdx.input.isKeyPressed(Keys.RIGHT))
      moveCamera(camMoveSpeed, 0);
    if (Gdx.input.isKeyPressed(Keys.UP))
      moveCamera(0, camMoveSpeed);
    if (Gdx.input.isKeyPressed(Keys.DOWN))
      moveCamera(0, -camMoveSpeed);
    if (Gdx.input.isKeyPressed(Keys.BACKSPACE))
      cameraHelper.setPosition(0, 0);
  }

  // Camera Controls (zoom)
  ...
}

@Override
public boolean keyUp (int keycode) {
  // Reset game world
  if (keycode == Keys.R) {
    init();
    Gdx.app.debug(TAG, "Game world resetted");
  }
  // Toggle camera follow
  else if (keycode == Keys.ENTER) {
    cameraHelper.setTarget(cameraHelper.hasTarget()
        ? null: level.bunnyHead);
    Gdx.app.debug(TAG, "Camera follow enabled: "
        + cameraHelper.hasTarget());
  }
  return false;
}
```

Now we can use the *Enter* key to toggle between the player and camera controls. What is still missing is the code that handles the input for the player character.

Add the following lines of code to `WorldController`:

```
private void handleInputGame (float deltaTime) {
  if (cameraHelper.hasTarget(level.bunnyHead)) {
    // Player Movement
    if (Gdx.input.isKeyPressed(Keys.LEFT)) {
      level.bunnyHead.velocity.x =
          -level.bunnyHead.terminalVelocity.x;
    } else if (Gdx.input.isKeyPressed(Keys.RIGHT)) {
      level.bunnyHead.velocity.x =
        level.bunnyHead.terminalVelocity.x;
    } else {
      // Execute auto-forward movement on non-desktop platform
      if (Gdx.app.getType() != ApplicationType.Desktop) {
        level.bunnyHead.velocity.x =
        level.bunnyHead.terminalVelocity.x;
      }
    }

    // Bunny Jump
    if (Gdx.input.isTouched() ||
      Gdx.input.isKeyPressed(Keys.SPACE))
      level.bunnyHead.setJumping(true);
    } else {
      level.bunnyHead.setJumping(false);
    }
  }
}
```

After that, simply call the new method in the `update()` method of `WorldController` as follows:

```
public void update (float deltaTime) {
  handleDebugInput(deltaTime);
  handleInputGame(deltaTime);
  level.update(deltaTime);
  testCollisions();
  cameraHelper.update(deltaTime);
}
```

The player is now controllable by using the left and right arrow keys to move in the corresponding direction. We also add an auto-forward moving behavior if the game is run on a non-desktop platform such as Android. Pressing either the Space bar or touching the display of your smartphone will trigger the player character to jump. You can now run the game once again and try to pick up the first items as well as try to carefully jump from rock to rock without falling from the edge. However, you may want to check what happens when you fall down. Obviously, nothing will happen in this case since we have not added any game logic yet to handle it properly. We also want to make the camera stop following the player character too far down the level to make it more clear to the player that the level ends at the height of the water and to avoid a graphical glitch.

 In a later chapter, we will have a closer look at a full-blown physics engine called Box2D that implements all the necessary features to detect a collision. However, we will not revise our implementation by replacing it with Box2D's one, because Canyon Bunny does not use physically accurate movements to make the game feel right. Trying to make real-world physics simulations do unrealistic physics can be a very hard and tedious task.

Losing lives, game over, and fixing the camera

Whenever the player falls into the water, it will cost one extra life. The game will be over as soon as there are no extra lives left and the player falls into the water once again. There will be a short delay of three seconds between the game over message and a complete restart of the game.

Add the following lines to Constants:

```
// Delay after game over
public static final float TIME_DELAY_GAME_OVER = 3;
```

Next, add the following lines to WorldController:

```
private float timeLeftGameOverDelay;

public boolean isGameOver () {
  return lives < 0;
}

public boolean isPlayerInWater () {
  return level.bunnyHead.position.y < -5;
}
```

In `isPlayerInWater()`, we test the bunny head's vertical position to find out if it fell down into the water. Since the water is placed at the bottom edge of the screen (y = 0), we simply need to check for a value smaller than this. In our example, we use -5 instead of 0 to also add a little delay in time. This is because travelling all the way down to the vertical position of -5 simply takes longer than it would do if we were using 0. The resulting effect is that the game will enforce a little pause on the player after each lost life.

After that, make the following modifications to `init()` and `update()` in `WorldController`:

```
private void init () {
  Gdx.input.setInputProcessor(this);
  cameraHelper = new CameraHelper();
  lives = Constants.LIVES_START;
  timeLeftGameOverDelay = 0;
  initLevel();
}

public void update (float deltaTime) {
  handleDebugInput(deltaTime);
  if (isGameOver()) {
    timeLeftGameOverDelay -= deltaTime;
    if (timeLeftGameOverDelay < 0) init();
  } else {
    handleInputGame(deltaTime);
  }
  level.update(deltaTime);
  testCollisions();
  cameraHelper.update(deltaTime);
  if (!isGameOver() && isPlayerInWater()) {
    lives--;
    if (isGameOver())
      timeLeftGameOverDelay = Constants.TIME_DELAY_GAME_OVER;
    else
      initLevel();
  }
}
```

The player character will now lose extra lives when falling down into the water. You can verify this by checking the top-right corner of the game screen. Each missing extra life will turn into a transparent bunny head icon. The game over delay and the restart of the game after that are also working now.

There is still one small modification needed to fix the camera follow behavior.

Change the update() method of CameraHelper as follows:

```
public void update (float deltaTime) {
  if (!hasTarget()) return;
  position.x = target.position.x + target.origin.x;
  position.y = target.position.y + target.origin.y;
  // Prevent camera from moving down too far
  position.y = Math.max(-1f, position.y);
}
```

Adding the game over text and the feather icon to the GUI

Add the following method to WorldRenderer:

```
private void renderGuiGameOverMessage (SpriteBatch batch) {
  float x = cameraGUI.viewportWidth / 2;
  float y = cameraGUI.viewportHeight / 2;
  if (worldController.isGameOver()) {
    BitmapFont fontGameOver = Assets.instance.fonts.defaultBig;
    fontGameOver.setColor(1, 0.75f, 0.25f, 1);
    fontGameOver.drawMultiLine(batch, "GAME OVER",
        x, y, 0, BitmapFont.HAlignment.CENTER);
    fontGameOver.setColor(1, 1, 1, 1);
  }
}
```

This method calculates the center of the GUI camera's viewport. The text is rendered using the big font from our assets. Its color is changed using the setColor() method of BitmapFont. The game over text is drawn using the drawMultiLine() method of BitmapFont, which takes a reference to SpriteBatch, the actual text to be displayed, a 2D position, a horizontal offset, and a constant for horizontal text alignment.

We could have used draw() instead of drawMultiLine(); however, draw() does not provide the horizontal text alignment parameter which we need to center the text around its 2D position. The text may contain newlines (\n) to display a multi-line text, which we do not use in the preceding code.

We are using the `BitmapFont.HAlignment.CENTER` constant to tell `BitmapFont` that we want it to draw the given text horizontally centered to the given position. The text message **GAME OVER** will only be visible if the `isGameOver()` method of `WorldController` returns `true`.

The following is a screenshot of a case where all the extra lives have been used up until the game was over:

Now, add the following method to `WorldRenderer`:

```
private void renderGuiFeatherPowerup (SpriteBatch batch) {
  float x = -15;
  float y = 30;
  float timeLeftFeatherPowerup =
      worldController.level.bunnyHead.timeLeftFeatherPowerup;
  if (timeLeftFeatherPowerup > 0) {
    // Start icon fade in/out if the left power-up time
    // is less than 4 seconds. The fade interval is set
    // to 5 changes per second.
    if (timeLeftFeatherPowerup < 4) {
      if (((int)(timeLeftFeatherPowerup * 5) % 2) != 0) {
        batch.setColor(1, 1, 1, 0.5f);
      }
```

```
        }
        batch.draw(Assets.instance.feather.feather,
            x, y, 50, 50, 100, 100, 0.35f, -0.35f, 0);
        batch.setColor(1, 1, 1, 1);
        Assets.instance.fonts.defaultSmall.draw(batch,
            "" + (int)timeLeftFeatherPowerup, x + 60, y + 57);
    }
}
```

This method first checks if there is still time left for the feather power-up effect to end. Only if this is the case, a feather icon is drawn in the top-left corner under the gold coin icon. A small number is drawn next to it that displays the rounded time that is still left until the effect vanishes. There is also some extra code that makes the feather icon fade back and forth when there are less than four seconds of the power-up effect to last.

The following is a screenshot where the feather power-up has been picked up and has six seconds left:

You can see this from the little number shown next to the feather icon in the top-left corner of the game screen.

As the final step for this chapter, both the new GUI render methods need to be added to the `renderGUI()` method of `WorldRenderer`:

```
private void renderGui (SpriteBatch batch) {
   batch.setProjectionMatrix(cameraGUI.combined);
   batch.begin();

   // draw collected gold coins icon + text
   // (anchored to top left edge)
   renderGuiScore(batch);
   // draw collected feather icon (anchored to top left edge)
   renderGuiFeatherPowerup(batch);
   // draw extra lives icon + text (anchored to top right edge)
   renderGuiExtraLive(batch);
   // draw FPS text (anchored to bottom right edge)
   renderGuiFpsCounter(batch);
   // draw game over text
   renderGuiGameOverMessage(batch);

   batch.end();
}
```

Summary

In this chapter, we learned how to implement the player character, platforms, and collectible items in conjunction with a basic yet functional physics simulation and collision detection code. Nonetheless, it should be mentioned that the physics simulation as well as the collision detection code both have their limitations. However, as long as our original requirements of the game do not change, we will be just fine.

Furthermore, we have completed the level loader and discussed how jumps for our player character work. Two conditions for losing extra lives and reaching game over have been added. The camera's position has been constrained in a way that it will never follow the player character below the height of the water. Finally, we have added a **GAME OVER** text message so that the player receives a visual feedback that all lives have been used up. The feather power-up also gives a visual feedback when collected and active by displaying a feather icon with a nice little countdown timer that shows the remaining time for the effect to last.

This concludes the basic implementation of the Canyon Bunny game, which also means that we have now implemented all the features that we had originally defined in our outline back in *Chapter 1, Introduction to Libgdx and Project Setup*.

In the next chapter, we will create a menu system to enrich the overall game experience.

7
Menus and Options

In this chapter we will create a menu for Canyon Bunny. There will be two buttons for the player to choose from. One of the buttons is the **Play** button, which will start a new game. The other button will show an options menu that contains a few changeable settings, such as sound and music volumes. All settings will be stored to and loaded from a Preferences file to make them permanent.

It is essential to have some sort of mechanism to manage multiple screens if we want to allow the player to switch between them. Libgdx provides a Game class which already supports such basic screen management.

You will also learn how to use Libgdx's scene graph called Scene2D to create and organize complex menu structures as well as how to handle events such as pressed buttons.

Managing multiple screens

We will now make some minor changes to our current class diagram to reflect the support for multiple screens that we want to add to our game.

You might want to take a peek at the previous class diagram of Canyon Bunny for a quick refresher. See *Chapter 3, Configuring the Game* for the diagram.

Take a look at the following updated class diagram:

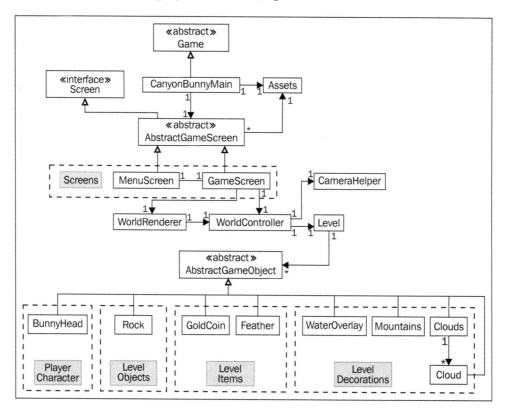

What has been changed here is that CanyonBunnyMain no longer implements the ApplicationListener interface that is used by Libgdx to control the flow of the application. Instead, CanyonBunnyMain now extends Libgdx's Game class, which in turn implements the ApplicationListener interface. The Game class provides a setScreen() method. Calling this method allows us to change the current screen to another one.

Every screen that we want to have in our game is encapsulated in a separate class and ends with *Screen. This is just a naming convention in this project and you are free to do it differently, of course. There are also three new classes shown in the preceding diagram, which are called AbstractGameScreen, MenuScreen, and GameScreen. The menu and the game screen classes extend AbstractGameScreen so that we can easily define the common actions that we want to be executed for all our screens. Additionally, AbstractGameScreen implements Libgdx's Screen interface, which introduces a show() and hide() method for each screen. These methods will be called by Game and will take the place of create() and dispose(), so we will have to move our existing code accordingly.

The diagram also shows that WorldController and WorldRenderer are no longer directly used by CanyonBunnyMain. Instead, GameScreen is using them from now on, since we will move all of the game-world-specific code from CanyonBunnyMain to GameScreen.

Create a new file for the AbstractGameScreen class and add the following code:

```
package com.packtpub.libgdx.canyonbunny.screens;

import com.badlogic.gdx.Game;
import com.badlogic.gdx.Screen;
import com.badlogic.gdx.assets.AssetManager;
import com.packtpub.libgdx.canyonbunny.game.Assets;

public abstract class AbstractGameScreen implements Screen {
  protected Game game;

  public AbstractGameScreen (Game game) {
    this.game = game;
  }

  public abstract void render (float deltaTime);
  public abstract void resize (int width, int height);
  public abstract void show ();
  public abstract void hide ();
  public abstract void pause ();

  public void resume () {
    Assets.instance.init(new AssetManager());
  }

  public void dispose () {
    Assets.instance.dispose();
  }
}
```

Each screen will take a reference to the instance of Game. This is necessary because each screen needs to be able to call the setScreen() method of the Game class. Apart from that, we have added two lines of code that will make sure that the game's assets will be correctly loaded and disposed as Libgdx sees fit.

Next, we will implement the two new screen classes. Create a new file for the MenuScreen class and add the following code:

```
package com.packtpub.libgdx.canyonbunny.screens;

import com.badlogic.gdx.Game;
import com.badlogic.gdx.Gdx;
import com.badlogic.gdx.graphics.GL10;

public class MenuScreen extends AbstractGameScreen {
  private static final String TAG = MenuScreen.class.getName();

  public MenuScreen (Game game) {
    super(game);
  }

  @Override
  public void render (float deltaTime) {
    Gdx.gl.glClearColor(0.0f, 0.0f, 0.0f, 1.0f);
    Gdx.gl.glClear(GL10.GL_COLOR_BUFFER_BIT);
    if (Gdx.input.isTouched())
      game.setScreen(new GameScreen(game));
  }

  @Override public void resize (int width, int height) { }
  @Override public void show () { }
  @Override public void hide () { }
  @Override public void pause () { }
}
```

This is still a very rough implementation of the menu screen, but it will serve us well for the moment. The render() method takes care of only two things. It constantly clears the screen by filling it with a solid black color and it looks for whether the screen has been touched, which also includes mouse clicks if the game is run on a desktop. As soon as a touch has been detected, the screen will be switched from the menu screen to the game screen showing our actual game world.

Next, create a new file for the GameScreen class and add the following code:

```
package com.packtpub.libgdx.canyonbunny.screens;

import com.badlogic.gdx.Game;
import com.badlogic.gdx.Gdx;
import com.badlogic.gdx.graphics.GL10;
import com.packtpub.libgdx.canyonbunny.game.WorldController;
import com.packtpub.libgdx.canyonbunny.game.WorldRenderer;

public class GameScreen extends AbstractGameScreen {
  private static final String TAG = GameScreen.class.getName();

  private WorldController worldController;
  private WorldRenderer worldRenderer;

  private boolean paused;

  public GameScreen (Game game) {
    super(game);
  }

  @Override
  public void render (float deltaTime) {
    // Do not update game world when paused.
    if (!paused) {
      // Update game world by the time that has passed
      // since last rendered frame.
      worldController.update(deltaTime);
    }
    // Sets the clear screen color to: Cornflower Blue
    Gdx.gl.glClearColor(0x64 / 255.0f,
                        0x95 / 255.0f,
                        0xed / 255.0f,
                        0xff / 255.0f);
    // Clears the screen
    Gdx.gl.glClear(GL10.GL_COLOR_BUFFER_BIT);
    // Render game world to screen
    worldRenderer.render();
  }
```

```
    @Override
    public void resize (int width, int height) {
      worldRenderer.resize(width, height);
    }

    @Override
    public void show () {
      worldController = new WorldController(game);
      worldRenderer = new WorldRenderer(worldController);
      Gdx.input.setCatchBackKey(true);
    }

    @Override
    public void hide () {
      worldRenderer.dispose();
      Gdx.input.setCatchBackKey(false);
    }

    @Override
    public void pause () {
      paused = true;
    }

    @Override
    public void resume () {
      super.resume();
      // Only called on Android!
      paused = false;
    }
  }
}
```

You should recognize most of the preceding code since it is merely a duplicate of the current CanyonBunnyMain class. However, some small changes have been made. First of all, the code that was in the create() and dispose() methods of CanyonBunnyMain have been moved over to the show() and hide() methods respectively to accommodate the Screen interface. Furthermore, catching Android's back key will be enabled when the game screen is shown and disabled again when the screen is hidden. This allows us to handle this event and execute a custom action (here, switch back to the menu screen) in place of the system's default action, which is to terminate the running application.

Now, let us fix CanyonBunnyMain. For clarity and brevity, we will just replace the whole class as most of its code has to be removed anyway.

Replace the current content of `CanyonBunnyMain` with the following code:

```
package com.packtpub.libgdx.canyonbunny;

import com.badlogic.gdx.Application;
import com.badlogic.gdx.Game;
import com.badlogic.gdx.Gdx;
import com.badlogic.gdx.assets.AssetManager;
import com.packtpub.libgdx.canyonbunny.game.Assets;
import com.packtpub.libgdx.canyonbunny.screens.MenuScreen;

public class CanyonBunnyMain extends Game {
  @Override
  public void create () {
    // Set Libgdx log level
    Gdx.app.setLogLevel(Application.LOG_DEBUG);
    // Load assets
    Assets.instance.init(new AssetManager());
    // Start game at menu screen
    setScreen(new MenuScreen(this));
  }
}
```

Our platform-independent entry point of the game has obviously become quite simple. Basically, `CanyonBunnyMain` has been reduced to only contain the `create()` method, which almost looks the same as before. What has changed inside this method is that after setting the log level and loading our assets, Libgdx is instructed through a call of the `setScreen()` method by the `Game` class to change the current screen. Since we want the game to start with the menu screen, we simply pass a new instance of `MenuScreen`.

One last change is required to finish our preparations for multiple screen management. The `WorldController` class holds our game logic and needs to initiate a switch back to the menu whenever the player has lost the game or if either the *Esc* key or the back button has been pressed.

Add the following two import lines to `WorldController`:

```
import com.badlogic.gdx.Game;
import com.packtpub.libgdx.canyonbunny.screens.MenuScreen;
```

After that, add the following code:

```
private Game game;

private void backToMenu () {
  // switch to menu screen
  game.setScreen(new MenuScreen(game));
}
```

This allows us to save a reference to the game instance which will enable us to switch to another screen. Additionally, a convenient method, backToMenu(), has also been added that will switch to the menu screen when called.

After that, make the following changes to WorldController:

```
public WorldController (Game game) {
  this.game = game;
  init();
}

public void update (float deltaTime) {
  handleDebugInput(deltaTime);
  if (isGameOver()) {
    timeLeftGameOverDelay -= deltaTime;
    if (timeLeftGameOverDelay < 0) backToMenu();
  } else {
    handleInputGame(deltaTime);
  }
  level.update(deltaTime);
  ...
}

@Override
public boolean keyUp (int keycode) {
  ...
  // Toggle camera follow
  else if (keycode == Keys.ENTER) {
    ...
  }
  // Back to Menu
  else if (keycode == Keys.ESCAPE || keycode == Keys.BACK) {
    backToMenu();
  }
  return false;
}
```

The constructor has been extended by taking a reference of the game instance as an argument, which is then stored for later reference when we need to switch the screen. In the update() method, a call to backToMenu() is initiated as soon as the game-over-delay timer has run out of time instead of restarting the game in the game world as has been the case before. As mentioned earlier, we want to handle Android's back key as well as the *Esc* key on the desktop ourselves, which is now done inside the keyUp() method.

You can now run the game and verify that you can switch back and forth between MenuScreen and GameScreen. Touch the black screen of the menu and try to get back to it by hitting either the *Esc* key or the back button, respectively. Losing all lives while still in the game screen should yield the same result and bring you back to the menu screen too.

Exploring Scene2D (UI), TableLayout, and skins

Libgdx comes with a great feature set to easily create scene graphs. A scene graph is a hierarchically organized structure of objects similar to files and folders on a hard disk. In Libgdx, such objects are called actors. Actors can be nested to create logical groups. Grouping actors is a very useful feature, since modifications applied to a parent actor will also affect its child actors. Furthermore, each actor has its own local coordinate system, which makes it very easy to define relative offsets inside a group of actors including position, angle of rotation, and scale.

Scene2D supports hit detection of rotated and scaled actors. Libgdx's flexible event system allows handling and routing inputs as needed so that the parent actors may intercept inputs before they reach the child actors. Finally, the built-in action system can be used to easily manipulate actors over time, creating complex effects that may execute in sequence, parallel, or in a combination of both. All of this described functionality is encapsulated in the Stage class, which contains the hierarchy and distributes user-generated events. Actors can be added to and removed from it at any time. The Stage class and the Actor class both contain an act() method, which takes a delta time as its argument to do some time-based action. Calling act() on a Stage instance will cause a call of act() on every actor in the scene graph. The act() methods of Stage and Actor are basically what we already know as the update() methods, only using a different name. For more information about Scene2D, check out the official documentation at https://code.google.com/p/libgdx/wiki/scene2d/.

Until now, we have not used any of Scene2D's functionality in our game. Naturally, we could have implemented the game world including its game objects with Scene2D. However, always keep in mind that using a scene graph comes with a certain amount of overhead. Libgdx tries its best to keep the overhead at a bare minimum, such as skipping complex calculations of transformation matrices if objects do not need to be rotated or scaled. So, it really depends on what your requirements are.

Since the user interface of the menu that we are going to create is rather complex, we want to make use of Libgdx's scene graph for this task. More precisely, we will use Scene2D UI. This is another implementation in Libgdx that builds on top of Scene2D and extends its functionality by providing a rich set of common and ready-to-use UI elements. In Libgdx, these UI elements are called widgets.

The following is a brief list of all the widgets currently available in Scene2D UI:

`Button`, `CheckBox`, `Dialog`, `Image`, `ImageButton`, `Label`, `List`, `ScrollPane`, `SelectBox`, `Slider`, `SplitPane`, `Stack`, `Window`, `TextButton`, `TextField`, `Touchpad`, and `Tree`.

Scene2D UI also supports the easy creation of new custom widgets. We will discuss a selected number of widgets as we implement them in our menu. For a complete list and description of each widget, check out the official documentation at `https://code.google.com/p/libgdx/wiki/scene2dui/`.

In addition to Scene2D UI, Libgdx also incorporates a separate project called `TableLayout`. `TableLayout` makes it very easy to create and maintain dynamic (read: resolution-independent) layouts using tables and also provides an intuitive API. A class called `Table` provides access to the functionality of `TableLayout`, which is also implemented as a widget, and therefore integrates seamlessly into the concept of Scene2D UI.

It is highly recommended to check out the official documentation at `https://code.google.com/p/table-layout/`.

One more important feature of Scene2D UI is the support of skins. A skin is a collection of resources which are used to style and display UI widgets. For example, resources can be texture regions, fonts, and colors. Typically, a skin uses texture regions which come from a texture atlas. The style definition of each widget is stored in a separate file using the JSON file format.

For more information, check out the official documentation at `https://code.google.com/p/libgdx/wiki/Skin`.

Using Libgdx's scene graph for the menu UI

We are now going to create the scene of the menu screen. The scene will feature a background image that fills the whole screen. There will be logos in the top-left and bottom-left corner of the screen and two clickable buttons anchored to the bottom-right corner that will trigger either a play or an options action. A gold coin and a huge image of the bunny head are also added to the scene.

The following is a screenshot of how the finished menu screen will look:

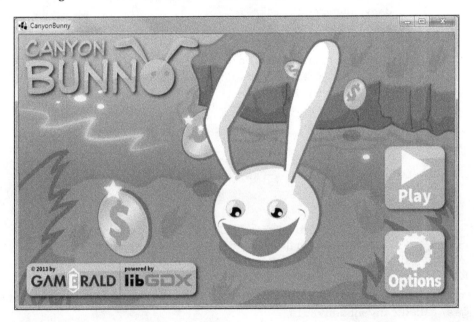

However, before we start to create this scene, we have to do some preparations in advance. First of all, we need to add the new images to our project and also make a small change to the automatic texture packing process so that we have a texture atlas for our UI.

Add a new subfolder in `CanyonBunny-desktop/assets-raw/` called `images-ui` and copy all of the new images into this directory. After that, make the following change to `Main`:

```
public static void main (String[] args) {
  if (rebuildAtlas) {
    Settings settings = new Settings();
    settings.maxWidth = 1024;
    settings.maxHeight = 1024;
    settings.debug = drawDebugOutline;
    TexturePacker2.process(settings, "assets-raw/images",
        "../CanyonBunny-android/assets/images",
        "canyonbunny.pack");
    TexturePacker2.process(settings, "assets-raw/images-ui",
        "../CanyonBunny-android/assets/images",
        "canyonbunny-ui.pack");
  }

  LwjglApplicationConfiguration cfg =
      new LwjglApplicationConfiguration();
  cfg.title = "CanyonBunny";
  cfg.useGL20 = false;
  cfg.width = 800;
  cfg.height = 480;

  new LwjglApplication(new CanyonBunnyMain(), cfg);
}
```

 You will need to set `rebuildAtlas` to `true` at least once and run the game on the desktop to let the texture packer create the required texture atlas.

The texture atlas for our UI will then be created in `CanyonBunny-android/assets/images/` called `canyonbunny-ui`.

The resulting texture atlas for our UI should look like the following screenshot:

Next, we will create a suitable JSON file to define the skin of our menu widgets.

Create a new file in CanyonBunny-android/assets/images/ called canyonbunny-ui.json and add the following lines:

```
{
com.badlogic.gdx.scenes.scene2d.ui.Button$ButtonStyle: {
  play: { down: play-dn, up: play-up },
  options: { down: options-dn, up: options-up }
},
com.badlogic.gdx.scenes.scene2d.ui.Image: {
  background: { drawable: background },
  logo: { drawable: logo },
  info: { drawable: info },
  coins: { drawable: coins },
  bunny: { drawable: bunny },
},
}
```

This definition file describes the type of widget to be used by specifying its completely qualified name. Inside the block of a widget definition, you can freely choose a name. Here we use play, options, background, and so on for our names. These names are then followed by a colon, followed by a comma-separated list of attributes enclosed in curly brackets that correspond exactly to the field names of the widget's class. For example, the Image widget has a field called drawable. Some widgets have an inner class which is denoted in the JSON file by appending a dollar sign followed by the name of the style class. Those style classes contain widget-specific fields. We are using such a definition type for the **Play** and **Options** buttons, which both have a down and up image assigned in their Button widget.

Lastly, add the following lines of code to Constants to finish our preparations:

```
public static final String TEXTURE_ATLAS_UI =
    "images/canyonbunny-ui.pack";
public static final String TEXTURE_ATLAS_LIBGDX_UI =
    "images/uiskin.atlas";

// Location of description file for skins
public static final String SKIN_LIBGDX_UI =
    "images/uiskin.json";
public static final String SKIN_CANYONBUNNY_UI =
    "images/canyonbunny-ui.json";
```

Building the scene for the menu screen

We will now begin with the actual implementation of the scene for the menu screen. First, take a look at the following diagram that shows the hierarchy of the UI scene graph that we are going to build step-by-step:

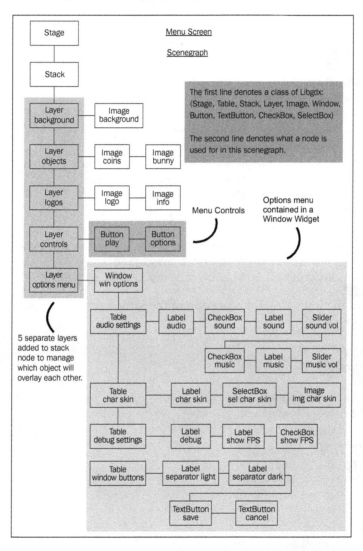

The scene graph starts with an empty `Stage`. Then, the first child actor added to the stage is a `Stack` widget. A `Stack` widget allows you to add actors that can overlay other actors. We will make use of this ability to create several layers. Each layer uses a `Table` widget as its parent actor. Using stacked tables enables us to layout actors in an easy and logical way.

In the first step we will add the basic structure of our stacked layers and some skeleton methods which we are going to fill in the subsequent steps.

Add the following import lines to `MenuScreen`:

```
import com.badlogic.gdx.graphics.Color;
import com.badlogic.gdx.graphics.g2d.TextureAtlas;
import com.badlogic.gdx.scenes.scene2d.Stage;
import com.badlogic.gdx.scenes.scene2d.ui.Button;
import com.badlogic.gdx.scenes.scene2d.ui.CheckBox;
import com.badlogic.gdx.scenes.scene2d.ui.Image;
import com.badlogic.gdx.scenes.scene2d.ui.Label;
import com.badlogic.gdx.scenes.scene2d.ui.Label.LabelStyle;
import com.badlogic.gdx.scenes.scene2d.ui.SelectBox;
import com.badlogic.gdx.scenes.scene2d.ui.Skin;
import com.badlogic.gdx.scenes.scene2d.ui.Slider;
import com.badlogic.gdx.scenes.scene2d.ui.Stack;
import com.badlogic.gdx.scenes.scene2d.ui.Table;
import com.badlogic.gdx.scenes.scene2d.ui.TextButton;
import com.badlogic.gdx.scenes.scene2d.ui.Window;
import com.badlogic.gdx.scenes.scene2d.utils.ChangeListener;
import com.packtpub.libgdx.canyonbunny.game.Assets;
import com.packtpub.libgdx.canyonbunny.util.Constants;
```

After that, add the following lines of code to the same class:

```
private Stage stage;
private Skin skinCanyonBunny;

// menu
private Image imgBackground;
private Image imgLogo;
private Image imgInfo;
private Image imgCoins;
private Image imgBunny;
private Button btnMenuPlay;
private Button btnMenuOptions;

// options
private Window winOptions;
private TextButton btnWinOptSave;
private TextButton btnWinOptCancel;
private CheckBox chkSound;
```

```
private Slider sldSound;
private CheckBox chkMusic;
private Slider sldMusic;
private SelectBox selCharSkin;
private Image imgCharSkin;
private CheckBox chkShowFpsCounter;

// debug
private final float DEBUG_REBUILD_INTERVAL = 5.0f;
private boolean debugEnabled = false;
private float debugRebuildStage;
```

We added new variables to store an instance of Stage called stage, an instance of Skin called skinCanyonBunny, and some more variables for the widgets of the menu screen and the **Options** window.

Next, add the following code to the same class:

```
private void rebuildStage () {
  skinCanyonBunny = new Skin(
      Gdx.files.internal(Constants.SKIN_CANYONBUNNY_UI),
      new TextureAtlas(Constants.TEXTURE_ATLAS_UI));

  // build all layers
  Table layerBackground = buildBackgroundLayer();
  Table layerObjects = buildObjectsLayer();
  Table layerLogos = buildLogosLayer();
  Table layerControls = buildControlsLayer();
  Table layerOptionsWindow = buildOptionsWindowLayer();

  // assemble stage for menu screen
  stage.clear();
  Stack stack = new Stack();
  stage.addActor(stack);
  stack.setSize(Constants.VIEWPORT_GUI_WIDTH,
              Constants.VIEWPORT_GUI_HEIGHT);
  stack.add(layerBackground);
  stack.add(layerObjects);
  stack.add(layerLogos);
  stack.add(layerControls);
  stage.addActor(layerOptionsWindow);
}
```

In rebuildStage(), we build everything that will make up the final scene of our menu screen. This method is implemented in a way so that it can be called in a repeated manner; hence the name rebuildStage. While we are implementing each of the layers, you may want to try and modify the code in each step to get a better understanding of how TableLayout behaves in certain situations.

Next, add the following code to the same class:

```
private Table buildBackgroundLayer () {
  Table layer = new Table();
  return layer;
}

private Table buildObjectsLayer () {
  Table layer = new Table();
  return layer;
}

private Table buildLogosLayer () {
  Table layer = new Table();
  return layer;
}

private Table buildControlsLayer () {
  Table layer = new Table();
  return layer;
}

private Table buildOptionsWindowLayer () {
  Table layer = new Table();
  return layer;
}
```

We have added five new methods that contain dummy implementations for now. They will be used to build each layer of the menu.

Next, make the following changes to the same class:

```
@Override
public void resize (int width, int height) {
  stage.setViewport(Constants.VIEWPORT_GUI_WIDTH,
                    Constants.VIEWPORT_GUI_HEIGHT, false);
}

@Override
```

```
public void hide () {
  stage.dispose();
  skinCanyonBunny.dispose();
}

@Override
public void show () {
  stage = new Stage();
  Gdx.input.setInputProcessor(stage);
  rebuildStage();
}
```

The show() method is called when the screen is shown. It initializes the stage, sets it as Libgdx's current input processor so that the stage will receive all the future inputs, and finally, the stage is (re)built by calling rebuildStage(). The hide() method will free the allocated resources when the screen is hidden. The resize() method sets the viewport size of the stage to our constants: VIEWPORT_GUI_WIDTH and VIEWPORT_GUI_HEIGHT for the GUI's width and height, respectively.

Lastly, make the following changes to the render() method in the same class:

```
@Override
public void render (float deltaTime) {
  Gdx.gl.glClearColor(0.0f, 0.0f, 0.0f, 1.0f);
  Gdx.gl.glClear(GL10.GL_COLOR_BUFFER_BIT);
  if (debugEnabled) {
    debugRebuildStage -= deltaTime;
    if (debugRebuildStage <= 0) {
      debugRebuildStage = DEBUG_REBUILD_INTERVAL;
      rebuildStage();
    }
  }
  stage.act(deltaTime);
  stage.draw();
  Table.drawDebug(stage);
}
```

The code in render() that would switch to the game screen when the screen is touched has been replaced by calls to update and render the stage. The statement Table.drawDebug() is a debugging feature of TableLayout which enables you to draw debug visuals in a scene. Additionally, you need to specify which Table widgets should draw debug lines by calling their debug() method.

The following hint might sound trivial, but this is such a big time saver that it is definitely worth pointing it out.

The code you just added to `MenuScreen` contains some additional debug code which will call `rebuildStage()` in periodic intervals defined in seconds by `DEBUG_REBUILD_INTERVAL`. You can enable periodic refreshing by simply setting `debugEnabled` to `true`. This will give you live updates at runtime, assuming that you are running the game in debug mode on the desktop, and will allow you to take advantage of JVM's awesome code hot swapping feature.

Adding the background layer

Make the following changes in `MenuScreen` to add the background layer:

```
private Table buildBackgroundLayer () {
  Table layer = new Table();
  // + Background
  imgBackground = new Image(skinCanyonBunny, "background");
  layer.add(imgBackground);
  return layer;
}
```

There will now be a background image drawn to the scene of the menu screen. The image is referenced by using the `background` name that we defined earlier in our skin file (`canyonbunny-ui.json`). If you change the size of the screen, the stage will adjust accordingly, along with the background layer and its `Image` widget.

Adding the objects layer

Make the following changes in `MenuScreen` to add the objects layer:

```
private Table buildObjectsLayer () {
  Table layer = new Table();
  // + Coins
  imgCoins = new Image(skinCanyonBunny, "coins");
  layer.addActor(imgCoins);
  imgCoins.setPosition(135, 80);
  // + Bunny
  imgBunny = new Image(skinCanyonBunny, "bunny");
  layer.addActor(imgBunny);
  imgBunny.setPosition(355, 40);
  return layer;
}
```

There will now be an image of some coins and another image of a huge bunny head, which are both drawn on top of the background layer. The positions of each actor are explicitly set to certain coordinates by calling setPosition() on each actor.

Adding the logos layer

Make the following changes in MenuScreen to add the logos layer:

```
private Table buildLogosLayer () {
  Table layer = new Table();
  layer.left().top();
  // + Game Logo
  imgLogo = new Image(skinCanyonBunny, "logo");
  layer.add(imgLogo);
  layer.row().expandY();
  // + Info Logos
  imgInfo = new Image(skinCanyonBunny, "info");
  layer.add(imgInfo).bottom();
  if (debugEnabled) layer.debug();
  return layer;
}
```

The logos layer is anchored to the top-left corner of the screen. After that, an image logo is added to the table followed by a call of the row() and expandY() methods. Every time you call add() on a Table widget, TableLayout will add a new column, which means the widget grows in a horizontal direction. So, if you want to start a new row, you can tell TableLayout about this by calling row(). The expandY() method expands the empty space in a vertical direction. The expansion is done by shifting the widgets to the bounds of the cell.

After that, another image information is added to the table, which is literally pushed down to the bottom edge due to the call of expandY().

Lastly, there is a call to layer.debug(), which is the way to tell TableLayout the object it should draw debug visuals for.

Adding the controls layer

Make the following changes in MenuScreen to add the controls layer:

```
private Table buildControlsLayer () {
  Table layer = new Table();
  layer.right().bottom();
  // + Play Button
```

```
btnMenuPlay = new Button(skinCanyonBunny, "play");
layer.add(btnMenuPlay);
btnMenuPlay.addListener(new ChangeListener() {
  @Override
  public void changed (ChangeEvent event, Actor actor) {
    onPlayClicked();
  }
});
layer.row();
// + Options Button
btnMenuOptions = new Button(skinCanyonBunny, "options");
layer.add(btnMenuOptions);
btnMenuOptions.addListener(new ChangeListener() {
  @Override
  public void changed (ChangeEvent event, Actor actor) {
    onOptionsClicked();
  }
});
if (debugEnabled) layer.debug();
return layer;
}
```

After that, add the following lines of code to the same class:

```
private void onPlayClicked () {
  game.setScreen(new GameScreen(game));
}


private void onOptionsClicked () { }
```

The controls layer is anchored to the bottom-right corner of the screen. A new button widget is added using the **Play** style. Next, a new ChangeListener is added to this button to define the action to be executed when the button is clicked on.

We are using ChangeListener to register new handlers for our button widgets. This is the recommended way of implementing handlers for widgets since most of them will fire ChangeEvent when changes occur. We could have also used ClickListener to accomplish the detection of clicks on button widgets, but doing so has a major drawback. The ClickListener method reacts on input events received by a widget, but does not know anything about widgets and their properties. Therefore, if a widget is set to be disabled, clicking on events will still be detected and handled by the listener.

After that, a new row is started in which the second button widget is added using the **Options** style. Each event handler calls a separate method to make it easier for us to maintain the code of the layer and the code for handling events. The `onPlayClicked()` method will switch to the game screen while the `onOptionsClicked()` method is intentionally left empty for the moment.

Adding the Options window layer

The **Options** window layer is going to be a lot more complex in comparison to all the other layers that we have implemented so far. There are also some further preparations required before we can continue to implement this layer.

Here is a screenshot to give you a better idea of how the finished **Options** window is going to look:

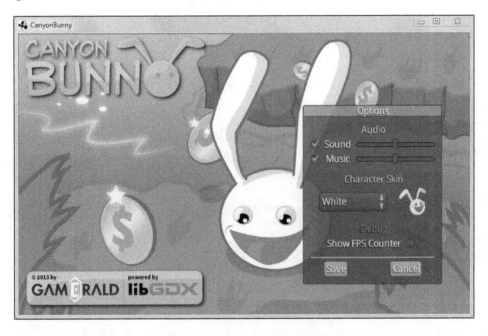

The **Options** window will be a small box that shows a title bar with text on it and which has some empty space to hold additional widgets. It can be dragged on the title bar to move it around in the scene. There will be a checkbox to enable and disable the **Sound** and **Music** effects as well as a slider to adjust the volume, respectively. A character skin can be chosen from a drop-down list. The current selection is shown next to it in a small preview image. The preview image is updated whenever a new selection in the drop-down list has been made to reflect the change. Lastly, there is another checkbox that toggles whether the FPS counter will be displayed in the game screen.

The menu controls, that is, the **Play** and **Options** buttons, will disappear when the **Options** window is shown. To close the **Options** window, the player has to choose between saving and cancelling any changes that have been made in the window. When the **Options** window is hidden, the menu controls will appear again.

Usually, we would have to draw all of these textures you see in the preceding screenshot to use all of the shown widgets. Luckily, we can take a shortcut here by taking a texture atlas, a suitable skin file, and a font definition file for the text to be displayed in these widgets from Libgdx's test repository. It contains much more than we need, so you may also want to take a closer look at the skin file to find out how certain widgets need to be defined that are not covered here.

You will need the following files from Libgdx's test repository and to put them into `CanyonBunny-android/assets/images/`:

- `uiskin.png`
- `uiskin.atlas`
- `uiskin.json`
- `default.fnt`

A copy of these files can be downloaded from `https://github.com/libgdx/libgdx/tree/master/tests/gdx-tests-android/assets/data/`.

This is how the image of the file `uiskin.png` should look like:

There are two more actions we will take in advance before we go back to implementing the actual layer for the options menu.

The first action is to create a new class that abstracts the process of loading and saving all of our game settings.

Create a new file called `GamePreferences` and add the following lines of code:

```
package com.packtpub.libgdx.canyonbunny.util;

import com.badlogic.gdx.Gdx;
```

```
import com.badlogic.gdx.Preferences;
import com.badlogic.gdx.math.MathUtils;

public class GamePreferences {
  public static final String TAG =
    GamePreferences.class.getName();

  public static final GamePreferences instance =
    new GamePreferences();

  public boolean sound;
  public boolean music;
  public float volSound;
  public float volMusic;
  public int charSkin;
  public boolean showFpsCounter;

  private Preferences prefs;

  // singleton: prevent instantiation from other classes
  private GamePreferences () {
    prefs = Gdx.app.getPreferences(Constants.PREFERENCES);
  }

  public void load () { }
  public void save () { }
}
```

This class is implemented as a singleton so we can call its load() and save() methods from virtually anywhere inside our project. The settings will be loaded from and saved to a preferences file defined in Constants.PREFERENCES.

Next, add the following code to the load() method of the same class:

```
public void load () {
  sound = prefs.getBoolean("sound", true);
  music = prefs.getBoolean("music", true);
  volSound = MathUtils.clamp(prefs.getFloat("volSound", 0.5f),
    0.0f, 1.0f);
  volMusic = MathUtils.clamp(prefs.getFloat("volMusic", 0.5f),
    0.0f, 1.0f);
  charSkin = MathUtils.clamp(prefs.getInteger("charSkin", 0),
    0, 2);
  showFpsCounter = prefs.getBoolean("showFpsCounter", false);
}
```

The `load()` method will always try its best to find a suitable and, more importantly, valid value. This is achieved by supplying default values to the `getter` methods of the `Preferences` class. For example, the call `getFloat("volSound", 0.5f)` will return a value of `0.5f` if there is no value found for the key named `volSound`. Before the value of the sound volume is finally stored, it is also passed to the `clamp()` utility method to ensure that the value is within the allowed range of values, which is `0.0f` and `1.0f` here.

Next, add the following code to the `save()` method of the same class:

```
public void save () {
    prefs.putBoolean("sound", sound);
    prefs.putBoolean("music", music);
    prefs.putFloat("volSound", volSound);
    prefs.putFloat("volMusic", volMusic);
    prefs.putInteger("charSkin", charSkin);
    prefs.putBoolean("showFpsCounter", showFpsCounter);
    prefs.flush();
}
```

The `save()` method is pretty straightforward as it just takes the current values of its public variables and puts them into the map of the preferences file. Finally, `flush()` is called on the preferences file to actually write the changed values into the file.

The second action is to create another class that abstracts all selectable character skins. Create a new file called `CharacterSkin` and add the following lines of code:

```
package com.packtpub.libgdx.canyonbunny.util;

import com.badlogic.gdx.graphics.Color;

public enum CharacterSkin {
    WHITE("White", 1.0f, 1.0f, 1.0f),
    GRAY("Gray", 0.7f, 0.7f, 0.7f),
    BROWN("Brown", 0.7f, 0.5f, 0.3f);

    private String name;
    private Color color = new Color();

    private CharacterSkin (String name, float r, float g, float b) {
        this.name = name;
        color.set(r, g, b, 1.0f);
    }

    @Override
```

```
    public String toString () {
      return name;
    }

    public Color getColor () {
      return color;
    }
  }
```

This class contains three distinct character skins: White, Gray, and Brown. All character skins are defined using a name that is used for display and RGB color values to describe a color which will be used to tint the image of the character player.

Building the Options window

Make the following changes in MenuScreen to add the **Options** window layer:

```
import com.packtpub.libgdx.canyonbunny.util.CharacterSkin;
import com.packtpub.libgdx.canyonbunny.util.GamePreferences;

private Skin skinLibgdx;

private void loadSettings() {
  GamePreferences prefs = GamePreferences.instance;
  prefs.load();
  chkSound.setChecked(prefs.sound);
  sldSound.setValue(prefs.volSound);
  chkMusic.setChecked(prefs.music);
  sldMusic.setValue(prefs.volMusic);
  selCharSkin.setSelection(prefs.charSkin);
  onCharSkinSelected(prefs.charSkin);
  chkShowFpsCounter.setChecked(prefs.showFpsCounter);
}

private void saveSettings() {
  GamePreferences prefs = GamePreferences.instance;
  prefs.sound = chkSound.isChecked();
  prefs.volSound = sldSound.getValue();
  prefs.music = chkMusic.isChecked();
  prefs.volMusic = sldMusic.getValue();
  prefs.charSkin = selCharSkin.getSelectionIndex();
  prefs.showFpsCounter = chkShowFpsCounter.isChecked();
```

```
    prefs.save();
  }

  private void onCharSkinSelected(int index) {
    CharacterSkin skin = CharacterSkin.values()[index];
    imgCharSkin.setColor(skin.getColor());
  }

  private void onSaveClicked() {
    saveSettings();
    onCancelClicked();
  }

  private void onCancelClicked() {
    btnMenuPlay.setVisible(true);
    btnMenuOptions.setVisible(true);
    winOptions.setVisible(false);
  }
```

The `loadSettings()` and `saveSettings()` methods are used to translate
back and forth between the values stored in the widgets and the instance of the
`GamePreferences` class. The methods starting with `on` in their name contain code
that we want to be executed at certain events. The `onCharSkinSelected()` method
will update the preview image. The `onSaveClicked()` method saves the current
settings of the **Options** window and swaps the **Options** window for the menu
controls. The `onCancelClicked()` method only swaps the widgets, which also
means that any changed settings will be discarded. The visibility of the menu
controls and the **Options** window is simply toggled by calling `setVisible()`
on the respective widgets.

Next, make the following changes to the same class:

```
  private void rebuildStage() {
    skinCanyonBunny = new Skin(
      Gdx.files.internal(Constants.SKIN_CANYONBUNNY_UI),
      new TextureAtlas(Constants.TEXTURE_ATLAS_UI));
    skinLibgdx = new Skin(
      Gdx.files.internal(Constants.SKIN_LIBGDX_UI),
      new TextureAtlas(Constants.TEXTURE_ATLAS_LIBGDX_UI));

    // build all layers
    ...
  }

  @Override
```

```
public void hide() {
    stage.dispose();
    skinCanyonBunny.dispose();
    skinLibgdx.dispose();
}
```

These changes enable us to use and add widgets defined in the Libgdx skin. Since the creation of all the widgets for the options menu involves quite a lot of code, we split it up into four separate build methods.

Now, add the `buildOptWinAudioSettings()` method to the same class:

```
private Table buildOptWinAudioSettings () {
    Table tbl = new Table();
    // + Title: "Audio"
    tbl.pad(10, 10, 0, 10);
    tbl.add(new Label("Audio", skinLibgdx, "default-font",
        Color.ORANGE)).colspan(3);
    tbl.row();
    tbl.columnDefaults(0).padRight(10);
    tbl.columnDefaults(1).padRight(10);
    // + Checkbox, "Sound" label, sound volume slider
    chkSound = new CheckBox("", skinLibgdx);
    tbl.add(chkSound);
    tbl.add(new Label("Sound", skinLibgdx));
    sldSound = new Slider(0.0f, 1.0f, 0.1f, false, skinLibgdx);
    tbl.add(sldSound);
    tbl.row();
    // + Checkbox, "Music" label, music volume slider
    chkMusic = new CheckBox("", skinLibgdx);
    tbl.add(chkMusic);
    tbl.add(new Label("Music", skinLibgdx));
    sldMusic = new Slider(0.0f, 1.0f, 0.1f, false, skinLibgdx);
    tbl.add(sldMusic);
    tbl.row();
    return tbl;
}
```

This method builds a table containing the audio settings. First, a label showing the text Audio in an orange color is added. Then, a checkbox, another label showing the text Sound, and a slider are added in the next row for the sound settings. This is also done for the music settings in the same way.

Next, add the `buildOptWinSkinSelection()` method to the same class:

```
private Table buildOptWinSkinSelection () {
  Table tbl = new Table();
  // + Title: "Character Skin"
  tbl.pad(10, 10, 0, 10);
  tbl.add(new Label("Character Skin", skinLibgdx,
  "default-font", Color.ORANGE)).colspan(2);
  tbl.row();
  // + Drop down box filled with skin items
  selCharSkin = new SelectBox(CharacterSkin.values(),
    skinLibgdx);
  selCharSkin.addListener(new ChangeListener() {
    @Override
    public void changed (ChangeEvent event, Actor actor) {
      onCharSkinSelected(
        ((SelectBox)actor).getSelectionIndex());
    }
  });
  tbl.add(selCharSkin).width(120).padRight(20);
  // + Skin preview image
  imgCharSkin = new Image(Assets.instance.bunny.head);
  tbl.add(imgCharSkin).width(50).height(50);
  return tbl;
}
```

This method builds a table containing the character skin selection via a drop-down box and a preview image next to it. A `ChangeListener` method is added to the drop-down widget `selCharSkin` so that the setting and preview image is updated by calling `onCharSkinSelected()` whenever a new selection occurs.

Next, add the `buildOptWinDebug()` method to the same class:

```
private Table buildOptWinDebug () {
  Table tbl = new Table();
  // + Title: "Debug"
  tbl.pad(10, 10, 0, 10);
  tbl.add(new Label("Debug", skinLibgdx, "default-font",
    Color.RED)).colspan(3);
  tbl.row();
  tbl.columnDefaults(0).padRight(10);
  tbl.columnDefaults(1).padRight(10);
  // + Checkbox, "Show FPS Counter" label
  chkShowFpsCounter = new CheckBox("", skinLibgdx);
  tbl.add(new Label("Show FPS Counter", skinLibgdx));
  tbl.add(chkShowFpsCounter);
  tbl.row();
  return tbl;
}
```

This method builds a table containing debug settings. At the moment, we only have one checkbox there that allows the player to toggle whether the FPS Counter is shown or not.

Next, add the `buildOptWinButtons()` method to the same class:

```
private Table buildOptWinButtons () {
  Table tbl = new Table();
  // + Separator
  Label lbl = null;
  lbl = new Label("", skinLibgdx);
  lbl.setColor(0.75f, 0.75f, 0.75f, 1);
  lbl.setStyle(new LabelStyle(lbl.getStyle()));
  lbl.getStyle().background = skinLibgdx.newDrawable("white");
  tbl.add(lbl).colspan(2).height(1).width(220).pad(0, 0, 0, 1);
  tbl.row();
  lbl = new Label("", skinLibgdx);
  lbl.setColor(0.5f, 0.5f, 0.5f, 1);
  lbl.setStyle(new LabelStyle(lbl.getStyle()));
  lbl.getStyle().background = skinLibgdx.newDrawable("white");
  tbl.add(lbl).colspan(2).height(1).width(220).pad(0, 1, 5, 0);
  tbl.row();
  // + Save Button with event handler
  btnWinOptSave = new TextButton("Save", skinLibgdx);
  tbl.add(btnWinOptSave).padRight(30);
  btnWinOptSave.addListener(new ChangeListener() {
    @Override
    public void changed (ChangeEvent event, Actor actor) {
      onSaveClicked();
    }
  });
  // + Cancel Button with event handler
  btnWinOptCancel = new TextButton("Cancel", skinLibgdx);
  tbl.add(btnWinOptCancel);
  btnWinOptCancel.addListener(new ChangeListener() {
    @Override
    public void changed (ChangeEvent event, Actor actor) {
      onCancelClicked();
    }
  });
  return tbl;
}
```

This method builds a table containing a separator and the **Save** and **Cancel** buttons at the bottom of the **Options** window. The **Save** and **Cancel** buttons use `ChangeListener`, which will call the `onSaveClicked()` and `onCancelClicked()` methods respectively whenever a click is detected.

Next, make the following changes to the `buildOptionsWindowLayer()` method:

```
private Table buildOptionsWindowLayer() {
    winOptions = new Window("Options", skinLibgdx);
    // + Audio Settings: Sound/Music CheckBox and Volume Slider
    winOptions.add(buildOptWinAudioSettings()).row();
    // + Character Skin: Selection Box (White, Gray, Brown)
    winOptions.add(buildOptWinSkinSelection()).row();
    // + Debug: Show FPS Counter
    winOptions.add(buildOptWinDebug()).row();
    // + Separator and Buttons (Save, Cancel)
    winOptions.add(buildOptWinButtons()).pad(10, 0, 10, 0);

    // Make options window slightly transparent
    winOptions.setColor(1, 1, 1, 0.8f);
    // Hide options window by default
    winOptions.setVisible(false);
    if (debugEnabled) winOptions.debug();
    // Let TableLayout recalculate widget sizes and positions
    winOptions.pack();
    // Move options window to bottom right corner
    winOptions.setPosition(
        Constants.VIEWPORT_GUI_WIDTH - winOptions.getWidth() - 50,
        50);
    return winOptions;
}
```

This method contains the code that initializes the **Options** window. It builds each part of the menu using the `build` methods that we just implemented before this one. The **Options** window is set to an opacity value of 80 percent. This makes the window appear slightly transparent, which adds a nice visual detail to it. The call of the `pack()` method of the `Window` widget makes sure that `TableLayout` recalculates the widget sizes and positions so that all added widgets will correctly fit into the window. After that, the window is moved to the bottom-right corner of the screen.

Last but not least, make the following changes to the `onOptionsClicked()` method:

```
private void onOptionsClicked() {
    loadSettings();
    btnMenuPlay.setVisible(false);
    btnMenuOptions.setVisible(false);
    winOptions.setVisible(true);
}
```

Finally, the added code allows the **Options** window to be opened. The settings are loaded before the **Options** window is shown so that the widgets will always be correctly initialized.

Here is a screenshot of the final **Options** window, menu screen, and the opened options window:

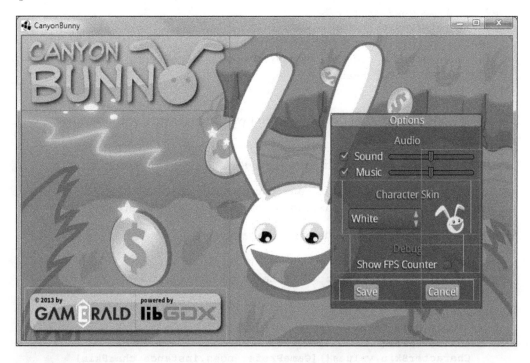

The thin pixel lines that are drawn all over the widgets are the enabled debug visuals of TableLayout.

The **Options** window is now fully functional. It shows up when the **Options** button is clicked on and hides when the **Save** or **Cancel** button is clicked on. Settings are only applied and saved with a click on the **Save** button.

Using the game settings

A lot of work went into the creation of our menu screen and also into the **Options** window to allow the change of certain game settings. What is still missing is the actual usage of the set values in our game. Luckily, this can be achieved very easily now with just a couple of additional lines of code.

Add the following import line to `GameScreen`:

```
import com.packtpub.libgdx.canyonbunny.util.GamePreferences;
```

After that, make the following changes to the same class:

```
@Override
public void show () {
  GamePreferences.instance.load();
  worldController = new WorldController(game);
  worldRenderer = new WorldRenderer(worldController);
  Gdx.input.setCatchBackKey(true);
}
```

The added code ensures that the game screen will always work with the latest game settings.

Next, add the following import lines to `BunnyHead`:

```
import com.packtpub.libgdx.canyonbunny.util.CharacterSkin;
import com.packtpub.libgdx.canyonbunny.util.GamePreferences;
```

After that, make the following change to the same class:

```
@Override
public void render (SpriteBatch batch) {
  TextureRegion reg = null;

  // Apply Skin Color
  batch.setColor(
    CharacterSkin.values()[GamePreferences.instance.charSkin]
    .getColor());

  // Set special color when game object has a feather power-up
  if (hasFeatherPowerup)
  batch.setColor(1.0f, 0.8f, 0.0f, 1.0f);

  // Draw image
  reg = regHead;
  batch.draw(reg.getTexture(),
    position.x, position.y,
    origin.x, origin.y,
    dimension.x, dimension.y,
```

```
    scale.x, scale.y,
    rotation,
    reg.getRegionX(), reg.getRegionY(),
    reg.getRegionWidth(), reg.getRegionHeight(),
    viewDirection == VIEW_DIRECTION.LEFT, false);

  // Reset color to white
  batch.setColor(1, 1, 1, 1);
}
```

This will apply the correct skin color by tinting the image of the bunny head.

Next, add the following import line to `WorldRenderer`:

```
import com.packtpub.libgdx.canyonbunny.util.GamePreferences;
```

After that, make the following change to the same class:

```
private void renderGui (SpriteBatch batch) {
  batch.setProjectionMatrix(cameraGUI.combined);
  batch.begin();

  // draw collected gold coins icon + text
  // (anchored to top left edge)
  renderGuiScore(batch);
  // draw collected feather icon (anchored to top left edge)
  renderGuiFeatherPowerup(batch);
  // draw extra lives icon + text (anchored to top right edge)
  renderGuiExtraLive(batch);
  // draw FPS text (anchored to bottom right edge)
  if (GamePreferences.instance.showFpsCounter)
  renderGuiFpsCounter(batch);
  // draw game over text
  renderGuiGameOverMessage(batch);

  batch.end();
}
```

This change will make the FPS counter appear only if the checkbox has been ticked in the **Options** window. Otherwise, the FPS counter will not be drawn to the scene.

Summary

In this chapter we have learned how to manage multiple screens and how to switch between them. We have discussed what a scene graph is and how it basically works in Libgdx in conjunction with Scene2D UI, TableLayout, and skins to create complex user interfaces like the one we have now implemented in Canyon Bunny. We have also learned how input events for widgets can be handled.

In the next chapter you will learn how to enhance the visual appearance of the game. Among others, we will use particle effects and interpolation algorithms to achieve special effects.

8
Special Effects

In this chapter you will learn how to add special effects to Canyon Bunny using Libgdx's particle system, and linear interpolation, and several other ways to enhance the visual appearance of the game. You will also design a custom particle effect in a graphical editor which is going to serve as "dust". This dust effect will be shown whenever the player character is running on rocks. You will be introduced to the concept of linear interpolation using examples of smoothing the camera's movement while it is following a set target as well as letting the rocks slowly bob up and down on the water.

In addition to this, you will implement a parallax scrolling effect for the displayed mountains in the background. The clouds will continuously move at random speeds from the right to the left of the level. The game's GUI will also be enhanced by adding some subtle effects for events where the player has lost a life or when the game score has increased.

Creating complex effects with particle systems

A particle system is a great way to simulate complex effects like fire, smoke, explosions, and so on. Basically, a particle system consists of a number of images which are rendered using either a normal (alpha masked) mode or an additive blending mode to create interesting results.

Take a look at the following diagram to see the difference between normal and additive blending modes:

Libgdx provides a sophisticated particle system through its `ParticleEffect` class. It is merely a container which allows you to easily work with your final effects on a high level such as setting the position or triggering or cancelling the designed particle effect.

The following is a brief description of the most important methods of `ParticleEffect`:

- `start()`: This starts the animation of the particle effect
- `reset()`: This resets and restarts the animation of the particle effect
- `update()`: This must be called to let the particle effect act in accordance to time
- `draw()`: This renders the particle effect at its current position
- `allowCompletion()`: This allows emitters to stop smoothly even if particle effects are set to play continuously
- `setDuration()`: This sets the overall duration the particle effect will run
- `setPosition()`: This sets the position to where it will be drawn
- `setFlip()`: This sets horizontal and vertical flip modes

- `save()`: This saves a particle effect with all its settings to a file
- `load()`: This loads a particle effect with all its settings from a saved file
- `dispose()`: This frees all resources allocated by the particle effect

Using an instance of `ParticleEffect` alone will not yield anything visible on the screen yet. This is because particles are represented as images and this class does not have such a reference to an image. Instead, an instance of the `ParticleEmitter` class is required, which among other attributes can take a reference to an image for the particles to be rendered. An emitter manages a group of particles that uses the same image. The particles of an emitter also share the same specific behavior, which is usually given in ranged values. These ranged values define the range for generating random values for each spawned particle, which will make the resulting effect look much more natural. If needed, several emitters can be added to a single effect to create more complex particle effects using multiple images and collective behavior.

The following code is an example of how to create a particle effect with one emitter:

```
ParticleEffect effect = new ParticleEffect();
ParticleEmitter emitter = new ParticleEmitter();
effect.getEmitters().add(emitter);
emitter.setAdditive(true);
emitter.getDelay().setActive(true);
emitter.getDelay().setLow(0.5f);
// ... more code for emitter initialization ...
```

While there is absolutely nothing wrong with this approach in general, it is not recommended to initialize particle emitters in code. Emitters contain roughly 20 attributes that can be played with, so it is quite obvious at this point that this approach will lead very quickly to a lot of code that is hard to understand and maintain. A much cleaner and also fun solution is to use Libgdx's graphical particle editor to create new or modify existing particle effects. The editor features a live preview of the current settings of the particle effect, which simplifies the design phase a lot. The preview gives direct feedback of the final result of the particle effect as well as how changed attributes alter the effect.

To run the editor, check out this Wiki article: `https://code.google.com/p/libgdx/wiki/ParticleEditor`.

The following screenshot shows the **Particle Editor** window right after it was started:

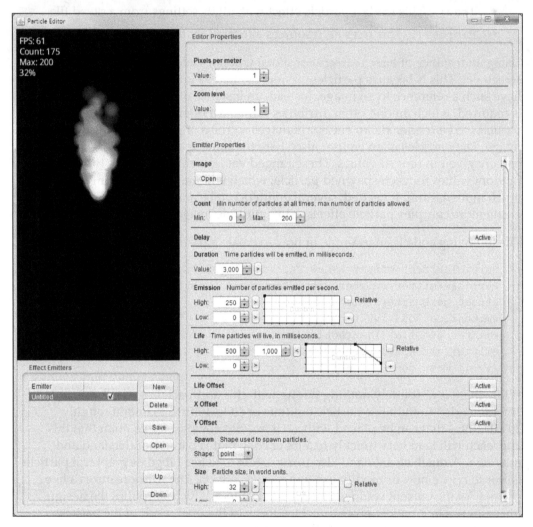

The live preview is located in the top-left corner and shows the current particle effect as well as some runtime information as follows:

- **FPS**: This gives the frames per second achieved
- **Count**: This gives the current number of particles in use
- **Max**: This gives the maximum number of simultaneously existing particles allowed
- **Percentage**: This gives the progress between the start (0 seconds) and the end (**Duration**)

The particle effect in the live preview can be moved around by clicking and dragging it with the mouse. This is a pretty neat feature not only because it allows adjustments to the effect's starting position, but also because it can be used to quickly check out how the effect behaves under non-stationary circumstances.

The bottom-left corner holds the already mentioned list of particle emitters. Emitters can be given a name but this is completely optional. The checkmark next to an emitter's name toggles its visibility. However, take note that this is just an editor-only setting to make the editing of complex effects with many emitters a bit easier. The state of the visibility checkmark is also not going to be saved to the particle effect file. The order of emitters can be changed using the **Up** and **Down** buttons to the right of the emitters list. The rendering of the emitters list runs from the top to the bottom. This means that the last emitter in the list is also going to be the last and therefore the most rendered emitter. New emitters can be added by clicking on the **New** button. Similarly, a click on the **Delete** button will remove the currently selected emitter from the emitters list.

The right side of the **Particle Editor** is split into two framed parts that contain two types of properties. The upper one is labeled **Editor Properties** which controls how the live preview is rendered. The **Pixels per meter** setting defines the dimensions just like we did for our game screen camera. The **Zoom level** setting is used to scale things either up or down depending on what can be seen in the live preview.

The last and biggest portion of the **Particle Editor** is contained in the frame labeled **Emitter Properties**. It controls everything about how particles of an emitter look, and how they will behave over time.

Here is a list of all the available properties and their meanings:

- **Image**: This is the image file that graphically represents the particle.
- **Count**: This is the minimum number of particles that will always exist at the start and the maximum number of particles that are allowed to exist at once. Keep in mind that the maximum value also affects the amount of preallocated memory.
- **Delay**: The emitter will pause for the given amount of time in milliseconds before it starts to emit particles. This setting must be activated in order to take effect.
- **Duration**: This is the amount of time in milliseconds during which particles will be emitted.
- **Emission**: This is the number of emitted particles per second.
- **Life**: This is the amount of time in milliseconds until a particle is destroyed.

- **Life Offset**: This is the amount of time in milliseconds that is used up of the particle's lifetime. This can be used, for example, to let a particle start at the middle of its life. All interim changes that would have normally been applied will be precalculated and set as the particle's starting state, such as the current displacement, the angle of rotation, and any change of color. This setting must be activated in order to take effect.

- **X Offset**: This is the horizontal displacement in world units of the particle from its emitter's position. This setting must be activated in order to take effect.

- **Y Offset**: This is the vertical displacement in world units of the particle from its emitter's position. This setting must be activated in order to take effect.

- **Spawn**: This defines the shape used to spawn particles. The available shapes are point, line, square, and ellipse. By default, it is point.

- **Size**: This is the particle's size in world units.

- **Velocity**: This is the particle's speed in world units per second. This setting must be activated in order to take effect.

- **Angle**: This is the particle's emission angle in degrees. This setting must be activated in order to take effect.

- **Rotation**: This is the particle's local rotation angle in degrees. This setting must be activated in order to take effect.

- **Wind**: This is the horizontal force applied to the particle in world units per second. This setting must be activated in order to take effect.

- **Gravity**: This is the vertical force applied to the particle in world units per second. This setting must be activated in order to take effect.

- **Tint**: This multiplies the colors of the particle's image with the set color. Therefore, using a monochrome-colored image is advisable for best tint results.

- **Transparency**: This is the particle's alpha or transparency value. This allows the particle to be anything between fully opaque and fully translucent. Moreover, multiple changes during a particle's life allow for fade-in and fade-out effects.

- **Options**: This contains five additional checkmarks to configure the emitter's behavior:

  - **Additive**: If checked, additive blending mode is enabled.

  - **Attached**: If checked, existing particles will follow the movement of their emitter.

- ◦ **Continuous**: If checked, the emitter will restart after its duration of time is over. Emitters that are not set to be continuous will only show up once at the beginning.

- ◦ **Aligned**: If checked, the particle's emission angle is added to its local rotation. This will turn the particle's image face in the same direction as it is moving.

- ◦ **Behind**: If checked, the corresponding marker flag is set to true. Otherwise, it is set to false. This is just a marker flag that can be queried by calling `isBehind()` to decide whether the emitter should be rendered behind or in front of something else.

Some of the emitter properties contain charts. The x axis in a chart always represents the lifetime of a particle, while the y axis represents the percentage of each emitter property's actual value. A click on the chart adds a new node. Double-clicking on a node removes it again. Clicking and dragging a node moves it inside the chart.

The following screenshot shows a portion of the emitter properties:

A chart can be expanded by clicking on the small **+** button next to it. A chart has a **High** and **Low** value which defines the absolute values of 100 percent and 0 percent on the y axis in the chart. Most value fields have a **>** button next to them. Clicking on this button shows a second value field which changes the single value to a ranged value. A ranged value has a minimum and a maximum value from which a random value is picked for each particle.

Adding a dust particle effect to the player character

We now want to create a dust particle effect which will appear whenever the player character is running on rocks. The effect is going to stop as soon as the player stops moving or if the player is no longer grounded on a platform.

First, we will need to design a custom particle effect that looks like dust.
The following screenshot is an example of what we are aiming for:

Open or restart the **Particle Editor** to begin with the default fire particle effect and apply the following modifications to the editor and emitter properties:

- In **Pixels per meter**, enter 200 for **Value:**
- In **Size**, enter 0.75 for **High:**; enter 0 for **Low:**; enter (0,0), (67,28), (100,0) for **Chart:**
- In **Velocity**, enter 1 to 5 for **High:**; enter -1 to -5 for **Low:**; enter (0,50) for **Chart:**
- In **Duration**, enter 100 for **Value:**
- In **Emission**, enter 200 for **High:**; enter 0 for **Low:**; enter (0,100) for **Chart:**
- In **Life**, enter 250 to 500 for **High:**; enter 0 for **Low:**; enter (0,100) for **Chart:**
- In **Angle**, enter 0 for **High:**; enter 0 for **Low:**; enter (0,100) for **Chart:**
- In **Gravity**, enter 5 for **High:**; enter -1 for **Low:**; enter (0,0), (67,28), (100,0) for **Chart:**
- In **Tint**, enter 107 for **R:**; enter 107 for **G:**; enter 107 for **B:**
- In **Transparency**, enter (0,100) (100,0) for **Chart:**
- In **Options**, select **off** for **Additive:**; select **on** for **Continuous:**

Next, click on the **Save** button to save the file and place it in `CanyonBunny-android/assets/particles/dust.pfx`.

There is no official file extension for particle effects in Libgdx. Nonetheless, it does not do any harm to make things explicit and name files after their intended purpose. Since **sfx** is a well-known abbreviation for **Sound Effect**, it makes sense to follow this scheme and adapt it for **Particle Effect**; hence the file extension used in this book is `.pfx`.

There is one more preparation required before we can start to implement the dust particle effect in Canyon Bunny. As you already know, particle effects are made out of images and so is our dust particle effect. You might have noticed that we skipped over that part to select a proper (another) image file for the dust particle in the editor. This is perfectly fine since we did not start from scratch but instead used the already existing particle image from the default fire particle effect. Its file is called `particle.png` and can be found in the `assets` folder of gdx tools. You can also download it from Libgdx's repository:

`https://raw.github.com/libgdx/libgdx/master/extensions/gdx-tools/assets/particle.png.`

The `particle.png` image basically contains just a small, white circle that smoothly fades out from the center. The image should look like this:

Place the `particle.png` file in `CanyonBunny-android/assets/particles/particle.png`.

Next, add the following two import lines to the `BunnyHead` class:

```
import com.badlogic.gdx.Gdx;
import com.badlogic.gdx.graphics.g2d.ParticleEffect;
```

After that, add the following new line to the same class:

```
public ParticleEffect dustParticles = new ParticleEffect();
```

This is the variable where we are going to hold a reference to our loaded and ready-to-fire dust particle effect.

Next, make the following modifications to the same class:

```
public void init () {
  ...
  // Power-ups
  hasFeatherPowerup = false;
  timeLeftFeatherPowerup = 0;

  // Particles
  dustParticles.load(Gdx.files.internal("particles/dust.pfx"),
    Gdx.files.internal("particles"));
}
```

```
@Override
public void update (float deltaTime) {
  super.update(deltaTime);
  ...
  dustParticles.update(deltaTime);
}

@Override
public void render (SpriteBatch batch) {
  TextureRegion reg = null;

  // Draw Particles
  dustParticles.draw(batch);

  // Apply Skin Color
  ...
}
```

As you can see, only a few changes were required to implement the dust particle effect in the game. The particle effect is loaded in init() and is continuously updated and rendered in update() and render(), respectively. However, calling draw() on a particle effect does not mean that it is always going to be rendered. The particle effect needs to be triggered first to start playing. Furthermore, if it is a continuous particle effect, it also needs to be stopped explicitly to become invisible again.

To take care of this, make the following changes to the code in updateMotionY():

```
@Override
protected void updateMotionY (float deltaTime) {
  switch (jumpState) {
    case GROUNDED:
      jumpState = JUMP_STATE.FALLING;
      if (velocity.x != 0) {
        dustParticles.setPosition(position.x + dimension.x / 2,
          position.y);
        dustParticles.start();
      }
      break;
      ...
  }
  if (jumpState != JUMP_STATE.GROUNDED) {
    dustParticles.allowCompletion();
    super.updateMotionY(deltaTime);
  }
}
```

Here is a screenshot of the result in the game:

Moving the clouds

Our next enhancement will be to make those clouds, which are just sitting there in the air, move to the left. The idea here is to simulate some kind of wind property in the game world while each cloud will also move at slightly different speeds to make their movement look more natural. In addition to this, there needs to be a condition to let more clouds appear at the right end of the level. Otherwise, the game will run out of clouds at some point. We could just go the easy route here and spawn a huge number, say, 1000 clouds, but this is not very clever performance-wise, and this also does not tackle our original problem that is the game will run out of clouds at some point. So, a better approach to solve our problem is to keep the maximum number of existing cloud objects to a minimum.

Make the following changes to the Clouds class:

```
private Cloud spawnCloud () {
   Cloud cloud = new Cloud();
   cloud.dimension.set(dimension);
   // select random cloud image
   cloud.setRegion(regClouds.random());
```

```
// position
Vector2 pos = new Vector2();
pos.x = length + 10; // position after end of level
pos.y += 1.75; // base position
// random additional position
pos.y += MathUtils.random(0.0f, 0.2f)
  * (MathUtils.randomBoolean() ? 1 : -1);
cloud.position.set(pos);
// speed
Vector2 speed = new Vector2();
speed.x += 0.5f; // base speed
// random additional speed
speed.x += MathUtils.random(0.0f, 0.75f);
cloud.terminalVelocity.set(speed);
speed.x *= -1; // move left
cloud.velocity.set(speed);
return cloud;
}
```

After that, add the following lines of code to the same class:

```
@Override
public void update (float deltaTime) {
  for (int i = clouds.size - 1; i >= 0; i--) {
    Cloud cloud = clouds.get(i);
    cloud.update(deltaTime);
    if (cloud.position.x < -10) {
      // cloud moved outside of world.
      // destroy and spawn new cloud at end of level.
      clouds.removeIndex(i);
      clouds.add(spawnCloud());
    }
  }
}
```

The spawnCloud() method will now create a new cloud that also makes use of our simple physics simulation code we implemented earlier. The update() method iterates through all existing clouds which in turn calls their update() method to let the physics move them. Afterwards, the cloud's new position is checked against a certain threshold. If a cloud fulfills this condition, it is removed from the list of current clouds and a new one is added and positioned at the right end of the level.

The list of clouds in update() is iterated in reverse on purpose to avoid a so-called mutating list. Normally, you should never modify a list you are currently iterating over. However, when iterating backwards from the last to the first element, the removal of an object like in our case will only happen to elements that have already been processed.

Smoothing with Linear interpolation (Lerp)

Linear interpolation (also known as **Lerp**) is a method to find unknown values between two known points. The unknown values are approximated through Linear interpolation by connecting these two known points with a straight line.

Lerp operations can also be used to smooth movements. We will show this using an example in which we will smooth the camera's target-following feature so the rocks will slightly move up and down to simulate that they are actually floating on the water.

First, add the following line to the `CameraHelper` class:

```
private final float FOLLOW_SPEED = 4.0f;
```

After that, make the following modifications to the same class:

```
public void update (float deltaTime) {
  if (!hasTarget()) return;

  position.lerp(target.position, FOLLOW_SPEED * deltaTime);

  // Prevent camera from moving down too far
  position.y = Math.max(-1f, position.y);
}
```

Luckily, Libgdx already provides a `lerp()` method in its `Vector2` class that makes it easy to execute Lerp operations. What happens here is that we call `lerp()` on the camera's current position vector, a 2D coordinate, and pass in a target position as well as a so-called alpha value. This alpha value describes the ratio between the current and the target positions. Remember that Lerp is virtually connecting the current and the target positions with a straight line and that the alpha value determines the point on this very line. If the alpha value is equal to 0.5, it means the new position is exactly in the middle of both the current and the target positions.

Since these Lerp operations are executed inside `update()`, we expect very small increments in movement. The value of `deltaTime` is usually something around 0.016 seconds (16 milliseconds or 1.6 percent if interpreted in the context of a Lerp operation). We actually just use the `deltaTime` variable to make the Lerp operation time-dependent. It is a common misconception that the usage of `deltaTime` here means that the interpolated movement will happen in one second. Instead, the movement will start fast and slows down over time as the distance between the current and the target positions becomes smaller and smaller. This is why we also use a speed factor `FOLLOW_SPEED` that needs to be multiplied with `deltaTime` to speed things up a bit.

Letting the rocks float on the water

We will do almost the same here, using Lerp operations to smoothly move all rocks up and down to create the illusion of rocks floating on the water.

Add the following two import lines to the `Rocks` class:

```
import com.badlogic.gdx.math.MathUtils;
import com.badlogic.gdx.math.Vector2;
```

After that, add the following lines of code to the same class:

```
private final float FLOAT_CYCLE_TIME = 2.0f;
private final float FLOAT_AMPLITUDE = 0.25f;
private float floatCycleTimeLeft;
private boolean floatingDownwards;
private Vector2 floatTargetPosition;
```

Next, make the following modifications to the same class:

```
private void init () {
  dimension.set(1, 1.5f);

  regEdge = Assets.instance.rock.edge;
  regMiddle = Assets.instance.rock.middle;

  // Start length of this rock
  setLength(1);

  floatingDownwards = false;
  floatCycleTimeLeft = MathUtils.random(0,
    FLOAT_CYCLE_TIME / 2);
  floatTargetPosition = null;
}
```

These changes make sure that the floating mechanism is correctly initialized. The starting value for the float direction is set to up; the cycle time is randomly picked between 0 and half of the maximum float cycle time. Using a random cycle time gives the floating effect a more natural look, because every rock seems to move just on its own. The `floatTargetPosition` variable is used to store the next target position:

```
@Override
public void update (float deltaTime) {
  super.update(deltaTime);

  floatCycleTimeLeft -= deltaTime;
  if (floatTargetPosition == null)
  floatTargetPosition = new Vector2(position);
  if (floatCycleTimeLeft <= 0) {
    floatCycleTimeLeft = FLOAT_CYCLE_TIME;
    floatingDownwards = !floatingDownwards;
    floatTargetPosition.y += FLOAT_AMPLITUDE
      * (floatingDownwards ? -1 : 1);
  }
  position.lerp(floatTargetPosition, deltaTime);
}
```

Adding parallax scrolling to the mountains in the background

Parallax scrolling is a special scrolling technique that creates the illusion of depth in a 2D scene. Therefore, the objects in the background move slower than the objects in the foreground when the camera moves by.

We will now implement a parallax scrolling effect for the mountains in the background of the game screen.

Add the following import line to the Mountains class:

```
import com.badlogic.gdx.math.Vector2;
```

After that, add the following lines of code to the same class:

```
public void updateScrollPosition (Vector2 camPosition) {
  position.set(camPosition.x, position.y);
}
```

Next, make the following changes to the same class:

```java
private void drawMountain (SpriteBatch batch, float offsetX, float
    offsetY, float tintColor, float parallaxSpeedX) {
  TextureRegion reg = null;
  batch.setColor(tintColor, tintColor, tintColor, 1);
  float xRel = dimension.x * offsetX;
  float yRel = dimension.y * offsetY;

  // mountains span the whole level
  int mountainLength = 0;
  mountainLength += MathUtils.ceil(
    length / (2 * dimension.x) * (1 - parallaxSpeedX));
  mountainLength += MathUtils.ceil(0.5f + offsetX);
  for (int i = 0; i < mountainLength; i++) {
    // mountain left
    reg = regMountainLeft;
    batch.draw(reg.getTexture(),
      origin.x + xRel + position.x * parallaxSpeedX,
      origin.y + yRel + position.y,
      origin.x, origin.y,
      dimension.x, dimension.y,
      scale.x, scale.y,
      rotation,
      reg.getRegionX(), reg.getRegionY(),
      reg.getRegionWidth(), reg.getRegionHeight(),
      false, false);
    xRel += dimension.x;
    // mountain right
    reg = regMountainRight;
    batch.draw(reg.getTexture(),
      origin.x + xRel + position.x * parallaxSpeedX,
      origin.y + yRel + position.y,
      origin.x, origin.y,
      dimension.x, dimension.y,
      scale.x, scale.y,
      rotation,
      reg.getRegionX(), reg.getRegionY(),
      reg.getRegionWidth(), reg.getRegionHeight(),
      false, false);
    xRel += dimension.x;
  }
  // reset color to white
  batch.setColor(1, 1, 1, 1);
}
```

```
@Override
public void render (SpriteBatch batch) {
  // 80% distant mountains (dark gray)
  drawMountain(batch, 0.5f, 0.5f, 0.5f, 0.8f);
  // 50% distant mountains (gray)
  drawMountain(batch, 0.25f, 0.25f, 0.7f, 0.5f);
  // 30% distant mountains (light gray)
  drawMountain(batch, 0.0f, 0.0f, 0.9f, 0.3f);
}
```

We have added a fifth parameter to `drawMountain()` that ranges between 0.0 and 1.0 describing the distance and its scrolling speed. The scrolling depends on the camera's current position, which is then multiplied with the distance factor. This is the reason why we have also added a new method called `updateScrollPosition()` which needs to be called in every update cycle where the camera can move.

Make the following changes to the `WorldController` class:

```
public void update (float deltaTime) {
  handleDebugInput(deltaTime);
  if (isGameOver()) {
    timeLeftGameOverDelay -= deltaTime;
    if (timeLeftGameOverDelay < 0) backToMenu();
  } else {
    handleInputGame(deltaTime);
  }
  level.update(deltaTime);
  testCollisions();
  cameraHelper.update(deltaTime);
  if (!isGameOver() && isPlayerInWater()) {
    lives--;
    if (isGameOver())
    timeLeftGameOverDelay = Constants.TIME_DELAY_GAME_OVER;
    else
    initLevel();
  }
  level.mountains.updateScrollPosition(
    cameraHelper.getPosition());
}
```

All three mountain layers will now scroll at different speeds: 30 percent, 50 percent, and 80 percent.

Enhancing the game screen's GUI

The last part of this chapter is dedicated to two enhancements of the game screen's GUI. Firstly, we will add a small animation that gives visual feedback to the player when a life is lost. Secondly, a counting-up animation for the player's score will be implemented.

Event – player lost a life

We want to play a small animation in the event that the player has just lost a life. The extra lives are shown as bunny heads in the top-right corner of the game screen. These icons become dark one after another as soon as another life has been lost. The animation we are aiming for is a temporary bunny head icon on top of the just lost extra life. The temporary icon is going to be scaled up, rotated, and will have a slightly red tint.

The following screenshot is an example of the animation:

Add the following line to the WorldController class:

```
public float livesVisual;
```

After that, make the following changes to the same class:

```
private void init () {
  Gdx.input.setInputProcessor(this);
  cameraHelper = new CameraHelper();
  lives = Constants.LIVES_START;
  livesVisual = lives;
  timeLeftGameOverDelay = 0;
  initLevel();
}

public void update (float deltaTime) {
  handleDebugInput(deltaTime);
```

```
    if (isGameOver()) {
      timeLeftGameOverDelay -= deltaTime;
      if (timeLeftGameOverDelay < 0) backToMenu();
    } else {
      handleInputGame(deltaTime);
    }
    level.update(deltaTime);
    testCollisions();
    cameraHelper.update(deltaTime);
    if (!isGameOver() && isPlayerInWater()) {
      lives--;
      if (isGameOver())
      timeLeftGameOverDelay = Constants.TIME_DELAY_GAME_OVER;
      else
      initLevel();
    }
    level.mountains.updateScrollPosition(
      cameraHelper.getPosition());
    if (livesVisual > lives)
    livesVisual = Math.max(lives, livesVisual - 1 * deltaTime);
  }
```

We have introduced a new variable livesVisual that will contain pretty much the same information as lives. However, livesVisual will only decrease slowly over time whenever lives is decreased. This enables us to play an animation as long as livesVisual has not yet reached the current value of lives.

Additionally, add the following import line to the WorldRenderer class:

```
import com.badlogic.gdx.math.MathUtils;
```

After that, make the following changes to the same class:

```
private void renderGuiExtraLive (SpriteBatch batch) {
  float x = cameraGUI.viewportWidth - 50
    Constants.LIVES_START * 50;
  float y = -15;
  for (int i = 0; i < Constants.LIVES_START; i++) {
    if (worldController.lives <= i)
    batch.setColor(0.5f, 0.5f, 0.5f, 0.5f);
    batch.draw(Assets.instance.bunny.head,
      x + i * 50, y,
      50, 50,
      120, 100,
      0.35f, -0.35f,
      0);
```

```
        batch.setColor(1, 1, 1, 1);
    }
    if (worldController.lives >= 0
      && worldController.livesVisual > worldController.lives) {
      int i = worldController.lives;
      float alphaColor = Math.max(0, worldController.livesVisual
        - worldController.lives - 0.5f);
      float alphaScale = 0.35f * (2 + worldController.lives
        - worldController.livesVisual) * 2;
      float alphaRotate = -45 * alphaColor;
      batch.setColor(1.0f, 0.7f, 0.7f, alphaColor);
      batch.draw(Assets.instance.bunny.head,
        x + i * 50, y,
        50, 50,
        120, 100,
        alphaScale, -alphaScale,
        alphaRotate);
      batch.setColor(1, 1, 1, 1);
    }
}
```

The added code will draw a temporary bunny head icon that is changed in its alpha color, scale, and rotation over time to create the animation. The progress of the animation is controlled by the current value in livesVisual.

Event – score increased

Every time the player collects an item, a reward is given that is added to the overall game score. The current score and a gold coin icon are shown in the top-right corner of the game screen. We want to add two subtle effects that begin to play when an increased score is detected. Firstly, we want the score to slowly add up to the new score. Secondly, the gold coin icon will shake a bit while the score is still adding up.

Here is a screenshot of the combined animation in five steps while some items have been collected:

Add the following line to the WorldController class:

```
public float scoreVisual;
```

After that, make the following changes to the same class:

```
private void initLevel () {
   score = 0;
   scoreVisual = score;
   level = new Level(Constants.LEVEL_01);
   cameraHelper.setTarget(level.bunnyHead);
}
```

```
public void update (float deltaTime) {
   ...
  level.mountains.updateScrollPosition(
    cameraHelper.getPosition());
  if (livesVisual > lives)
  livesVisual = Math.max(lives, livesVisual - 1 * deltaTime);
  if (scoreVisual < score)
  scoreVisual = Math.min(score, scoreVisual
    + 250 * deltaTime);
}
```

We introduced the new variable `scoreVisual` which serves the same purpose as `livesVisual` does to control the progress of the score animation.

Additionally, make the following changes to the `WorldRenderer` class:

```
private void renderGuiScore (SpriteBatch batch) {
  float x = -15;
  float y = -15;
  float offsetX = 50;
  float offsetY = 50;
  if (worldController.scoreVisual < worldController.score) {
    long shakeAlpha = System.currentTimeMillis() % 360;
    float shakeDist = 1.5f;
    offsetX += MathUtils.sinDeg(shakeAlpha * 2.2f) * shakeDist;
    offsetY += MathUtils.sinDeg(shakeAlpha * 2.9f) * shakeDist;
  }
  batch.draw(Assets.instance.goldCoin.goldCoin,
    x, y,
    offsetX, offsetY,
    100, 100,
    0.35f, -0.35f,
    0);
  Assets.instance.fonts.defaultBig.draw(batch,
    "" + (int)worldController.scoreVisual,
    x + 75, y + 37);
}
```

The value in `scoreVisual` is cast to an integer value to cut off the fraction. The resulting intermediate value will be the score that is shown in the GUI for the counting-up animation. To let the coin icon shake, we use a sine function with different factors as input angles to find the offset for the temporary displacement of the icon.

Summary

In this chapter we have used a variety of approaches for adding our special effects which let the game come more and more alive. We have learned about particle systems and how they work in Libgdx. Particle effects can be easily designed using the powerful **Particle Editor**, and it is recommended to use this instead of working them out in code. We have learned how a finished particle effect can be incorporated and controlled in our existing game. We have also learned how to achieve a wind effect using our simple physics simulation to animate the clouds in the game world with just a few changes. An introduction to Linear interpolation has been given and how this can be applied to create smooth movements for the game's camera and rocks that now appear to float on the water. Parallax scrolling has been added to the mountains in the background to increase the game immersion even further. As a final touch, the game screen's GUI has been enhanced with subtle effects.

In the next chapter, we will enhance the multiple screens management that was introduced in *Chapter 7, Menus and Options*. Therefore, we will implement a flexible system to easily create smoothly animated screen transitions that will upgrade the screen switching.

Screen Transitions

9

In this chapter you will learn about screen transitions, a technique to create a smooth user experience, while switching from one screen to another over a certain period of time. You will be introduced to a technique known as **Render to Texture (RTT)** that allows easy composition of two individually rendered screens. Normally, transition effects make use of linear and nonlinear interpolation to create interesting and natural-looking results. Libgdx provides a class that implements a wide variety of common interpolation algorithms, which are suitable not only for transition effects, but also for any values that should follow a certain behavior over time.

Moreover, in *Chapter 7*, *Menus and Options*, we learned how to create and manage several screens that can be shown and hidden using Libgdx's Game class. We will expand on this idea in this chapter by adding a feature to use transition effects for switching our screens. With reference to our game, Canyon Bunny, we are going to implement three distinct transition effects: fade, slide, and slice.

Adding the screen transition capability

We need to use an interface that all our screen transitions will implement. This will allow us to easily add new transition effects later on a modular basis.

Create a new file for the ScreenTransition interface and add the following code:

```
package com.packtpub.libgdx.canyonbunny.screens.transitions;

import com.badlogic.gdx.graphics.Texture;
import com.badlogic.gdx.graphics.g2d.SpriteBatch;

public interface ScreenTransition {
  public float getDuration ();

  public void render (SpriteBatch batch,
```

```
                        Texture currScreen,
                        Texture nextScreen,
                        float alpha);

    }
```

The preceding interface allows us to query the duration of a transition effect and enables us to let it render its effect using two supplied textures that contain the images of the current and the next screen. In addition to this, the `alpha` value is used to describe the current state of progress of the transition effect that is to be rendered. Using an `alpha` value of `0.0`, for example, will render the effect at the very beginning, while a value of, say, `0.25`, will render it when the effect has progressed to 25 percent.

You might wonder why the `render()` method takes two instances of `Texture` instead of `AbstractGameScreen`. This is because in general, a transition effect should not depend on the contents of the screens that it is working with. Therefore, both the screens, the current and the next one, need to be transformed into two self-contained units. This can be achieved by rendering each screen to its own in-memory texture. This technique is also known as RTT.

OpenGL has a feature called **Framebuffer Objects (FBO)**, which allows this kind of offscreen rendering to textures present in memory. FBOs can be used by instantiating new objects of Libgdx's `Framebuffer` class.

The following is an example of how FBOs should be used in general:

```
// ...
Framebuffer fbo;
fbo = new Framebuffer(Format.RGB888, width, height, false);
fbo.begin(); // set render target to FBO's texture buffer
Gdx.gl.glClearColor(0.0f, 0.0f, 0.0f, 1.0f); // solid black
Gdx.gl.glClear(GL10.GL_COLOR_BUFFER_BIT); // clear FBO batch.
draw(someTextureRegion, 0, 0); // draw (to FBO)
fbo.end(); // revert render target back to normal
// retrieve result
Texture fboTexture = fbo.getColorBufferTexture();
// ...
```

A new FBO is initialized by passing in a format, a width and height, and a flag indicating whether an attached depth buffer is needed. The passed format and dimensions are used to initialize the FBO's texture that will serve as its render target. The flag for the depth buffer, also referred to as the Z-buffer, enables the sorting of pixels in 3D space. Since we are creating a game in 2D space and also have taken care of the rendering order by ourselves, there is no need to enable this buffer which would just waste precious memory.

As you can see in the preceding code example, rendering to an FBO is just a matter of calling its begin() method to temporarily redirect all subsequent draw calls to the FBO's texture buffer. The rendering to an FBO must always be finished by calling its end() method. Afterwards, the resulting texture can be retrieved by simply calling the getColorBufferTexture() method.

In order to work with FBOs, you need to explicitly tell Libgdx to initialize your application in the OpenGL ES 2.0 mode. However, Libgdx will fall back to GLES 1.x if GLES 2.0 is not supported on the device. You may want to implement two render paths for this case: one for GLES 1.x and another for GLES 2.0. Libgdx's graphics module can be queried to find out which OpenGL mode is currently available as shown in the following line of code:

```
Gdx.graphics.isGL11Available(); // Using GLES 1.x mode?
Gdx.graphics.isGL20Available(); // Using GLES 2.0 mode?
```

Remember that these methods do not return any information about available hardware support, but they instead check if the tested OpenGL mode was (successfully) initialized by Libgdx on startup.

For simplicity, we assume full hardware support for GLES 2.0 in this book.

We will now make some mandatory changes to our platform-specific projects wherever needed to enable the OpenGL ES 2.0 mode so that we can use FBOs.

For a desktop platform, make the following modification to the Main class of the CanyonBunny-desktop project:

```
public static void main (String[] args) {
    ...
    cfg.title = "CanyonBunny";
    cfg.useGL20 = true;
    cfg.width = 800;
    cfg.height = 480;

    new LwjglApplication(new CanyonBunnyMain(), cfg);
}
```

Next, for the Android platform, make the following changes to the AndroidManifest.xml file of the CanyonBunny-android project:

```
<?xml version="1.0" encoding="utf-8"?>
<manifest
    xmlns:android="http://schemas.android.com/apk/res/android"
    package="com.packtpub.libgdx.canyonbunny"
```

```
    android:versionCode="1"
    android:versionName="1.0" >

    <uses-sdk android:minSdkVersion="5"
            android:targetSdkVersion="8" />

    <uses-feature android:glEsVersion="0x00020000"
            android:required="true" />
    ...
</manifest>
```

After this, also make the following changes to the `MainActivity` class:

```
public class MainActivity extends AndroidApplication {
    @Override
    public void onCreate(Bundle savedInstanceState) {
        super.onCreate(savedInstanceState);

        AndroidApplicationConfiguration cfg =
            new AndroidApplicationConfiguration();
        cfg.useGL20 = true;

        initialize(new CanyonBunnyMain(), cfg);
    }
}
```

 For the HTML5 project, no extra modifications need to be made as GWT always renders in OpenGL ES 2.0 mode.

In *Chapter 7, Menus and Options*, we learned about Libgdx's `Game` class and used it to manage and switch, back and forth, between screens. We are now going to build a new class that expands on the idea of the `Game` class to support screen switching as well as an optional screen transition.

Create a new file for the `DirectedGame` class and add the following code:

```
package com.packtpub.libgdx.canyonbunny.screens;

import com.badlogic.gdx.ApplicationListener;
import com.badlogic.gdx.Gdx;
import com.badlogic.gdx.graphics.Pixmap.Format;
import com.badlogic.gdx.graphics.g2d.SpriteBatch;
import com.badlogic.gdx.graphics.glutils.FrameBuffer;
import com.packtpub.libgdx.canyonbunny.screens.transitions
```

```
    .ScreenTransition;

public abstract class DirectedGame implements ApplicationListener {
  private boolean init;
  private AbstractGameScreen currScreen;
  private AbstractGameScreen nextScreen;
  private FrameBuffer currFbo;
  private FrameBuffer nextFbo;
  private SpriteBatch batch;
  private float t;
  private ScreenTransition screenTransition;

  public void setScreen (AbstractGameScreen screen) {
    setScreen(screen, null);
  }

  public void setScreen (AbstractGameScreen screen,
      ScreenTransition screenTransition) {
    int w = Gdx.graphics.getWidth();
    int h = Gdx.graphics.getHeight();
    if (!init) {
      currFbo = new FrameBuffer(Format.RGB888, w, h, false);
      nextFbo = new FrameBuffer(Format.RGB888, w, h, false);
      batch = new SpriteBatch();
      init = true;
    }
    // start new transition
    nextScreen = screen;
    nextScreen.show(); // activate next screen
    nextScreen.resize(w, h);
    nextScreen.render(0); // let screen update() once
    if (currScreen != null) currScreen.pause();
    nextScreen.pause();
    Gdx.input.setInputProcessor(null); // disable input
    this.screenTransition = screenTransition;
    t = 0;
  }
}
```

This new class is meant to work in a similar way to Libgdx's Game class. Therefore, DirectedGame implements the same interface (ApplicationListener) with its corresponding methods as well as the setScreen() method, which we are already using to switch our screens. Actually, there are two variants of this method in this new class: one that allows changing to a new screen with a transition effect and one without any effect similar to the original screen.

The `setScreen()` method, which takes an instance of `ScreenTransition`, initializes two FBOs for the current and the next screen on its first call. Then, a new transition is started by storing the next-to-be screen in `nextScreen`, which in turn is activated and initialized so that it becomes renderable.

Next, add the following code to the same class to implement the `render()` method of the `ApplicationListener` interface:

```
@Override
public void render () {
  // get delta time and ensure an upper limit of one 60th second
  float deltaTime = Math.min(Gdx.graphics.getDeltaTime(),
                               1.0f / 60.0f);
  if (nextScreen == null) {
    // no ongoing transition
    if (currScreen != null) currScreen.render(deltaTime);
  } else {
    // ongoing transition
    float duration = 0;
    if (screenTransition != null)
      duration = screenTransition.getDuration();
    // update progress of ongoing transition
    t = Math.min(t + deltaTime, duration);
    if (screenTransition == null || t >= duration) {
      //no transition effect set or transition has just finished
      if (currScreen != null) currScreen.hide();
      nextScreen.resume();
      // enable input for next screen
      Gdx.input.setInputProcessor(
          nextScreen.getInputProcessor());
      // switch screens
      currScreen = nextScreen;
      nextScreen = null;
      screenTransition = null;
    } else {
      // render screens to FBOs
      currFbo.begin();
      if (currScreen != null) currScreen.render(deltaTime);
      currFbo.end();
      nextFbo.begin();
      nextScreen.render(deltaTime);
      nextFbo.end();
      // render transition effect to screen
      float alpha = t / duration;
```

```
        screenTransition.render(batch,
                                currFbo.getColorBufferTexture(),
                                nextFbo.getColorBufferTexture(),
                                alpha);
      }
    }
  }
```

Notice that the call to the next screen's `render()` method to which a delta time of 0 is passed. This allows the next screen to update its internal state once for initialization purposes. After this, both screens are paused so that they do not make any progress in time as long as the transition effect has not finished. Also, the input processor is set to `null` to avoid any interference from a potential user input during a running transition. The desired transition effect, if any, is stored in `screenTransition` for future reference. Finally, the `t` variable is used to keep a track of the effect's elapsed time and always needs to be reset to 0 to let new transitions start from the beginning.

There are basically two ways by which the `render()` method works. In the first case, it will simply call the `render()` method of the currently set screen. This holds true as long as no next screen is set, which implicates no ongoing transition effect. Otherwise, it is assumed that there is an ongoing transition. In this case, `t` is increased by the current delta time to let the transition effect progress correctly in time. After this, the current and next screens are rendered to their designated FBOs. Then, the resulting two textures are eventually passed on to the transition effect's `render()` method to do something fancy with it. Finally, the screens are switched and the input processor is reactivated as soon as the value of `t` has reached the transition effect's duration. Also, `nextScreen` is set back to `null` so that the first way of rendering is used again.

The delta time in the `render()` method of our new `DirectedGame` class is constrained to a maximum value of one one-sixtieth of a second to ensure **semi-fixed time steps** in all our screens. We will use this from now on to avoid potential time-related problems that may arise from using **variable time steps**, which we used before.

For a thorough explanation about various time stepping strategies, check out the following article on Glen Fiedler's blog: `http://gafferongames.com/game-physics/fix-your-timestep/`

After this, add the following code to the same class to implement the remaining parts of the `ApplicationListener` interface:

```
@Override
public void resize (int width, int height) {
  if (currScreen != null) currScreen.resize(width, height);
  if (nextScreen != null) nextScreen.resize(width, height);
}

@Override
public void pause () {
  if (currScreen != null) currScreen.pause();
}

@Override
public void resume () {
  if (currScreen != null) currScreen.resume();
}

@Override
public void dispose () {
  if (currScreen != null) currScreen.hide();
  if (nextScreen != null) nextScreen.hide();
  if (init) {
    currFbo.dispose();
    currScreen = null;
    nextFbo.dispose();
    nextScreen = null;
    batch.dispose();
    init = false;
  }
}
```

The preceding code ensures that the current and the next screen will be informed about the occurring events and that the screens, the sprite batch, and the FBOs will be correctly disposed off when they are no longer needed.

As a last step, we now want to rewire some parts of Canyon Bunny to use the added screen transition capability, which we just implemented. Therefore, we are going to make some minor modifications in those places where we are still using Libgdx's Game class and replace it with our own class, `DirectedGame`.

Add the following import line to `AbstractGameScreen`:

```
import com.badlogic.gdx.InputProcessor;
```

After this, add the following line to the same class:

```
public abstract InputProcessor getInputProcessor ();
```

Next, make the following changes to the same class:

```
protected DirectedGame game;

    public AbstractGameScreen (DirectedGame game) {
    this.game = game;
}
```

These changes introduce a new method called `getInputProcessor()`, which also needs to be implemented in `MenuScreen` and `GameScreen`. This is necessary to allow `DirectedGame` to route and control the flow of input processing as needed. As mentioned earlier, this will avoid any interference with the user input during a running transition.

Now, add the following import line to `CanyonBunnyMain`:

```
import com.packtpub.libgdx.canyonbunny.screens.DirectedGame;
```

After this, make the following changes to the same class:

```
public class CanyonBunnyMain extends DirectedGame {
    ...
}
```

Next, we are going to move on to `MenuScreen`. Make the following changes to this class:

```
public MenuScreen (DirectedGame game) {
    super(game);
}
```

After this, add the following code to the same class:

```
import com.badlogic.gdx.InputProcessor;

@Override
public InputProcessor getInputProcessor () {
    return stage;
}
```

Finally, remove the line that sets the input processor in `show()` so that it now looks as follows:

```
@Override
public void show () {
   stage = new Stage();
   rebuildStage();
}
```

Next, we are going to move on to `GameScreen`. Make the following changes to this class:

```
public GameScreen (DirectedGame game) {
   super(game);
}
```

After this, add the following code to the same class:

```
import com.badlogic.gdx.InputProcessor;

@Override
public InputProcessor getInputProcessor () {
   return worldController;
}
```

Lastly, we are going to move on to `WorldController`. Add the following import line to this class:

```
import com.packtpub.libgdx.canyonbunny.screens.DirectedGame;
```

After this, make the following changes to the same class:

```
private DirectedGame game;

public WorldController (DirectedGame game) {
   this.game = game;
   init();
}
```

Finally, remove the line that sets the input processor in `init()` so that it now looks like this:

```
private void init () {
    cameraHelper = new CameraHelper();
    lives = Constants.LIVES_START;
    livesVisual = lives;
    timeLeftGameOverDelay = 0;
    initLevel();
}
```

Admittedly, the game code has been subjected to a number of small but important changes, which has led us to having a generic way of handling any kind of screen transition. You might want to test run the game just to verify that screen switching is still working the same as before.

Implementing transition effects

Now that we have established a generic way to describe and use screen transitions, we can now start to implement the transition effects that we want. However, let us take a quick look at interpolation first as this will greatly improve the overall look and feel of our transition effects.

Knowing about interpolation algorithms

In *Chapter 8, Special Effects*, we have already seen an interpolation algorithm called Lerp which stands for Linear Interpolation. As the name implies, it calculates its interpolated values in an equal stepping from start to end. This works very well for any kind of constant movement. However, if we want to create more complex effects such as acceleration, deceleration, or maybe even both in a combination, we will need to use formulas that express those progressions as nonlinear curves. Luckily, Libgdx provides an `Interpolation` class that already implements many useful linear and non-linear interpolation algorithms so that we can happily skip the math involved and just use it.

Take a look at the following diagram that shows individual graphs of each available interpolation algorithm:

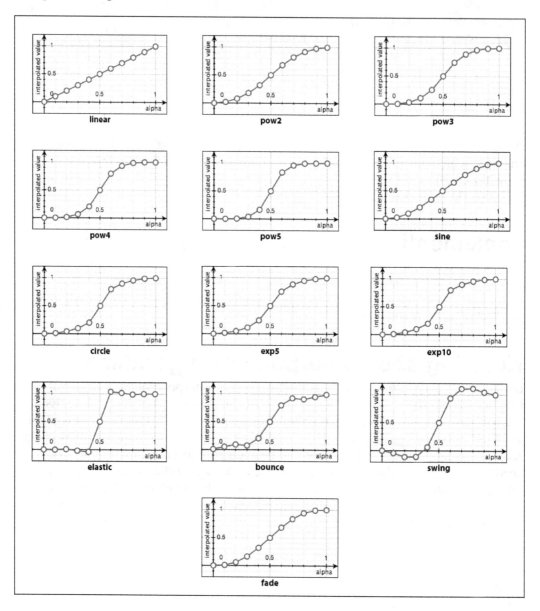

In Layman's terms, what can be seen in each graph is a kind of lookup table. The function of one of these algorithms takes the `alpha` value (x axis) as its input and outputs the corresponding interpolated value (y axis). The actual output simply depends on the algorithm's curve and what `alpha` value is used. The label below each graph also denotes the name of the method which you will find in `Interpolation`. Also, note that each algorithm reverses its effect at an `alpha` value of `0.5`. There are variants of each method for an algorithm in case you may want to apply a certain effect on the first half (`alpha` from `0.0` to `0.5`) or on the second one (`alpha` from `0.5` to `1.0`) only. This can be achieved by using the `In` or `Out` suffix respectively, such as `fadeIn`, `pow4In`, and `swingOut`.

The basic usage of `Interpolation` looks as follows:

```
float alpha = 0.25f;
float interpolatedValue = Interpolation.elastic.apply(alpha);
```

This code example finds the interpolated value (y axis) for a given `alpha` value (x axis) of `0.25` using the `elastic` algorithm. Remember, the `alpha` value can also be interpreted as progress (here: 25 percent) of the overall effect.

With this in mind, we will now start to implement three distinct effects: fade, slide, and slice.

Creating a fade transition effect

We will now create a fade transition effect that we will use for switching from the menu screen to the game screen. In this effect, the next screen overlays the current screen while gradually increasing the next screen's opacity. The opacity will start at 0 percent (fully translucent) and end at 100 percent (fully opaque).

The following sequence of screenshots shows this effect:

Now, create a new file for the ScreenTransitionFade class and add the following code:

```java
package com.packtpub.libgdx.canyonbunny.screens.transitions;

import com.badlogic.gdx.Gdx;
import com.badlogic.gdx.graphics.GL10;
import com.badlogic.gdx.graphics.Texture;
import com.badlogic.gdx.graphics.g2d.SpriteBatch;
import com.badlogic.gdx.math.Interpolation;

public class ScreenTransitionFade implements ScreenTransition {
  private static final ScreenTransitionFade instance =
      new ScreenTransitionFade();

  private float duration;

  public static ScreenTransitionFade init (float duration) {
    instance.duration = duration;
    return instance;
  }

  @Override
  public float getDuration () {
    return duration;
  }

  @Override
  public void render (SpriteBatch batch, Texture currScreen,
      Texture nextScreen, float alpha) {
    float w = currScreen.getWidth();
    float h = currScreen.getHeight();
    alpha = Interpolation.fade.apply(alpha);

    Gdx.gl.glClearColor(0.0f, 0.0f, 0.0f, 1.0f);
    Gdx.gl.glClear(GL10.GL_COLOR_BUFFER_BIT);
    batch.begin();
    batch.setColor(1, 1, 1, 1);
    batch.draw(currScreen, 0, 0, 0, 0, w, h, 1, 1, 0, 0, 0,
        currScreen.getWidth(), currScreen.getHeight(),
        false, true);
    batch.setColor(1, 1, 1, alpha);
    batch.draw(nextScreen, 0, 0, 0, 0, w, h, 1, 1, 0, 0, 0,
        nextScreen.getWidth(), nextScreen.getHeight(),
        false, true);
    batch.end();
  }
}
```

First of all, notice how we were able to tuck away the render logic of our new transition effect in such a nice and compact manner. The `ScreenTransitionFade` class is built as a singleton so that it can be easily accessed from anywhere in the code without having to create and keep multiple instances of it. The `init()` method should be called before it is used. It takes one argument to define the duration of the effect. The `render()` method uses both the supplied textures to create the desired effect. It is achieved by first clearing the screen, followed by drawing the current screen's texture, and lastly by drawing the next screen's texture on top of the other. However, prior to the `draw` call of the next screen, we also change the drawing color. It is set to full white, and the `alpha` channel, which controls the opacity for each of the following `draw` calls is set to `alpha`. The `alpha` variable contains the interpolated value where we have chosen to use the `fade` algorithm.

Finally, let the menu screen use the fade transition effect when the player has clicked on the **Play** button. Add the following import lines to the `MenuScreen` class:

```
import com.packtpub.libgdx.canyonbunny.screens.transitions
    .ScreenTransition;
import com.packtpub.libgdx.canyonbunny.screens.transitions
    .ScreenTransitionFade;
```

After this, make the following changes to the same class:

```
private void onPlayClicked () {
    ScreenTransition transition = ScreenTransitionFade.init(0.75f);
    game.setScreen(new GameScreen(game), transition);
}
```

With these changes, the transition from the menu screen to the game screen will last for 0.75 seconds or 750 milliseconds until finished. You can start the game now and watch the transition live in action. Change the transition's duration to either slow down or speed up the effect.

Creating a slide transition effect

We will now create a slide transition effect that we will use for switching from the game screen to the menu screen. In this effect, the next screen slides in from the top edge and moves downwards until it is entirely visible.

The following sequence of screenshots illustrates this effect:

Now, create a new file for the ScreenTransitionSlide class and add the following code:

```java
package com.packtpub.libgdx.canyonbunny.screens.transitions;

import com.badlogic.gdx.Gdx;
import com.badlogic.gdx.graphics.GL10;
import com.badlogic.gdx.graphics.Texture;
import com.badlogic.gdx.graphics.g2d.SpriteBatch;
import com.badlogic.gdx.math.Interpolation;

public class ScreenTransitionSlide implements ScreenTransition {
  public static final int LEFT = 1;
  public static final int RIGHT = 2;
  public static final int UP = 3;
  public static final int DOWN = 4;

  private static final ScreenTransitionSlide instance =
      new ScreenTransitionSlide();

  private float duration;
  private int direction;
  private boolean slideOut;
  private Interpolation easing;

  public static ScreenTransitionSlide init (float duration,
      int direction, boolean slideOut, Interpolation easing) {
    instance.duration = duration;
    instance.direction = direction;
    instance.slideOut = slideOut;
    instance.easing = easing;
    return instance;
  }
```

```
   @Override
   public float getDuration () {
      return duration;
   }
}
```

The second transition effect is implemented in the same way as we did for "fade" as a singleton class. As you will see in a moment, this class is a little bit heavier because it not only allows sliding in another screen from the top edge, but also allows sliding out the current screen to define the direction of movement. The init() method allows you to specify all these settings and also takes an interpolation algorithm that should be used.

Next, add the following code to the same class to implement the render() method of the ScreenTransition interface:

```
   @Override
   public void render (SpriteBatch batch, Texture currScreen,
         Texture nextScreen, float alpha) {
      float w = currScreen.getWidth();
      float h = currScreen.getHeight();
      float x = 0;
      float y = 0;
      if (easing != null) alpha = easing.apply(alpha);

      // calculate position offset
      switch (direction) {
      case LEFT:
         x = -w * alpha;
         if (!slideOut) x += w;
         break;
      case RIGHT:
         x = w * alpha;
         if (!slideOut) x -= w;
         break;
      case UP:
         y = h * alpha;
         if (!slideOut) y -= h;
         break;
      case DOWN:
         y = -h * alpha;
         if (!slideOut) y += h;
         break;
      }
```

```
// drawing order depends on slide type ('in' or 'out')
Texture texBottom = slideOut ? nextScreen : currScreen;
Texture texTop = slideOut ? currScreen : nextScreen;

// finally, draw both screens
Gdx.gl.glClearColor(0.0f, 0.0f, 0.0f, 1.0f);
Gdx.gl.glClear(GL10.GL_COLOR_BUFFER_BIT);
batch.begin();
batch.draw(texBottom, 0, 0, 0, 0, w, h, 1, 1, 0, 0, 0,
    currScreen.getWidth(), currScreen.getHeight(),
    false, true);
batch.draw(texTop, x, y, 0, 0, w, h, 1, 1, 0, 0, 0,
    nextScreen.getWidth(), nextScreen.getHeight(),
    false, true);
batch.end();
}
```

The `render()` method of this transition effect calculates the drawing order and position offsets for the current and the next screens using the `direction`, `slideOut`, and `alpha` variables. The value in `alpha` might be altered before it is used for calculations if an interpolation algorithm is set.

Finally, let the game screen use the slide transition effect when it wants to go back to the menu screen. Add the following import lines to the `WorldController` class:

```
import com.badlogic.gdx.math.Interpolation;
import com.packtpub.libgdx.canyonbunny.screens.transitions
    .ScreenTransition;
import com.packtpub.libgdx.canyonbunny.screens.transitions
    .ScreenTransitionSlide;
```

After this, make the following changes to the same class:

```
private void backToMenu () {
    // switch to menu screen
    ScreenTransition transition = ScreenTransitionSlide.init(0.75f,
        ScreenTransitionSlide.DOWN, false, Interpolation.bounceOut);
    game.setScreen(new MenuScreen(game), transition);
}
```

It is highly recommended to take some time and play around with the constants for UP, DOWN, LEFT, and RIGHT, as well as to try different combinations of interpolation algorithms either doing a slide-in or slide-out movement.

Creating a slice transition effect

We will now create a slice transition effect that we will use at the start of the game. As you will see in a moment, we can also start a transition without a current screen to another (first) one, which is exactly what we are going to do when the game starts. In this effect, the next screen is cut in a number of vertical slices. These slices are then vertically moved off the screen to their respective starting positions. The starting position alternates between the top and bottom edge. Finally, each slice is moved in and over the current screen until it is entirely visible.

The following sequence of screenshots illustrates this effect:

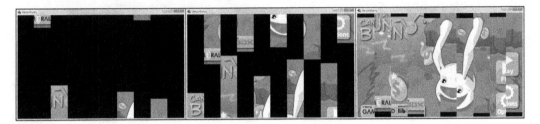

Now, create a new file for the ScreenTransitionSlice class and add the following code:

```
package com.packtpub.libgdx.canyonbunny.screens.transitions;

import com.badlogic.gdx.Gdx;
import com.badlogic.gdx.graphics.GL10;
import com.badlogic.gdx.graphics.Texture;
import com.badlogic.gdx.graphics.g2d.SpriteBatch;
import com.badlogic.gdx.math.Interpolation;
import com.badlogic.gdx.utils.Array;

public class ScreenTransitionSlice implements ScreenTransition {
    public static final int UP = 1;
    public static final int DOWN = 2;
    public static final int UP_DOWN = 3;

    private static final ScreenTransitionSlice instance =
        new ScreenTransitionSlice();

    private float duration;
    private int direction;
    private Interpolation easing;
    private Array<Integer> sliceIndex = new Array<Integer>();
```

```
public static ScreenTransitionSlice init (float duration,
    int direction, int numSlices, Interpolation easing) {
  instance.duration = duration;
  instance.direction = direction;
  instance.easing = easing;
  // create shuffled list of slice indices which determines
  // the order of slice animation
  instance.sliceIndex.clear();
  for (int i = 0; i < numSlices; i++)
    instance.sliceIndex.add(i);
  instance.sliceIndex.shuffle();
  return instance;
}

@Override
public float getDuration () {
  return duration;
}

@Override
public void render (SpriteBatch batch, Texture currScreen,
    Texture nextScreen, float alpha) {
  float w = currScreen.getWidth();
  float h = currScreen.getHeight();
  float x = 0;
  float y = 0;
  int sliceWidth = (int)(w / sliceIndex.size);

  Gdx.gl.glClearColor(0.0f, 0.0f, 0.0f, 1.0f);
  Gdx.gl.glClear(GL10.GL_COLOR_BUFFER_BIT);
  batch.begin();
  batch.draw(currScreen, 0, 0, 0, 0, w, h, 1, 1, 0, 0, 0,
      currScreen.getWidth(), currScreen.getHeight(),
      false, true);
  if (easing != null) alpha = easing.apply(alpha);
  for (int i = 0; i < sliceIndex.size; i++) {
    // current slice/column
    x = i * sliceWidth;
    // vertical displacement using randomized
    // list of slice indices
    float offsetY = h * (1 + sliceIndex.get(i)
                        / (float)sliceIndex.size);
    switch (direction) {
    case UP:
```

```
          y = -offsetY + offsetY * alpha;
          break;
        case DOWN:
          y = offsetY - offsetY * alpha;
          break;
        case UP_DOWN:
          if (i % 2 == 0) {
            y = -offsetY + offsetY * alpha;
          } else {
            y = offsetY - offsetY * alpha;
          }
          break;
        }
        batch.draw(nextScreen, x, y, 0, 0, sliceWidth, h, 1, 1, 0,
            i * sliceWidth, 0, sliceWidth, nextScreen.getHeight(),
            false, true);
      }
      batch.end();
    }
  }
```

The effect builds a random list of indices for each slice. The randomization is used to create a small vertical displacement for the slices so that they arrive at their target location at different times.

Finally, let the main class of Canyon Bunny use the slice transition effect when the game is started. Add the following import lines to the `CanyonBunnyMain` class:

```
import com.badlogic.gdx.math.Interpolation;
import com.packtpub.libgdx.canyonbunny.screens.transitions
    .ScreenTransition;
import com.packtpub.libgdx.canyonbunny.screens.transitions
    .ScreenTransitionSlice;
```

After this, make the following changes to the same class:

```
    @Override
    public void create () {
      // Set Libgdx log level
      Gdx.app.setLogLevel(Application.LOG_DEBUG);

      // Load assets
      Assets.instance.init(new AssetManager());

      // Start game at menu screen
      ScreenTransition transition = ScreenTransitionSlice.init(2,
          ScreenTransitionSlice.UP_DOWN, 10, Interpolation.pow5Out);
      setScreen(new MenuScreen(this), transition);
    }
```

Summary

In this chapter we have learned how to manage screen transitions in a generic way by separating the implementation details of the transition effects from the actual screens that should be rendered. We have learned about OpenGL's FBOs, which allow us to render multiple screens to in-memory textures (RTT). Then, with the knowledge gained on how to use FBOs, we created a screen transition system that can apply any kind of transition effect while being completely independent of the screen's contents. We have used Libgdx's `Interpolation` class, which comes with a pool of 13 ready-to-use interpolation algorithms. Finally, we have discussed and implemented the three transition effects.

In the next chapter, we will learn how to create sound effects using several sound generators. Furthermore, we will add background music and create an audio manager using the Libgdx Audio API to easily manage music and sound effects in the game.

10
Managing Music and Sound Effects

In this chapter you will learn how to manage your music and sound effects. Libgdx provides four interfaces to handle different types of audio data. The first two interfaces that we will discuss are targeted at playing back prerecorded audio files. The two remaining interfaces give us even more low-level access to the audio device. They can be used to record and play back raw samples of audio data, which is a so-called **PCM (Pulse-Code Modulation)**-encoded audio signal. After that, we will take a look at the great world of sound generators. These tools are extremely handy as they allow you to quickly create new sound effects in a short period of time.

Lastly, looping background music and some sound effects for certain in-game events will be added to Canyon Bunny. The game's audio settings can be changed in the options menu of the menu screen through two new checkboxes and sliders for music and sound effects.

Playing back music and sound effects

Libgdx provides cross-platform audio playback for prerecorded audio files of the following three supported file formats:

- .wav **(RIFF WAVE)**
- .mp3 **(MPEG-2 Audio Layer III)**
- .ogg **(Ogg Vorbis)**

There are two interfaces called Music and Sound. They serve two different use cases of playing back audio files. In terms of Libgdx, sounds are audio files that usually play no longer than one second; think of laser or machine gun sounds. Audio files used as Sound objects are loaded and decoded so that they can be directly sent to the audio device. Obviously, the decoded audio data kept in memory can heavily increase the overall memory usage. On the contrary, audio files used as Music objects are streamed, which means that only the necessary portion of it is decoded and held in memory. Therefore, Music objects should be used for playing long audio files like background music.

 Music objects may require more CPU cycles because the streamed audio data needs to be decoded before it can be sent to the audio device. This is not the case with Sound objects because they are already decoded upon loading. So, it is simply a trade-off between performance and memory usage.

The following sections will give you an overview of Libgdx's Sound and Music interfaces.

Exploring the Sound interface

The Sound interface is suitable for playing back short audio files. New sound instances can be requested from Libgdx's Gdx.audio module using the newSound() method as follows:

```
Sound sound = Gdx.audio.newSound(
  Gdx.files.internal("sound.wav"));
```

This line of code will allocate new memory for the decoded audio data of the sound. wav file. The Sound interface also makes use of the Disposable interface, which implicates that the allocated resources need to be disposed manually using the respective dispose() method when a sound instance is no longer needed.

```
sound.dispose(); // free allocated memory
```

Calling the play() method of a sound instance will start the playback of its audio data and will return an ID that is associated with the sound that is being played. A sound ID can be used to refer to a specific playing sound. This allows controlling sounds at a later time, such as stopping the playback and changing the volume, pitch, and pan.

Libgdx will silently ignore any requests to a referred sound if that sound is no longer playing.

There are several overloaded methods to start playing a sound for a single time or in an endless loop. Optionally, values for the sound's volume, pitch, and pan can also be passed.

```
long play();
long play(float volume);
long play(float volume, float pitch, float pan);
long loop();
long loop(float volume);
long loop(float volume, float pitch, float pan);
```

The value for `volume` ranges between 0.0 and 1.0, where higher values result in louder audio signals. Sounds can be pitched up and down resulting in lower or higher frequency audio signals, respectively. A pitch value of 1.0 will play the sound at its normal speed. Pitch values above 1.0 will let the sound play faster, while values below 1.0 will result in slower playback. A pan value of 0.0 will play the sound equally loud on the left and right audio channel, which is also referred to as the center. Negative pan values will play the sound only on the left audio channel whereas positive pan values will achieve the opposite.

Consider a scenario where we have two sounds, one for a cat and one for a dog. Both sounds will be loaded in Libgdx as separate sound instances that can be used to play back several copies of them in parallel. To stop all playing copies of a (cat or dog) sound instance, the `stop()` method can be called. Alternatively, a sound ID can be passed to the `stop()` method to stop a specific copy of the (cat or dog) sound instance only.

```
void stop();
void stop(long soundId);
```

Sounds that are currently playing can be modified using their sound ID and one of the following methods:

```
void setVolume(long soundId, float volume);
void setPan(long soundId, float pan, float volume);
void setPitch(long soundId, float pitch);
void setLooping(long soundId, boolean looping);
```

Exploring the Music interface

The Music interface is suitable for playing back long audio files and is designed in a very similar way when compared with the Sound interface. Therefore, new music instances can also be requested from Libgdx's Gdx.audio module; however, the method is called newMusic().

```
Music music = Gdx.audio.newMusic(
    Gdx.files.internal("music.mp3"));
```

The Music interface also makes use of the Disposable interface. The music instances that are no longer needed should always be disposed to free the allocated memory.

```
music.dispose(); // free allocated memory
```

Apart from that, the interface provides the expected method to control music playback as follows:

```
void play();
void pause();
void stop();
```

Additionally, there are some methods to modify the music being played as shown in the following listing:

```
void setPan(float pan, float volume);
void setVolume(float volume);
void setLooping(boolean isLooping);
```

At times, it might be useful to query the music for its state, such as its current position (in milliseconds) and whether it is still playing or not.

```
boolean isPlaying();
float getPosition();
```

Accessing the audio device directly

In addition to the Music and Sound interfaces Libgdx also provides two more low-level audio interfaces that enable direct access to the audio device. They can be used for recording and playback of raw samples of audio data. Those samples are stored as a PCM-encoded audio signal.

These direct access features are currently unavailable in HTML5/GWT applications.

Exploring the AudioDevice interface

The AudioDevice interface allows you to send PCM-encoded audio samples directly to the audio device. For this to work, a new audio device can be requested using Libgdx's Gdx.audio module and called by its newAudioDevice() method as follows:

```
AudioDevice audioDevice =
    Gdx.audio.newAudioDevice(44100, false);
```

The preceding line of code allocates a new instance of an audio device with a sample rate of 44.1 kHz in stereo mode. Requested instances of AudioDevice need to be disposed using the dispose() method when they are no longer needed in order to avoid memory leaks.

```
audioDevice.dispose(); // free allocated memory
```

New audio data can be sent to an audio device either using an array of floats or an array of 16-bit signed shorts.

```
void writeSamples(float[] samples, int offset, int numSamples);
void writeSamples(short[] samples, int offset, int numSamples);
```

The offset (start) and numSamples (length) parameters are used to define the range of samples that will be sent to the audio device.

 Using an audio device with stereo mode enabled implies that the amount of samples needs to be doubled, as there are two separate audio channels to be fed with audio data. Stereo samples are interleaved starting with the left channel followed by the right channel; for example, to create a sound that will last for exactly one second at a sample rate of 44.1 kHz will require a total number of 44100 samples in mono mode and 88200 samples in stereo mode.

Exploring the AudioRecorder interface

The `AudioRecorder` interface allows you to record samples in a 16-bit PCM format using a connected microphone. New instances of `AudioRecorder` can be requested using Libgdx's `Gdx.audio` module and by calling its `newAudioRecorder()` method as follows:

```
AudioRecorder audioRecordedr =
  Gdx.audio.newAudioRecorder(44100, false);
```

Basically, `AudioRecorder` works nearly the same as `AudioDevice` except that it captures samples. As always, unused instances need to be disposed in order to avoid memory leaks.

```
audioRecorder.dispose(); // free allocated memory
```

To record samples with the audio recorder, all that is needed is an array into which the captured samples will be stored.

```
void read(short[] samples, int offset, int numSamples);
```

The `offset` (start) and `numSamples` (length) parameters are used to define which samples in the `samples` target array will be overwritten with new data.

Using sound generators

So, we have learned about direct access to the audio device in Libgdx, and we know now know to write audio samples to it. Sure enough, we could now (try to) write our own sound generator class from here and feed one of Libgdx's audio device instances with the resulting audio samples. However, audio programming is beyond the scope of this book, and it is also a very advanced topic even for seasoned programmers.

A viable solution to get hold of some nice sound effects is to use one of the existing sound generators which are free and open source. One of these sound generators is called **sfxr**, which was originally developed by Tomas "DrPetter" Pettersson in 2007. Over time, several sfxr variants have emerged, such as bfxr, cfxr, and as3sfxr.

About the sfxr generator

The sfxr sound generator quickly became widespread among independent game developers everywhere because it simplified the creation of new sounds just by clicking on the **RANDOMIZE** button. Naturally, all other parameters used to create a sound are tweakable to allow fine-tuning. Also, simple means are provided to get basic sound effects into games through presets as buttons to the left of the program GUI, such as **PICKUP/COIN**, **LASER/SHOOT**, **EXPLOSION**, **POWERUP**, **HIT/HURT**, **JUMP**, and **BLIP/SELECT**. If you like a generated sound effect, you can export it to a .wav file to be used in your game.

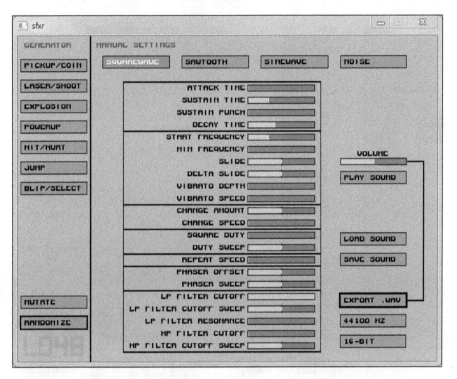

The official source code repository of sfxr can be found at
https://code.google.com/p/sfxr/.

About the cfxr generator

The cfxr sound generator was originally developed by Joachim Bengtsson in 2008. It is based on sfxr and was ported to Mac OS as a native Cocoa application, hence the name **cfxr (Cocoa sfxr)**. A history list was added with the possibility to rate each generated sound effect by the user. This also allows you to easily flip through a couple of sounds and jump back to previous ones if needed.

The official source code repository of cfxr can be found at https://github.com/nevyn/cfxr/.

About the bfxr generator

This sound generator was originally developed by Stephen "increpare" Lavelle. It appears to be the most advanced version of that time. Some additional waveforms as well as a mixer have been added to create more complex sounds. The created sounds can be saved to and loaded from files, which is a useful feature that is available in neither sfxr nor cfxr. Additionally, the lock symbol next to each parameter can be used to avoid any further changes to them while using the **Randomize** and **Mutation** buttons.

The official source code repository of bfxr can be found at https://github.com/increpare/bfxr/.

Adding music and sounds to Canyon Bunny

Let us now add some music and sound effects to our game. First, we need to know what audio files are needed and then copy them to our `assets` folder.

 All assets shown and discussed in this book, including any other project files, can be downloaded from Packt's website at `http://www.packtpub.com/learning-libgdx-game-development/book`.

The following tables contain descriptions of each audio file and their function in Canyon Bunny:

- Sounds (generated with bfxr):

Filename	Event
jump.wav	When player jumps
jump_with_feather.wav	When player jumps in mid-air (requires active feather power-up)
pickup_coin.wav	When player picks up a gold coin
pickup_feather.wav	When player picks up a feather power-up
live_lost.wav	When player loses a life (for example, player falls down into the water)

- Music (provided by Klaus "keith303" Spang):

Filename	Event
keith303_-_brand_new_highscore.mp3	When application starts (indefinitely looping background music)

Now add all these files to `CanyonBunny-android/assets/`. Split up the audio files by placing them either in the `music` or `sound` subfolder. The following screenshot shows how the final structure of your `assets` folder should look:

After this, we need to update our `Assets` class in order to make the audio files accessible in the same way as the rest of our assets. We will also use `AssetManager` to let Libgdx handle the loading and unloading process of the music and sound files.

Add the following two import lines to the `Assets` class:

```
import com.badlogic.gdx.audio.Music;
import com.badlogic.gdx.audio.Sound;
```

Then, add the following code to the same class:

```
public AssetSounds sounds;
public AssetMusic music;

public class AssetSounds {
   public final Sound jump;
   public final Sound jumpWithFeather;
   public final Sound pickupCoin;
   public final Sound pickupFeather;
   public final Sound liveLost;
```

```
    public AssetSounds (AssetManager am) {
        jump = am.get("sounds/jump.wav", Sound.class);
        jumpWithFeather = am.get("sounds/jump_with_feather.wav",
            Sound.class);
        pickupCoin = am.get("sounds/pickup_coin.wav", Sound.class);
        pickupFeather = am.get("sounds/pickup_feather.wav",
            Sound.class);
        liveLost = am.get("sounds/live_lost.wav", Sound.class);
    }
}


public class AssetMusic {
    public final Music song01;

    public AssetMusic (AssetManager am) {
        song01 = am.get("music/keith303_-_brand_new_highscore.mp3",
            Music.class);
    }
}
```

This adds the two new inner classes, AssetSounds and AssetMusic, which will
hold the loaded instances of the music and sound effects. Next, make the following
changes to the same class:

```
public void init (AssetManager assetManager) {
    this.assetManager = assetManager;
    // set asset manager error handler
    assetManager.setErrorListener(this);
    // load texture atlas
    assetManager.load(Constants.TEXTURE_ATLAS_OBJECTS,
        TextureAtlas.class);
    // load sounds
    assetManager.load("sounds/jump.wav", Sound.class);
    assetManager.load("sounds/jump_with_feather.wav", Sound.class);
    assetManager.load("sounds/pickup_coin.wav", Sound.class);
    assetManager.load("sounds/pickup_feather.wav", Sound.class);
    assetManager.load("sounds/live_lost.wav", Sound.class);
    // load music
    assetManager.load("music/keith303_-_brand_new_highscore.mp3",
        Music.class);
    // start loading assets and wait until finished
    assetManager.finishLoading();
```

```
    Gdx.app.debug(TAG, "# of assets loaded: "
      + assetManager.getAssetNames().size);
    for (String a : assetManager.getAssetNames())
    Gdx.app.debug(TAG, "asset: " + a);

    TextureAtlas atlas =
      assetManager.get(Constants.TEXTURE_ATLAS_OBJECTS);

    // enable texture filtering for pixel smoothing
    for (Texture t : atlas.getTextures())
    t.setFilter(TextureFilter.Linear, TextureFilter.Linear);

    // create game resource objects
    fonts = new AssetFonts();
    bunny = new AssetBunny(atlas);
    rock = new AssetRock(atlas);
    goldCoin = new AssetGoldCoin(atlas);
    feather = new AssetFeather(atlas);
    levelDecoration = new AssetLevelDecoration(atlas);
    sounds = new AssetSounds(assetManager);
    music = new AssetMusic(assetManager);
  }
```

These changes tell the asset manager to load and manage every audio file that we want to use in the game. We are now all set to play back our audio files. However, the game should also respect the current audio settings that are available in the **Options** menu of the menu screen.

At this point, it would seem logical to just call `play()` on the sound and music instances in the game code where needed. However, this approach poses an issue in terms of clean code with regard to the game settings, as the current game settings need to be checked every time an audio file is played. So, it would be ideal to have an audio manager as a centralized point of control over the game's audio playback. Since Libgdx does not provide an audio manager, we will build one of our own.

Create a new file for the `AudioManager` class and add the following code:

```
package com.packtpub.libgdx.canyonbunny.util;

import com.badlogic.gdx.audio.Music;
import com.badlogic.gdx.audio.Sound;

public class AudioManager {
  public static final AudioManager instance = new AudioManager();

  private Music playingMusic;

  // singleton: prevent instantiation from other classes
  private AudioManager () { }

  public void play (Sound sound) {
    play(sound, 1);
  }

  public void play (Sound sound, float volume) {
    play(sound, volume, 1);
  }

  public void play (Sound sound, float volume, float pitch) {
    play(sound, volume, pitch, 0);
  }

  public void play (Sound sound, float volume, float pitch,
    float pan) {
    if (!GamePreferences.instance.sound) return;
    sound.play(GamePreferences.instance.volSound * volume,
      pitch, pan);
  }
}
```

The `AudioManager` class is a singleton class, so we can access it from anywhere in the code. It features a couple of overloaded `play()` methods just like the original `Sound` and `Music` interfaces. The advantage of overloading these methods is that you can make some parameters optional. The methods in this class check against the values in `GamePreferences`, which holds the currently loaded audio settings among others. If the checkbox for sounds is not selected in the **Options** menu, `GamePrefernces.instance.sound` will return `false`, and therefore any call of `AudioManager`'s `play()` will be aborted before the actual `play()` call of a sound is executed.

Next, add the following code to the same class:

```
public void play (Music music) {
  stopMusic();
  playingMusic = music;
  if (GamePreferences.instance.music) {
    music.setLooping(true);
    music.setVolume(GamePreferences.instance.volMusic);
    music.play();
  }
}

  public void stopMusic () {
    if (playingMusic != null) playingMusic.stop();
  }

public void onSettingsUpdated () {
  if (playingMusic == null) return;
  playingMusic.setVolume(GamePreferences.instance.volMusic);
  if (GamePreferences.instance.music) {
    if (!playingMusic.isPlaying()) playingMusic.play();
  } else {
    playingMusic.pause();
  }
}
```

This code adds another overloaded `play()` method which takes an instance of `Music` that shall be played. If some music is already playing, it is stopped first. Then, the new music is initialized for playback and started if **Music** is enabled in the game settings. The `onSettingsUpdated()` method is used to allow the **Options** menu to inform `AudioManager` when settings have changed to execute appropriate actions, such as setting a new music volume.

Now let us connect the audio manager with the **Options** menu in the menu screen and the rest of the game.

Add the following import line to `MenuScreen`:

```
import com.packtpub.libgdx.canyonbunny.util.AudioManager;
```

After that, make the following changes to the same class:

```
private void onSaveClicked () {
  saveSettings();
  onCancelClicked();
  AudioManager.instance.onSettingsUpdated();
}

private void onCancelClicked () {
  btnMenuPlay.setVisible(true);
  btnMenuOptions.setVisible(true);
  winOptions.setVisible(false);
  AudioManager.instance.onSettingsUpdated();
}
```

These changes make sure that when the **Options** menu is closed, the audio manager will start or stop the music depending on the current audio settings.

Next, add the following import lines to the `CanyonBunnyMain` class:

```
import com.packtpub.libgdx.canyonbunny.util.AudioManager;
import com.packtpub.libgdx.canyonbunny.util.GamePreferences;
```

After that, make the following changes to the same class:

```
@Override
public void create () {
  // Set Libgdx log level
  Gdx.app.setLogLevel(Application.LOG_DEBUG);

  // Load assets
  Assets.instance.init(new AssetManager());

  // Load preferences for audio settings and start playing music
  GamePreferences.instance.load();
  AudioManager.instance.play(Assets.instance.music.song01);

  // Start game at menu screen
  ScreenTransition transition = ScreenTransitionSlice.init(2,
    ScreenTransitionSlice.UP_DOWN, 10, Interpolation.pow5Out);
  setScreen(new MenuScreen(this), transition);
}
```

These changes will make sure that after the assets and game preferences have been loaded, the music starts playing. This is done using the play() method of AudioManager, which takes care of checking the current audio settings, setting the correct music volume, and potentially starting the playback of the music file.

 Libgdx automatically handles the task of pausing and resuming for any instances of playing music. Therefore, no extra code is required to handle these cases in the game code.

Next, add the following import line to the WorldController class:

```
import com.packtpub.libgdx.canyonbunny.util.AudioManager;
```

After that, make the following changes to the same class:

```
public void update (float deltaTime) {
  handleDebugInput(deltaTime);
  if (isGameOver()) {
    timeLeftGameOverDelay -= deltaTime;
    if (timeLeftGameOverDelay < 0) backToMenu();
  } else {
    handleInputGame(deltaTime);
  }
  level.update(deltaTime);
  testCollisions();
  cameraHelper.update(deltaTime);
  if (!isGameOver() && isPlayerInWater()) {
    AudioManager.instance.play(Assets.instance.sounds.liveLost);
    lives--;
    if (isGameOver())
    timeLeftGameOverDelay = Constants.TIME_DELAY_GAME_OVER;
    else
    initLevel();
  }
  level.mountains.updateScrollPosition(
    cameraHelper.getPosition());
  if (livesVisual > lives)
  livesVisual = Math.max(lives, livesVisual - 1 * deltaTime);
  if (scoreVisual < score)
  scoreVisual = Math.min(score, scoreVisual +250 * deltaTime);
}

private void onCollisionBunnyWithGoldCoin (GoldCoin goldcoin) {
  goldcoin.collected = true;
```

```
      AudioManager.instance.play(Assets.instance.sounds.pickupCoin);
      score += goldcoin.getScore();
      Gdx.app.log(TAG, "Gold coin collected");
    }

    private void onCollisionBunnyWithFeather (Feather feather) {
      feather.collected = true;
      AudioManager.instance.play(Assets.instance.sounds.pickupFeather);
      score += feather.getScore();
      level.bunnyHead.setFeatherPowerup(true);
      Gdx.app.log(TAG, "Feather collected");
    }
```

These changes add the code to trigger the sound effects for the Life Lost,
Picked up Gold Coin, and Picked up Feather events at the right time.

Next, add the following two import lines to the BunnyHead class:

```
    import com.badlogic.gdx.math.MathUtils;
    import com.packtpub.libgdx.canyonbunny.util.AudioManager;
```

After that, make the following changes to the same class:

```
    public void setJumping (boolean jumpKeyPressed) {
      switch (jumpState) {
        case GROUNDED: // Character is standing on a platform
        if (jumpKeyPressed) {
          AudioManager.instance.play(Assets.instance.sounds.jump);
          // Start counting jump time from the beginning
          timeJumping = 0;
          jumpState = JUMP_STATE.JUMP_RISING;
        }
        break;
        case JUMP_RISING: // Rising in the air
        if (!jumpKeyPressed) {
          jumpState = JUMP_STATE.JUMP_FALLING;
        }
        break;
        case FALLING:// Falling down
        case JUMP_FALLING: // Falling down after jump
        if (jumpKeyPressed && hasFeatherPowerup) {
          AudioManager.instance.play(
            Assets.instance.sounds.jumpWithFeather, 1,
            MathUtils.random(1.0f, 1.1f));
          timeJumping = JUMP_TIME_OFFSET_FLYING;
          jumpState = JUMP_STATE.JUMP_RISING;
        }
        break;
      }
    }
```

The changes in the code for `BunnyHead` trigger the sound effects for the jumped and jumped-in-mid-air events at the right time. The `jumpWithFeather` sound is played using a different `play()` method of the `AudioManager` class. It is also provided with a random pitch value in the range of `1.0` to `1.1` which adds a little change in the frequency, rendering the rapidly repeated sound effect more interesting.

 Currently, sound pitching does not work in the GWT backend that is used in Libgdx to support the WebGL target platform. The sound will just play at its normal rate if pitching is used.

These were the last changes and thus we conclude this chapter about working with audio in Libgdx and how to use it in Canyon Bunny.

Summary

In this chapter, we have learned how to use Libgdx's four audio interfaces, `Sound`, `Music`, `AudioDevice`, and `AudioRecorder`, and about their specific use cases. We have taken a look at freely available and open source sound generators and used one of them to create sound effects that can be used in Canyon Bunny. We have also added background music to the game and understood that Libgdx takes care of when a music instance being played needs to be paused and resumed in terms of the Life-Cycle in a Libgdx application. A manager class called `AudioManager` has been created to gain centralized control over any audio-related actions. Finally, playing music and sounds turned out to be a very straightforward process in conjunction with the use of our audio manager. We had to add just a few new lines of code to trigger the music and sound effects at the right time for each event.

In the next chapter, we will have a look at some advanced programming techniques. This includes using a physics engine suitable for 2D game objects, creating a shader program to apply a simple monochrome filter effect, and querying the accelerometer hardware to implement an alternative input method.

11
Advanced Programming Techniques

In this chapter we will take a look at Box2D, a physics engine for simulating realistic-looking physics of the objects in 2D space. After we have covered the basics of how to use Box2D, we will move on and create a little physics simulation that is going to be triggered at the end of the level. For this to work, we will also need to add a new level object that represents the level's end.

After that, we will look into the topic of shader programs. Shaders, in general, are simple programs that are going to be executed on the **Graphics Processing Unit (GPU)**. We will create our own shader program consisting of a vertex and a fragment shader to achieve a simple monochrome filter effect.

Physics engines, such as Box2D and programming shaders, are very complex topics. Each deserves at least one book on their own to get hold of their gist. Nonetheless, this chapter is meant to give you a first push in the right direction on how to approach these broad topics.

Today's smartphones have an integrated accelerometer. This can be used to detect the spatial position of the device, which is delivered by the accelerometer as one value for each of the three axes. We will query the accelerometer hardware and use the read values to translate them into the player movement in Canyon Bunny.

Simulating physics with Box2D

Box2D was created by *Erin Catto* and is an open source physics engine for simulating rigid bodies in 2D space. It is written in platform-independent C++ code that has encouraged ports to several frameworks, game engines, and programming languages in general.

You should really check out at least one of the following popular games if you have never seen Box2D in action before: Angry Birds, Limbo, Tiny Wings, and Crayon Physics Deluxe.

Libgdx integrates Box2D, similar to other frameworks, through a thin wrapper API that is congruent with Box2D's original API. This approach makes it pleasantly easy to transfer existing knowledge about Box2D by following tutorials and examples that are not based on Libgdx, and, of course, by using the official Box2D manual.

For more information, check out the official website of Box2D at: http://www.box2d.org/

For Box2D tutorials, check out the following websites:

- C++: http://www.iforce2d.net/b2dtut/
- Objective-C: http://www.raywenderlich.com/28602/intro-to-box2d-with-cocos2d-2-x-tutorial-bouncing-balls
- Flash: http://www.emanueleferonato.com/category/box2d/
- JavaScript: http://blog.sethladd.com/2011/09/box2d-collision-damage-for-javascript.html

Exploring the concepts of Box2D

We will now shed some light on the basic ideas behind Box2D, and find out how it allows us to define virtual worlds that can be used to simulate believable physics with rigid bodies.

Understanding rigid bodies

First of all, let us clarify what this seemingly mysterious term *rigid body* means. A body, in the sense of physics, is just a collection of matter with some attributes assigned to it, such as its position and orientation. It is what we usually call an object in our real world. Now, a so-called rigid body describes an idealized body, which is assumed to be solid and thus incapable of being deformed by the exerting forces. From now on, we will use the shorter term, body, for brevity, since Box2D has only support for rigid bodies anyway.

Libgdx also integrates a second open source physics engine named **Bullet**. In contrast to Box2D, which is limited to 2D space and rigid body support only, Bullet features a full-fledged 3D physics simulation as well as support for both rigid and soft bodies. However, we will solely focus on Box2D in this chapter, as 3D physics is an even more advanced topic.

For more information, check out the official website of Bullet at: http://bulletphysics.org/

In addition to the (2D) position and orientation attributes, a body also has the following features:

- A mass given in kilograms
- A velocity (directed speed) given in meters per second (m/s)
- An angular velocity (rotational speed) given in radian per second (rad/s)

Choosing body types

There are three different body types to choose from. They are as follows:

- **Static**: It is a stationary body. It does not collide with other static or kinematic bodies. It is useful for floors, walls, non-moving platforms, and so on.
- **Kinematic**: It is a movable body. The position can be manually updated or changed according to its velocity, which is the preferred and more reliable method. Kinematic bodies do not collide with other static or kinematic bodies. It is useful for moving platforms (for example, elevators), reflecting dynamic bodies, and so on.
- **Dynamic**: It is a movable body. The position can be manually updated or changed according to forces, which is the preferred and more reliable method. Dynamic bodies can collide with all body types. It is useful for players, enemies, items, and so on.

 Kinematic bodies do not respond to forces. They will only move according to their set velocity.

Using shapes

Shapes describe the 2D objects in a geometrical way using radiuses for circles, widths and heights for rectangles, or a certain number of points (also vertices) for more complex shapes using polygons. So, those shapes define areas that can be tested for collisions with other shapes later on. For more information about creating polygon shapes, see the Box2D manual, *4.4 Polygon Shapes*.

Using fixtures

A fixture uses exactly one shape to which it adds material properties, such as density, friction, and restitution. The shape defined in a fixture is then attached to a body by adding the fixture to it. So it plays an important role in how bodies interact with each other. For more information about using fixtures, see the Box2D manual, *6.2 Fixture Creation*.

Simulating physics in the world

The world is the virtual sandbox inside which the physics simulation takes place. Each body, including their fixtures and shapes, needs to be inserted into the world to be included in the simulation.

Box2D is a very feature-rich engine, and thus contains a lot more features, such as Constraints, Joints, Sensors, and Contact Listener just to name a few, but which are not in the scope of this chapter.

For more in-depth information, consult the official manual of Box2D at:
`http://www.box2d.org/manual.pdf`

Physics body editor

The creation of bodies for images with complex shapes can be a very time-consuming task. The Physics body editor, created by *Aurélien Ribon*, lets you build bodies in a graphical editor and comes with many useful features, such as decomposition of concave shapes into convex polygons, tracing outlines of images, and a built-in collision tester.

Check out the official project website at:
`https://code.google.com/p/box2d-editor/`

A screenshot from the project's website that shows the editor in action is as follows:

Preparing Canyon Bunny for raining carrots

What, raining carrots? Absolutely! We are going to add two new game objects to Canyon Bunny. One will act as the end point or goal of a level, while the other is a regular carrot that we will be using later in our physics simulation. To be able to place the goal game object in our level, we will also have to do some minor changes to the level image and level loader.

So, a screenshot to give you a better impression of what we are aiming for, while we are working on it step-by-step, is as follows:

In the preceding screenshot, you see the running physics simulation of raining carrots, which is kicked off as soon as the player character passes the goal (golden carrot statue). Lots of carrots will fall down from the sky, nicely bounce off the ground, and eventually pile up on each other.

Adding the new assets

Firstly, copy the two new images `carrot.png` and `goal.png` to CanyonBunny-desktop/assets-raw/images/. Also, do not forget to rebuild your texture atlas. After that, let us add them to our global assets class for easier access.

Add the following lines to the inner class `AssetLevelDecoration` of the `Assets` class:

```
public final AtlasRegion carrot;
public final AtlasRegion goal;
```

Next, make the following changes to the same (inner) class so that the new images will become available for later use:

```
public AssetLevelDecoration (TextureAtlas atlas) {
  waterOverlay = atlas.findRegion("water_overlay");
  carrot = atlas.findRegion("carrot");
  goal = atlas.findRegion("goal");
}
```

Adding the carrot game object

The carrot is just a normal game object like any other that we have created for Canyon Bunny so far.

Create a new file for the `Carrot` class and add the following code:

```
package com.packtpub.libgdx.canyonbunny.game.objects;

import com.badlogic.gdx.graphics.g2d.SpriteBatch;
import com.badlogic.gdx.graphics.g2d.TextureRegion;
import com.packtpub.libgdx.canyonbunny.game.Assets;

public class Carrot extends AbstractGameObject {
  private TextureRegion regCarrot;

  public Carrot () {
    init();
  }

  private void init () {
    dimension.set(0.25f, 0.5f);

    regCarrot = Assets.instance.levelDecoration.carrot;

    // Set bounding box for collision detection
    bounds.set(0, 0, dimension.x, dimension.y);
    origin.set(dimension.x / 2, dimension.y / 2);
  }
```

```
public void render (SpriteBatch batch) {
  TextureRegion reg = null;

  reg = regCarrot;
  batch.draw(reg.getTexture(), position.x - origin.x,
    position.y - origin.y, origin.x, origin.y, dimension.x,
      dimension.y, scale.x, scale.y, rotation, reg.getRegionX(),
        reg.getRegionY(), reg.getRegionWidth(),
          reg.getRegionHeight(), false, false);
  }
}
```

Adding the goal game object

The goal game object will be used to mark the end of a level.

Create a new file for the Goal class and add the following code:

```
package com.packtpub.libgdx.canyonbunny.game.objects;

import com.badlogic.gdx.graphics.g2d.SpriteBatch;
import com.badlogic.gdx.graphics.g2d.TextureRegion;
import com.packtpub.libgdx.canyonbunny.game.Assets;

public class Goal extends AbstractGameObject {
  private TextureRegion regGoal;

  public Goal () {
```

```
      init();
   }

   private void init () {
      dimension.set(3.0f, 3.0f);
      regGoal = Assets.instance.levelDecoration.goal;

      // Set bounding box for collision detection
      bounds.set(1, Float.MIN_VALUE, 10, Float.MAX_VALUE);
      origin.set(dimension.x / 2.0f, 0.0f);
   }

   public void render (SpriteBatch batch) {
      TextureRegion reg = null;

      reg = regGoal;
      batch.draw(reg.getTexture(), position.x - origin.x,
         position.y - origin.y, origin.x, origin.y, dimension.x,
            dimension.y, scale.x, scale.y, rotation,
               reg.getRegionX(), reg.getRegionY(),
                  reg.getRegionWidth(), reg.getRegionHeight(),
                     false, false);
   }
}
```

There is one specialty about this game object that is important enough to be mentioned. We have set the bounds of the goal to values that make it almost infinitely tall in relation to other objects in the game world. This ensures that the player character will always collide with the goal and trigger the corresponding event.

Extending the level

The next step is to include the goal game object in the level image. Remember that each pixel color represents a certain game object in the world of Canyon Bunny. For the goal game object, we choose red as the pixel color (R=255, G=0, B=0).

Add the new red pixel marked as **Goal** to the level image. Use the following screenshot for reference:

Obviously, the goal should be placed at the far right to make it harder to reach for the player. In our example level, this is the elongated platform right after the arrow that is made out of gold coins.

Now, we need to tell the level loader about the new pixel and game object to let it handle it correctly.

Add the following import lines to the `Level` class:

```
import com.packtpub.libgdx.canyonbunny.game.objects.Carrot;
import com.packtpub.libgdx.canyonbunny.game.objects.Goal;
```

After that, add the following code to the same class:

```
public Array<Carrot> carrots;
public Goal goal;
```

Furthermore, add the following constant to the `BLOCK_TYPE` enumeration that defines the goal's red pixel color:

```
GOAL(255, 0, 0), // red
```

Next, make the following changes to the `init()` method in which we want to initialize a new array for the carrot game objects, and create a new goal game object if the corresponding pixel color was found in the level image:

```
private void init (String filename) {

  // objects
  rocks = new Array<Rock>();
  goldcoins = new Array<GoldCoin>();
  feathers = new Array<Feather>();
```

```
carrots = new Array<Carrot>();

// load image file that represents the level data
Pixmap pixmap = new Pixmap(Gdx.files.internal(filename));
// scan pixels from top-left to bottom-right
int lastPixel = -1;
for (int pixelY = 0; pixelY < pixmap.getHeight(); pixelY++) {
  for (int pixelX = 0; pixelX < pixmap.getWidth(); pixelX++) {

    // gold coin
    else if
    (BLOCK_TYPE.ITEM_GOLD_COIN.sameColor(currentPixel)) {
      ...
    }
    // goal
    else if (BLOCK_TYPE.GOAL.sameColor(currentPixel)) {
      obj = new Goal();
      offsetHeight = -7.0f;
      obj.position.set(pixelX, baseHeight + offsetHeight);
      goal = (Goal)obj;
    }
    // unknown object/pixel color
    else {

    }
    lastPixel = currentPixel;
  }
 }
}
```

Finally, make the following changes to the update() and render() methods in the same class to let each carrot update correctly, as well as render the goal and the carrot game objects in the right order on the screen, as follows:

```
public void update (float deltaTime) {
  // Feathers
  for (Feather feather : feathers)
    feather.update(deltaTime);
  for (Carrot carrot : carrots)
    carrot.update(deltaTime);
  // Clouds
```

```
        clouds.update(deltaTime);
      }

  public void render (SpriteBatch batch) {
    // Draw Mountains
    mountains.render(batch);
    // Draw Goal
    goal.render(batch);
    // Draw Rocks
    for (Rock rock : rocks)
      rock.render(batch);

    for (Feather feather : feathers)
      feather.render(batch);
    // Draw Carrots
    for (Carrot carrot : carrots)
      carrot.render(batch);
    // Draw Player Character
    bunnyHead.render(batch);
      }
```

You may want to run the game now and verify that the goal game object is visible at the end of the level. However, nothing will happen when the player character passes it. We will address the implementation details for the event handling and physics simulation next.

Letting it rain carrots

We will now focus on the implementation details, where we actually make use of Box2D in Canyon Bunny. Remember that we have created our own simple physics simulation for the game objects before. We do not want to replace this implementation, but in fact allow using either one of them as it suits our needs. In other words, we want to keep the existing implementation that is doing collision detection and physics for the game objects, and just add a coexisting alternative that uses Box2D.

Add the following import line to the `AbstractGameObject` class:

```
import com.badlogic.gdx.physics.box2d.Body;
```

After that, add the following line to the same class:

```
public Body body;
```

The (rigid) `Body` class directly relates to what we have discussed at the beginning of this chapter. Next, make the following changes to the `update()` method in the same class:

```
public void update (float deltaTime) {
  if (body == null) {
    updateMotionX(deltaTime);
    updateMotionY(deltaTime);

    // Move to the new position
    position.x + = velocity.x * deltaTime;
    position.y + = velocity.y * deltaTime;
    } else {
    position.set(body.getPosition());
    rotation = body.getAngle() * MathUtils.radiansToDegrees;
    }
  }
}
```

The idea here is that each game object will be using our simple physics as long as there is no Box2D body defined in the `body` variable. Otherwise, the current position and angle of rotation is simply taken from the body and applied to the game object to reflect the state of Box2D's calculations. In conclusion, this means that we have given Box2D full control over the movement parameters for those game objects.

Next, add the following import lines to the `WorldController` class:

```
import com.badlogic.gdx.math.MathUtils;
import com.badlogic.gdx.math.Vector2;
import com.badlogic.gdx.physics.box2d.Body;
import com.badlogic.gdx.physics.box2d.BodyDef;
import com.badlogic.gdx.physics.box2d.BodyDef.BodyType;
import com.badlogic.gdx.physics.box2d.FixtureDef;
import com.badlogic.gdx.physics.box2d.PolygonShape;
import com.badlogic.gdx.physics.box2d.World;
import com.packtpub.libgdx.canyonbunny.game.objects.Carrot;
```

Then, add the following lines of code to the same class:

```
private boolean goalReached;
public World b2world;

private void initPhysics () {
  if (b2world ! = null) b2world.dispose();
```

```
b2world = new World(new Vector2(0, -9.81f), true);
// Rocks
Vector2 origin = new Vector2();
for (Rock rock : level.rocks) {
  BodyDef bodyDef = new BodyDef();
  bodyDef.type = BodyType.KinematicBody;
  bodyDef.position.set(rock.position);
  Body body = b2world.createBody(bodyDef);
  rock.body = body;
  PolygonShape polygonShape = new PolygonShape();
  origin.x = rock.bounds.width / 2.0f;
  origin.y = rock.bounds.height / 2.0f;
  polygonShape.setAsBox(rock.bounds.width / 2.0f,
    rock.bounds.height / 2.0f, origin, 0);
  FixtureDef fixtureDef = new FixtureDef();
  fixtureDef.shape = polygonShape;
  body.createFixture(fixtureDef);
  polygonShape.dispose();
  }
}
```

The `goalReached` variable is used to keep track of the game's state whether or not the player has already managed to reach the goal. The `World` class directly relates to the description at the beginning of this chapter. In the `initPhysics()` method, we create a new instance of `World`, and store it in the `b2world` variable for later reference. The constructor of `World` takes an instance of `Vector2` for the world's simulated gravity, and a second parameter that controls whether bodies in Box2D can become inactive. Usually, this flag should be enabled to reduce the CPU load and in particular to preserve some battery power on mobile devices. In our case, we create a world with a gravity, pulling down objects at 9.81 meters per second squared, which is the same acceleration as we experience in real life on earth.

 Remember to always call the `dispose()` method of `World` when it is no longer needed. This is also true for all the Box2D shape classes, for example, `PolygonShape`, `CircleShape`, and so on.

After the Box2D world is created, we loop through the level's list of rocks, and create the corresponding Box2D bodies that are mapped to the same position and size as defined in the loaded level. Thus, both worlds, the Box2D one and our level, will start in a synchronized model state for each rock. Creating bodies for the rocks is a necessary step, because Box2D will have to take each rock into account in its calculations. Otherwise, the carrot game objects will fall through everything in the level because there simply is nothing to collide with from Box2D's point of view.

Box2D requires using separate definition classes to create new instances of `Body` and `Fixture`, which are named `BodyDef` and `FixtureDef`, respectively. The instance in the `bodyDef` variable is configured to describe a kinematic body type whose initial position is set to the same position as the rock instance. After that, we call the `createBody()` method of `b2world`, and pass in the body definition to create and add the new body at once. The method returns the reference of the newly created body, which is then stored in the rock instance to activate the Box2D physics handling, according to the changes we just made in our `update()` method of `AbstractGameObject`.

The created body also needs a shape to allow interaction with other bodies. So we create a shape using the `PolygonShape` class and call its `setAsBox()` helper method to define a rectangle. Shapes cannot be directly attached to bodies, thus we create a new instance of the `Fixture` class, bind our shape to it, and eventually attach the fixture to the body of the rock by calling the `createFixture()` method of the `body` instance. Now, the shape is no longer needed as its information has been processed in the new fixture. This is why we can safely call the `dispose()` method on the shape to free the memory that was allocated by this shape.

A screenshot of Box2D's view of the rock bodies is as follows:

The thin blue lines forming a rectangle visualize how (the shape) and where (the position) Box2D sees each rock. These lines have been rendered with the help of Box2D's `Box2DDebugRenderer` class. Let us add this feature to the game code so that it can be quickly enabled when needed.

Add the following import line to the `WorldRenderer` class:

```
import com.badlogic.gdx.physics.box2d.Box2DDebugRenderer;
```

After that, add the following lines of code to the same class:

```
private static final boolean DEBUG_DRAW_BOX2D_WORLD = false;
private Box2DDebugRenderer b2debugRenderer;
```

Then, make the following changes to the same class:

```
private void init () {
  batch = new SpriteBatch();
  camera = new OrthographicCamera(Constants.VIEWPORT_WIDTH,
    Constants.VIEWPORT_HEIGHT);
  camera.position.set(0, 0, 0);
  camera.update();
  cameraGUI = new OrthographicCamera(Constants.VIEWPORT_GUI_WIDTH,
    Constants.VIEWPORT_GUI_HEIGHT);
  cameraGUI.position.set(0, 0, 0);
  cameraGUI.setToOrtho(true);
  // flip y-axis
  cameraGUI.update();
  b2debugRenderer = new Box2DDebugRenderer();
}

private void renderWorld (SpriteBatch batch) {
  worldController.cameraHelper.applyTo(camera);
  batch.setProjectionMatrix(camera.combined);
  batch.begin();
  worldController.level.render(batch);
  batch.end();
  if (DEBUG_DRAW_BOX2D_WORLD) {
    b2debugRenderer.render(worldController.b2world,
      camera.combined);
  }
}
```

Now, we can easily toggle the debug view for Box2D, by setting `DEBUG_DRAW_`
`BOX2D_WORLD` to `true` or `false`.

Next, add the following lines of code to the `Constants` class:

```
// Number of carrots to spawn
public static final int CARROTS_SPAWN_MAX = 100;

// Spawn radius for carrots
public static final float CARROTS_SPAWN_RADIUS = 3.5f;

// Delay after game finished
public static final float TIME_DELAY_GAME_FINISHED = 6;
```

We will use these new constants to control the number of carrots to spawn and
the delay time before the game switches back to the menu screen after the goal was
reached by the player. In this particular case, we use a value of `100` carrots and a
delay of `6` seconds.

Next, add the following lines of code to the `WorldController` class:

```
private void spawnCarrots (Vector2 pos, int numCarrots,
  float radius) {
  float carrotShapeScale = 0.5f;
  // create carrots with box2d body and fixture
  for (int i = 0; i < numCarrots; i++) {
    Carrot carrot = new Carrot();
    // calculate random spawn position, rotation, and scale
    float x = MathUtils.random(-radius, radius);
    float y = MathUtils.random(5.0f, 15.0f);
    float rotation = MathUtils.random(0.0f, 360.0f)
    * MathUtils.degreesToRadians;
    float carrotScale = MathUtils.random(0.5f, 1.5f);
    carrot.scale.set(carrotScale, carrotScale);
    // create box2d body for carrot with start position
    // and angle of rotation
    BodyDef bodyDef = new BodyDef();
    bodyDef.position.set(pos);
    bodyDef.position.add(x, y);
    bodyDef.angle = rotation;
    Body body = b2world.createBody(bodyDef);
    body.setType(BodyType.DynamicBody);
    carrot.body = body;
    // create rectangular shape for carrot to allow
    // interactions (collisions) with other objects
    PolygonShape polygonShape = new PolygonShape();
```

```
float halfWidth = carrot.bounds.width / 2.0f * carrotScale;
float halfHeight = carrot.bounds.height /2.0f * carrotScale;
polygonShape.setAsBox(halfWidth * carrotShapeScale,
  halfHeight * carrotShapeScale);
// set physics attributes
FixtureDef fixtureDef = new FixtureDef();
fixtureDef.shape = polygonShape;
fixtureDef.density = 50;
fixtureDef.restitution = 0.5f;
fixtureDef.friction = 0.5f;
body.createFixture(fixtureDef);
polygonShape.dispose();
// finally, add new carrot to list for updating/rendering
level.carrots.add(carrot);
    }
}
```

The spawnCarrots() method contains the logic to create a variable number (numCarrots) of the new carrot game objects at a specific location (pos) in the game world. Inside the loop, a new carrot game object is created for which random values are calculated for the starting position (x, y), angle of rotation (rotation), and scale (carrotScale). The location that is passed in the pos variable is used as the center spawn point. The third parameter, radius, is used to distribute the carrots around the center spawn point of the horizontal starting position. The vertical starting position is randomly chosen in the range between 5 and 15 to ensure that the carrots will always spawn outside the game camera's view. Also, this range helps to create a more rain-like effect, by distributing the carrots in a column full of carrots, so that they will hit the ground at different points in time. The random rotation values are chosen within a range of a full circle (0 to 360 degrees), which simply means that any angle of rotation can occur. The random scale values are chosen within the range of half below or above the carrot's original size, which gives the overall effect a more natural touch as carrots are not of the same size in real life either.

Similar to what we did for the rock game object, a Box2D body, fixture, and shape must be created for each carrot game object. It should be noted once more that the reference of a Box2D body is stored in the body variable of the carrot instance to activate the Box2D update mechanism for the game object. Also notice that the fixture is set to have a density of 50, which affects the object's calculated mass data, and thus controls whether it is a light or a heavy object. Furthermore, restitution is set to 0.5, which means that the carrot will be half-elastic to allow some rebound to happen until it comes to rest eventually. A friction value of 0.5 lets the carrots skid down on each other. Using a value of 1 or higher for friction would make the object look sticky when getting into contact with other objects.

As a last tweak, each Box2D shape is shrunk to half the size (carrotShapeScale = 0.5f) of the carrot game object to eliminate small gaps between adjacent carrots. Finally, each new carrot with its corresponding Box2D body is added to the level's list of carrots for updating and rendering.

Next, add the following lines of code to the WorldController class:

```
private void onCollisionBunnyWithGoal () {
  goalReached = true;
  timeLeftGameOverDelay = Constants.TIME_DELAY_GAME_FINISHED;
  Vector2 centerPosBunnyHead =
    new Vector2 (level.bunnyHead.position);
  centerPosBunnyHead.x + = level.bunnyHead.bounds.width;
  spawnCarrots(centerPosBunnyHead, Constants.CARROTS_SPAWN_MAX,
    Constants.CARROTS_SPAWN_RADIUS);
}
```

This new method will handle the event when the player passes the goal-level object. The goalReached flag is set to true, which will be used to avoid unnecessary collision tests and start the countdown that will switch back to the menu screen. The countdown starts at the value that is taken from the new constant TIME_DELAY_GAME_FINISHED. Then, the spawnCarrots() method is called with the player's current position, the number of carrots, and the spawn radius.

Now, make the following changes to the WorldController class:

```
private void initLevel () {
  score = 0;
  scoreVisual = score;
  goalReached = false;
  level = new Level(Constants.LEVEL_01);
  cameraHelper.setTarget(level.bunnyHead);
  initPhysics();
}

private void testCollisions (float deltaTIme) {
  r1.set(level.bunnyHead.position.x, level.bunnyHead.position.y,
    level.bunnyHead.bounds.width, level.bunnyHead.bounds.height);

  // Test collision: Bunny Head <-> Rocks
  ...

  // Test collision: Bunny Head <-> Gold Coins
  ...

  // Test collision: Bunny Head <-> Feathers
  ...
```

```
      // Test collision: Bunny Head <-> Goal
      if (goalReached) {
        r2.set(level.goal.bounds);
        r2.x += level.goal.position.x;
        r2.y += level.goal.position.y;
        if (r1.overlaps(r2)) onCollisionBunnyWithGoal();
        }
  }

  public void update (float deltaTime) {
    handleDebugInput(deltaTime);
    if (isGameOver() || goalReached) {
      timeLeftGameOverDelay -= deltaTime;
      if (timeLeftGameOverDelay < 0) backToMenu();
      } else {
      handleInputGame(deltaTime);
      }
    level.update(deltaTime);
    testCollisions();
    b2world.step(deltaTime, 8, 3);
    cameraHelper.update(deltaTime);
    }
```

At the end of the initLevel() method, right after the level is loaded, we now also call the initPhysics() method. It is important to do it in this particular order, because initPhysics() works with the list of rocks of the loaded level. The testCollisions() method is extended by another check that will call the onCollisionBunnyWithGoal() method as soon as it detects a collision between the player and the goal game objects.

In the update() method, we have added the goalReached flag as an alternative condition to the isGameover() condition. So, from now on, a delayed switchback to the menu screen will be executed, if either condition is met.

Lastly, the Box2D world instance stored in b2world needs to be updated just like the rest of the game to make any progress. This is done by calling its step() method and passing in the delta time. The last two parameters denote the number of iterations Box2D is allowed to execute for its velocity and position calculations. Using higher values for these parameters may increase the precision of the simulation as well as the computational workload. However, Box2D is not going to always use up the maximum number of iterations if it decides that the errors in the simulation are small enough to go unnoticed.

Box2D suggests an iteration count of 8 for velocities and 3 for positions. See *2.4 Simulating the World (of Box2D)* in the official manual.

There are only two more, but not less important, changes to fully complete our new game feature.

Make the following changes to the Rock class:

```
@Override
public void update (float deltaTime) {
  super.update(deltaTime);

  floatCycleTimeLeft -= deltaTime;
  if (floatCycleTimeLeft <= 0) {
    floatCycleTimeLeft = FLOAT_CYCLE_TIME;
    floatingDownwards = !floatingDownwards;
    body.setLinearVelocity(0, FLOAT_AMPLITUDE
      * (floatingDownwards ? -1 : 1));
  } else {
    body.setLinearVelocity(body.getLinearVelocity().mul(0.98f));
  }
}
```

These changes represent an almost direct translation from our own physics simulation to Box2D's one for the rock's floating-on-water effect. It is crucial to understand why we have to change this part or else you will probably spend a lot of time hunting down nasty problems in conjunction with Box2D.

In our previous implementation, the rock's movement was achieved by directly modifying its position vector. Since rocks are now controlled by Box2D, we would have to change the position of the rock's body using the setTransform() method instead. Usually, this is a really bad idea as it can confuse Box2D when a manual change of a body position results in two or more overlapping shapes. Those overlapping shapes, then, can cause quite unpredictable effects such as extreme accelerations or a disruption of resting objects. So, additional care needs to be taken if the position and/or angle of the rotation of a body are set directly.

As you can see in the preceding changed code, we are actually not using setTransform(), but setLinearVelocity(). So the general rule to avoid the mentioned problems is to tell Box2D about the physical cause to get the desired effect. This means that we have to express changes in the world through forces, which in turn are translated into velocities.

After all this, the last modification is to free the allocated memory when appropriate.

Add the following import line to the WorldController class:

```
import com.badlogic.gdx.utils.Disposable;
```

Next, let the same class implement the Disposable interface as follows:

```
public class WorldController extends InputAdapter
implements Disposable {
...
}
```

Then, add the following lines of code to the same class:

```
@Override
public void dispose () {
   if (b2world != null) b2world.dispose();
}
```

Finally, make the following changes to the GameScreen class:

```
@Override
public void hide () {
   worldController.dispose();
   worldRenderer.dispose();
   Gdx.input.setCatchBackKey(false);
}
```

Memory that is allocated by a Box2D's world instance is now going to be freed correctly when it is no longer needed.

Now, run the game, and finish the level by passing the goal to marvel at the awesome rain of carrots. A screenshot of what you should see is as follows:

The screenshot shows the spawned carrots that have already come to rest, as well as the debug overlay drawn by the Box2D debug renderer. If you take a closer look at the shape's location of each carrot, you will probably come to the conclusion that it must be misaligned, though the simulation appears to be perfectly fine.

Fortunately, there is no real issue at all, because it is just an illusion due to the transparent area and the green leaves of the carrot. An isolated view that only shows a couple of carrots and two debug boxes is shown in the following figure:

The inner box is still drawn using the Box2D debug render. The outer box, however, is the real border of the image used for the carrot game object. You can try this yourself by enabling the debug outline for the texture packer and rebuilding the texture atlas afterwards.

Working with shaders in Libgdx

Let us now turn our attention to the topic of shaders. This is a feature that is available in OpenGL (ES) 2.0 only, as it makes use of the so-called **Programmable Pipeline**. Shaders are usually small programs, which allow us to take over control of certain stages in the rendering process to define the way how a scene should be rendered by the graphics processor. In consequence, shaders are an important building block in today's computer graphics and are also an extremely powerful tool to create all sorts of (special) effects that would be very hard to realize otherwise. For the sake of simplicity, we will only discuss vertex and fragment shaders here.

 Fragment shaders are also called pixel shaders. Unfortunately, this is a bit misleading as this type of shader actually operates on fragments instead of pixels.

Consider the following list of reasons as to why shaders are generally useful and highly recommended to be in the toolkit of every (graphics) programmer:

- Programmability of the GPU rendering pipeline via shaders to create arbitrary complex effects. This means a high degree of flexibility for all sorts of special effects expressible through mathematical formulas.
- Shaders are run on the GPU, which saves CPU time that can be spent on other tasks, such as doing physics and general game logic.
- Heavy mathematical computations are usually done faster on GPUs than on CPUs.
- GPUs are able to parallelize the processing of vertices and fragments.

Vertex shaders operate on each vertex given to the GPU. A vertex is a point in 3D space with attributes, such as a position, a color, and texture coordinates. These values can then be manipulated through the shader to achieve effects, for example, the deformation of an object. The output for each vertex computed by the vertex shader is then passed along in the rendering pipeline as the input for the next rendering stage.

Fragment shaders compute the color of a pixel for each fragment. For this, many factors may be taken into account to simulate different kinds of materials. Some of them are values for lighting, translucency, shadows, and so on.

The combination of a vertex and fragment shader is called a shader program.

Shaders are usually written in an API-specific high-level language, such as **OpenGL Shading Language** (GLSL) for OpenGL, which uses syntax for the code like C does. Take a look at the last two pages of the OpenGL ES 2.0 Reference Card at: `http://www.khronos.org/opengles/sdk/docs/reference_cards/OpenGL-ES-2_0-Reference-card.pdf`

This should give a quick overview of the available feature set in GLSL.

For more details about the specifications of OpenGL (ES) 2.0, GLSL as well as the Programmable Pipeline, check out the official website of the Khronos Group at: `http://www.khronos.org/opengles/2_X/`

Also, the following list contains some links to the GLSL tutorials and websites with collections of shader examples ranging from beginners to experts:

- `https://github.com/mattdesl/lwjgl-basics/wiki/Shaders`
- `http://devmaster.net/posts/tags/shaders/`
- `http://www.lighthouse3d.com/tutorials/glsl-tutorial/`
- `http://glsl.heroku.com/`
- `https://www.shadertoy.com/`

Creating a monochrome filter shader program

We now want to create a new pair of vertex and fragment shaders to form a shader program. Its purpose will be to act as a color filter that renders everything it is applied to in a beautiful grayscale.

Let us start with the vertex shader. Create a new subdirectory in CanyonBunny-android/assets named shaders. Then, create a new file monochrome.vs in the shaders directory, and add the following code:

```
attribute vec4 a_position;
attribute vec4 a_color;
attribute vec2 a_texCoord0;
varying vec4 v_color;
varying vec2 v_texCoords;
uniform mat4 u_projTrans;

void main() {
  v_color = a_color;
  v_texCoords = a_texCoord0;
  gl_Position = u_projTrans * a_position;
}
```

The first six lines in the vertex shader declare the variables of different data types using so-called storage qualifiers in terms of GLSL. The data types vec2 and vec4 stand for the float vectors with two and four components, respectively, while mat4 stands for a square matrix of order four of floats. The attribute qualifier is only available in the vertex shader and denotes the inputs that are passed from the vertex arrays sent by the application. As mentioned before, these inputs are the position, color, and texture coordinates of one vertex at a time. The varying qualifier denotes the variables that are readable and writeable in the context of the vertex shader, but read-only to the fragment shader. Thus, the variables using this qualifier allow the transfer of additional information from the vertex shader to the fragment shader. Last but not least, the uniform qualifier denotes the variables that are known to be constant during multiple executions of the shader in the same draw call. The variable u_projTrans is automatically set to the combined projection-modelview matrix by the Libgdx's Spritebatch class.

The next step is the declaration of the main() function. It is the entry point of the shader where the execution begins. In this vertex shader, we pass the input values of the color and texture coordinates via varying variables to the fragment shader for later use. The variable gl_Position is a predefined GLSL output variable (see GLES2 Reference Card) that holds the projected position vector and is computed by the multiplication of the combined projection-model view matrix (u_projTrans) and the position vector (a_position) of the current vertex.

Next, create another new file `monochrome.fs` in the `shaders` directory and add the following code:

```
#ifdef GL_ES
precision mediump float;
#endif
varying vec4 v_color;
varying vec2 v_texCoords;
uniform sampler2D u_texture;
uniform float u_amount;

void main() {
  vec4 color = v_color * texture2D(u_texture, v_texCoords);
  float grayscale = dot(color.rgb, vec3(0.222, 0.707, 0.071));
  color.rgb = mix(color.rgb, vec3(grayscale), u_amount);
  gl_FragColor = color;
}
```

In the first three lines, we use a GLSL macro to set `precision` of the float values to `medium` for devices that use OpenGL ES. In the next lines, you may have already recognized our two `varying` variables that we pass from within our vertex shader to this one.

 Be sure to always match the name and data type of each `varying` variable passed from a vertex shader to the corresponding fragment shader.

The data type `sampler2D` stands for a two-dimensional texture. The `u_amount` variable is meant to be set by the application code to control the amount of grayscale that should be applied. The first line inside the `main()` function of the fragment shader computes a combined color value between the original vertex color and the color value of the texture referenced in `u_texture` using the coordinates passed in `v_texCoords`. Now, to find an appropriate grayscale value, we compute the dot product of our color vector and another vector containing varying color weights that match best with the sensitivity of typical human eyesight as suggested in the book *GPU Gems* in *Chapter 22.3.1, Grayscale Conversion*.

This book is publicly available on nVidia's developer zone at:
`http://http.developer.nvidia.com/GPUGems/gpugems_ch22.html`

Then, we use the `mix()` function, which applies a linear interpolation between the original color vector and the grayscale vector using the `u_amount` variable. `gl_FragColor` is another predefined output variable of GLSL that determines the final pixel color of the fragment that is currently being processed.

Using the monochrome filter shader program in Canyon Bunny

Now that we have created our monochrome filter shader program it is time to put it to use in Canyon Bunny. We want to use the shader's effect in the game screen, and apply it to the game world. This means that the GUI will remain colored like before. In addition to that, the shader program can be switched on and off with a new checkbox added to the debug section of the menu screen's **Options** dialog.

First, add these new constants to the Constants class that point to the files of our new shader program:

```
// Shader
public static final String shaderMonochromeVertex =
    "shaders/monochrome.vs";
public static final String shaderMonochromeFragment =
    "shaders/monochrome.fs";
```

After that, add the following line to the GamePreferences class:

```
public boolean useMonochromeShader;
```

Next, make the following changes to the same class:

```
public void load () {
    showFpsCounter = prefs.getBoolean("showFpsCounter", false);
    useMonochromeShader = prefs.getBoolean("useMonochromeShader",
        false);
}

public void save () {
    prefs.putBoolean("showFpsCounter", showFpsCounter);
    prefs.putBoolean("useMonochromeShader", useMonochromeShader);
    prefs.flush();
}
```

Then, add the following line to the MenuScreen class:

```
private CheckBox chkUseMonochromeShader;
```

After that, make the following changes to the same class:

```
private Table buildOptWinDebug () {
    Table tbl = new Table();
    // + Title: "Debug"

    // + Checkbox, "Show FPS Counter" label
```

```
    // + Checkbox, "Use Monochrome Shader" label
    chkUseMonochromeShader = new CheckBox("", skinLibgdx);
    tbl.add(new Label("Use Monochrome Shader", skinLibgdx));
    tbl.add(chkUseMonochromeShader);
    tbl.row();
    return tbl;
  }

  private void loadSettings () {
    chkShowFpsCounter.setChecked(prefs.showFpsCounter);
    chkUseMonochromeShader.setChecked(prefs.useMonochromeShader);
  }

  private void saveSettings () {
    prefs.showFpsCounter = chkShowFpsCounter.isChecked();
    prefs.useMonochromeShader = chkUseMonochromeShader.isChecked();
    prefs.save();
  }
```

The last modifications to `GamePreferences` and `MenuScreen` just extended the settings handling by a new boolean flag, which can now be toggled via the new checkbox added to the debug section of the options dialog in the menu screen.

Next, add the following import lines to the `WorldRenderer` class:

```
import com.badlogic.gdx.graphics.glutils.ShaderProgram;
import com.badlogic.gdx.utils.GdxRuntimeException;
```

After that, add the following line to the same class:

```
private ShaderProgram shaderMonochrome;
```

Also make the following changes to the same class:

```
private void init () {
  batch = new SpriteBatch();
  camera = new OrthographicCamera(Constants.VIEWPORT_WIDTH,
    Constants.VIEWPORT_HEIGHT);
  camera.position.set(0, 0, 0);
  camera.update();
  cameraGUI = new OrthographicCamera(Constants.VIEWPORT_GUI_WIDTH,
    Constants.VIEWPORT_GUI_HEIGHT);
  cameraGUI.position.set(0, 0, 0);
  cameraGUI.setToOrtho(true); // flip y-axis
  cameraGUI.update();
  b2debugRenderer = new Box2DDebugRenderer();
```

```
  shaderMonochrome = new ShaderProgram(
    Gdx.files.internal(Constants.shaderMonochromeVertex),
      Gdx.files.internal(Constants.shaderMonochromeFragment));
  if (!shaderMonochrome.isCompiled()) {
    String msg = "Could not compile shader program: "
      + shaderMonochrome.getLog();
    throw new GdxRuntimeException(msg);
    }
  }

private void renderWorld (SpriteBatch batch) {
  worldController.cameraHelper.applyTo(camera);
  batch.setProjectionMatrix(camera.combined);
  batch.begin();
  if (GamePreferences.instance.useMonochromeShader) {
    batch.setShader(shaderMonochrome);
    shaderMonochrome.setUniformf("u_amount", 1.0f);
    }
  worldController.level.render(batch);
  batch.setShader(null);
  batch.end();
  if (DEBUG_DRAW_BOX2D_WORLD) {
    b2debugRenderer.render(worldController.b2world,
      camera.combined);
    }
  }

@Override
public void dispose () {
  batch.dispose();
  shaderMonochrome.dispose();
  }
```

To load and initialize our shader program in the `init()` method, we pass both shader files to the constructor of a new instance of `ShaderProgram`, which is then stored in the `shaderMonochrome` variable for later reference. It is good practice to ask a new shader program instance, whether it could be successfully compiled by calling its `isCompiled()` method. If this is not the case, the corresponding log message of the compile error can be retrieved by calling the `getLog()` method.

In the `renderWorld()` method, we wrapped the call that renders the actual game world with two `setShader()` calls. The first call activates our monochrome filter shader program, while the next call passes null for the shader, which makes `SpriteBatch` switch back to Libgdx's default shader. Calling the `setUniformf()` method of an instance of a shader program allows to set a float value for a uniform variable by name. There are many more of those setter methods for different combinations of storage qualifiers and data types. We set the value of the uniform float variable named `u_amount` to a value of `1.0f`. According to our code in the fragment shader, the linear interpolation will apply the grayscale effect in full to its target pixels.

Finally, we take care that the shader program's `dispose()` method is called to free any allocated memory when it is no longer needed.

Now, run the game, go to the options dialog, and tick the checkbox to activate the monochrome filter shader program. The game screen should show up in a beautiful grayscale tone as soon as the game is started.

A screenshot of the game with the enabled monochrome filter shader program is as follows:

The blue background color, which is actually created by using OpenGL's clear color, is not affected by our shader program. The reason behind this is that the shader's effect is only applied during the rendering of the game world where it is temporarily set in the sprite batch. Moreover, the game world is rendered on top of the (blue) clear color, which back then appeared to be a good idea just because it was an easy and cheap way of making the clear color a part of the scene and get a sky for free.

Adding alternative input controls

The last and rather short topic in this chapter will show you how to use the peripheral devices using the example of accelerometers, which are very common types of sensors in today's smartphones and tablets. Accelerometers are subsystems that reliably and accurately detect and measure acceleration, tilt, shock, and vibration. Basically, we just need to read the sensor data that is being measured by the accelerometer hardware and later translate the data into values and/or ranges suitable for our game.

Accelerometers in Android devices are exposed by Libgdx using the three axes x, y, and z, which can be queried via the Gdx.input module. For instance, the current acceleration value for the x axis can be easily retrieved as follows:

```
float ax = Gdx.input.getAccelerometerX();
```

This is great, but what does the value that we just stored in ax actually mean? Moreover, what will influence it? So, to better understand how sensors work, we need to know what exactly is measured.

Let us start with the range of values. In the documentations of Android and Libgdx, the values for accelerometers are said to range within -10.0f and 10.0f. This roughly resembles a value of what we know as the constant for gravity on earth, approximately 9.81 meters per square second. However, what we still do not know about is the internal orientation of the sensor hardware inside a device. This poses a problem to us, because we cannot tell which axis is which. Luckily, Libgdx comes to the aid and is able to make an educated guess that is also reliable. There is a blog post by *Mario Zechner* that describes the issue about different so-called native orientations in more detail at: http://www.badlogicgames.com/wordpress/?p=2041

All we have to remember is that Libgdx will make sure that the y axis always coincides with the bigger side, while the x axis coincides with the smaller one. The z axis comes out of the screen.

An image taken from Android's SDK developer website that nicely illustrates the sensor coordinate system is as follows:

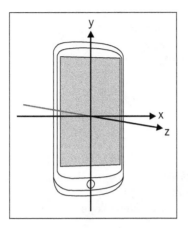

We will now move on to Canyon Bunny and implement alternative input controls using the accelerometer. The screen needs to be rotated by 90 degrees to the left in order to be able to play Canyon Bunny on a smartphone, since it is using the so-called landscape mode for displaying. It is important to understand that the orientation of the sensors will always remain the same no matter how the smartphone is moved and rotated around.

The new controls will allow tilting the screen to the left and right side to move into the very same direction. The tilt angle for the y axis will determine the maximum velocity of the player character.

Add the following new constants to the Constants class:

```
// Angle of rotation for dead zone (no movement)
public static final float ACCEL_ANGLE_DEAD_ZONE = 5.0f;

// Max angle of rotation needed to gain max movement velocity
public static final float ACCEL_MAX_ANGLE_MAX_MOVEMENT = 20.0f;
```

Then, add this line of code to the WorldController class:

```
private boolean accelerometerAvailable;
```

After that, make the following changes to the same class:

```
private void init () {
  accelerometerAvailable = Gdx.input.isPeripheralAvailable(
    Peripheral.Accelerometer);
  cameraHelper = new CameraHelper();
  lives = Constants.LIVES_START;
  livesVisual = lives;
  timeLeftGameOverDelay = 0;
  initLevel();
}

private void handleInputGame (float deltaTime) {
  if (cameraHelper.hasTarget(level.bunnyHead)) {
    // Player Movement
    if (Gdx.input.isKeyPressed(Keys.LEFT)) {
      ...
    } else {
      // Use accelerometer for movement if available
      if (accelerometerAvailable) {
        // normalize accelerometer values from [-10, 10] to [-1, 1]
        // which translate to rotations of [-90, 90] degrees
        float amount = Gdx.input.getAccelerometerY() / 10.0f;
        amount *= 90.0f;
        // is angle of rotation inside dead zone?
        if (Math.abs(amount) < Constants.ACCEL_ANGLE_DEAD_ZONE) {
          amount = 0;
        } else {
          // use the defined max angle of rotation instead of
          // the full 90 degrees for maximum velocity
          amount /= Constants.ACCEL_MAX_ANGLE_MAX_MOVEMENT;
        }
        level.bunnyHead.velocity.x =
          level.bunnyHead.terminalVelocity.x * amount;
      }
      // Execute auto-forward movement on non-desktop platform
      else if (Gdx.app.getType() != ApplicationType.Desktop) {
        level.bunnyHead.velocity.x =
          level.bunnyHead.terminalVelocity.x;
      }
    }
  }
}
```

The new variable `accelerometerAvailable` is set once in the `init()` method, which in turn is used to select the input mode in `handleInputGame()`. If an accelerometer hardware is detected, the alternative input controls for player movement will be used. In this case, however, we first normalize the accelerometer values to make them stay in a range between `-1.0f` and `1.0f`, which can now also be interpreted by us as the percentage of desired movement in relation to the amount of tilt. The sign of the percentage does also nicely describe the direction of the horizontal movement. A negative sign means movement to the left, whereas a positive sign means movement to the opposite direction. The percentage currently maps a movement of 100 percent in one direction to 90 degrees of tilting the screen in the same direction. It is very inconvenient to have to turn the device over the full range of 180 degrees, which also prevents fast player reactions.

This is why we introduced a new constant named `ACCEL_MAX_ANGLE_MAX_MOVEMENT` that allows defining the maximum tilt angle that is needed to reach maximum velocity. The other new constant `ACCEL_ANGLE_DEAD_ZONE` is used to define a dead zone (here 5.0 degrees) in the positive and negative direction where no movement will occur. So the dead zone makes it easier for the player to find a neutral position to let the bunny head stand still. Finally, we end up with a percentage of the desired movement stored in `amount` that is simply multiplied with the terminal velocity to calculate the correct velocity value.

Summary

In this chapter we covered the basics of the Box2D rigid body physics engine, and thereafter, applied the newly gained knowledge including all the individual parts (rigid body, body type, shape, fixture, and world) by creating a believable physics simulation of raining carrots. Also, two new game objects were added, which represented the carrot for physics simulations and a huge golden carrot statue symbolizing a level's goal or exit.

Then, we went down the graphics pipeline, more precisely the Programmable Pipeline of OpenGL (ES) 2.0 to explore the use of shaders. We created our own shader program to apply a monochrome filter effect of arbitrary intensity through a uniform variable that can be passed to the shader program at runtime in the application code. We learned about GLSL and created a simple pair of vertex and fragment shaders that is used in Canyon Bunny.

Finally, we learned how to use and work with peripheral devices using the example of an accelerometer. We also learned how to transform the data provided by a sensor into more suitable values. These values were then used as input to create an alternative way to control the player's movement just by tilting the screen to the left or to the right.

In the next and final chapter, we are going to add animations to the game.

12
Animations

In this chapter you will learn how to create and manage different kinds of animations using Libgdx's `Actions` and `Animation` classes. We will exemplify their usage by animating certain parts of the menu and game screen.

In regard to the menu screen, we will create time-based and event-based animations including moving, scaling, and fading `Actor` objects via so-called actions of the `Actions` class. Additionally, interpolation algorithms provided by Libgdx's `Interpolation` class will be used for added effects and for the smoothing of those animations.

The game screen, in a sense, is already animated according to the game logic, which takes care of coordinating the movement of every game object. However, each game object is rendered using a still image. In terms of animations, this is equivalent to a one-frame animation. With the help of the `Animation` class, we will define several sequences of individual frames to form animations for our game objects.

Manipulating actors through actions

The `Actions` class offers a large collection of common actions to easily manipulate `Actor` objects. Besides action-specific parameters such as the position for a move action, some actions also allow you to specify the duration as well as the interpolation algorithm to be used. An action will always complete in an instant if the duration is either omitted or set to `0`. Interpolation algorithms are provided by Libgdx's `Interpolation` class.

 For a quick overview of the available interpolation algorithms in Libgdx, check out *Chapter 9, Screen Transitions*.

The following example illustrates the typical method signatures of two actions:

```
moveTo (x, y);
moveTo (x, y, duration);
moveTo (x, y, duration, interpolation);

rotateTo (rotation);
rotateTo (rotation, duration);
rotateTo (rotation, duration, interpolation);
```

The `moveTo()` and `rotateTo()` actions both have their action-specific parameters x, y, and `rotation` respectively, which are the absolute minimum requirement. In this case, both actions can also take an optional `duration` and `interpolation` parameter if needed.

The methods of the `Actions` class are intended for static import. There are mainly two reasons for this: convenience and increased readability when chaining together multiple actions. The preceding example code and each following code using the `Actions` class will assume the use of static imports.

In Java, a static import can be used to make static methods of one class available in the namespace of another class, thus removing the need to use the class qualification in order to call such methods.

For more information about static imports, check out http://docs.oracle.com/javase/1.5.0/docs/guide/language/static-import.html.

Now, to add one or more actions to an actor, we simply need to call its `addAction()` method as follows:

```
Actor actor = new Actor();
float x = 100.0f, y = 100.0f, rotation = 0.0f, duration = 1.0f;
actor.addAction(sequence(
    moveTo(x, y),
    rotateTo(rotation),
    delay(duration),
    parallel(
        moveBy(50.0f, 0.0f, 5.0f),
        rotateBy(90.0f, 5.0f, Interpolation.swingOut))));
```

This example code shows a fictional actor which is completely initialized and manipulated via a chain of nested actions only. In this case, the added chain of actions starts as a sequence of more actions. That being said, the sequence is comprised of an absolute move action using `moveTo()` to a given point (`100, 100`), followed by an absolute rotation using `rotateTo()` (`0` degrees), followed by a short delay of `1` second, and finally followed by a parallel action that contains a list of even more actions. Those parallel actions are a relative move using `moveBy()` (`50, 0`) and a relative rotation using `rotateBy()` (`90` degrees). Additionally, both actions use a duration of `5` seconds. Moreover, the relative rotation uses the `swingOut` interpolation algorithm.

So, the combined use of the `Actor` and `Actions` classes provide a very powerful way for us to express quite complex actor behaviors with relatively little code.

The following sections contain two lists with descriptions of the actions that are currently available.

Actions for manipulating actors

This list describes actions that are useful to manipulate actors:

- `add()`: This adds an action to an actor.
- `alpha()`: This sets the alpha value of an actor's color.
- `color()`: This sets the color of an actor.
- `fadeIn()` and `fadeOut()`: These are convenience actions to set the alpha value of an actor's color to 1 or 0, respectively.
- `hide()`: This sets the visibility of an actor to false.
- `layout()`: This sets the actor's layout to enabled or disabled.
- `moveBy()` and `moveTo()`: These move an actor by a relative amount or to a specific location.
- `removeActor()`: This removes the actor to which this action is attached. Alternatively, another actor that is to be removed can be specified.
- `rotateBy()` and `rotateTo()`: These rotate an actor by a relative amount or to a specific angle of rotation.
- `run()`: This runs a `Runnable` (the code will be executed in a separate thread).
- `scaleBy()` and `scaleTo()`: These scale an actor by a relative amount or to a specific scale.

- `show()`: This sets the visibility of an actor to true.
- `sizeBy()` and `sizeTo()`: These resize an actor by a relative amount or to a specific size.
- `touchable()`: This sets the touchability of an actor (refer to *Touchable enumerator*).
- `visible()`: This sets the visibility of an actor.

Controlling the order and time of execution

This list describes actions that are useful for controlling the order and time of execution of other actions:

- `after()`: This waits for other actions of an actor to finish before its action is executed. Note that this action will only wait for other actions that were already added to an actor prior to this.
- `delay()`: This delays the execution of an action.
- `forever()`: This repeats an action forever.
- `parallel()`:This executes a list of actions at the same time.
- `repeat()`: This repeats an action for a given number of times.
- `sequence()`: This executes a list of actions one after another.

Animating the menu screen

Let us now discuss what we are actually going to animate in the menu screen. Basically, the first two bits of our animated menu involve the gold coins and the large bunny head.

Take a look at the following screenshot:

In this screenshot you can see a rough sketch of the final animation divided in to four essential steps. The following lists the actions that need to be taken for the shown steps:

1. The gold coins and bunny head are invisible at the beginning.

2. The gold coins fade in and scale up from 0 percent to 100 percent from the center screen as if they are jumping out of the water.

3. After a short pause, the bunny head appears in the top-right corner which moves slightly until it reaches the edge of the rock that is visible in the background.

4. The bunny head moves as if it was jumping over to the other rock in front of it.

Animating the gold coins and bunny head actors

Add the following (static) import lines to the MenuScreen class:

```
import static com.badlogic.gdx.scenes.scene2d.actions.Actions.*;

import com.badlogic.gdx.math.Interpolation;
```

After that, make the following changes to the same class:

```
private Table buildObjectsLayer () {
  Table layer = new Table();
  // + Coins
  imgCoins = new Image(skinCanyonBunny, "coins");
  layer.addActor(imgCoins);
  imgCoins.setOrigin(imgCoins.getWidth() / 2,
    imgCoins.getHeight() / 2);
  imgCoins.addAction(sequence(
    moveTo(135, -20),
    scaleTo(0, 0),
    fadeOut(0),
    delay(2.5f),
    parallel(moveBy(0, 100, 0.5f, Interpolation.swingOut),
      scaleTo(1.0f, 1.0f, 0.25f, Interpolation.linear),
      alpha(1.0f, 0.5f))));
  // + Bunny
  imgBunny = new Image(skinCanyonBunny, "bunny");
  layer.addActor(imgBunny);
  imgBunny.addAction(sequence(
    moveTo(655, 510),
    delay(4.0f),
    moveBy(-70, -100, 0.5f, Interpolation.fade),
    moveBy(-100, -50, 0.5f, Interpolation.fade),
    moveBy(-150, -300, 1.0f, Interpolation.elasticIn)));
  return layer;
}
```

All of the four steps are now expressed as actions in the code of the buildObjectLayer() method. The origin of the gold coin's image that is stored in imgCoins needs to be adjusted so that it now points to its center. In this way, the image does not only grow or shrink when scaled but it will never move away from its original position. The first action of imgCoins is a sequence() that merely groups all other actions. Then, the animation is initialized through the first three actions: moveTo(), scaleTo(), and fadeOut(). Next, a delay() action follows that creates a short delay of 2.5 seconds before the parallel action is executed.

The parallel action contains three more actions, `moveBy()`, `scaleTo()`, and `alpha()`, which are all executed at the same time. These three actions, when played together, create the impression that the gold coins appear to jump out of the water by moving them a bit downwards as well as fading them in and scaling them up from 0 percent to 100 percent. Interpolations are also used to support this effect. Choosing the right interpolation algorithm is usually a little trial-and-error at first, but after a while, you will have a better understanding and feel for which one could work best for certain kinds of effects.

The animation for the bunny head is not that much different to the gold coins. It starts with a grouping `sequence()` that is comprised of an initializing `moveTo()` action followed by a `delay()` of 4 seconds. Then, three subsequent `moveBy()` actions are executed that describe the complete movement we discussed earlier in our screenshot.

Animating the menu buttons and options window

Now, for a final touch to the menu screen, let us animate the menu buttons in the bottom-right corner of the scene as well as the **Options** window that appears when the **Options** button is clicked. We want to let both buttons move out of the scene when the **Options** button is clicked on and let them move back into the scene after the **Options** window is closed again.

Add the following import lines to the `MenuScreen` class:

```
import com.badlogic.gdx.scenes.scene2d.actions.SequenceAction;
import com.badlogic.gdx.scenes.scene2d.Touchable;
```

Next, add the following lines of code to the same class:

```
private void showMenuButtons (boolean visible) {
  float moveDuration = 1.0f;
  Interpolation moveEasing = Interpolation.swing;
  float delayOptionsButton = 0.25f;

  float moveX = 300 * (visible ? -1 : 1);
  float moveY = 0 * (visible ? -1 : 1);
  final Touchable touchEnabled = visible ? Touchable.enabled
    : Touchable.disabled;
  btnMenuPlay.addAction(
    moveBy(moveX, moveY, moveDuration, moveEasing));

  btnMenuOptions.addAction(sequence(
```

```
        delay(delayOptionsButton),
        moveBy(moveX, moveY, moveDuration, moveEasing)));

    SequenceAction seq = sequence();
    if (visible)
    seq.addAction(delay(delayOptionsButton + moveDuration));
    seq.addAction(run(new Runnable() {
      public void run () {
        btnMenuPlay.setTouchable(touchEnabled);
        btnMenuOptions.setTouchable(touchEnabled);
      }
    }));
    stage.addAction(seq);
}

  private void showOptionsWindow (boolean visible,
      boolean animated) {
    float alphaTo = visible ? 0.8f : 0.0f;
    float duration = animated ? 1.0f : 0.0f;
    Touchable touchEnabled = visible ? Touchable.enabled
      : Touchable.disabled;
    winOptions.addAction(sequence(
      touchable(touchEnabled),
      alpha(alphaTo, duration)));
}
```

The two new methods `showMenuButtons()` and `showOptionsWindow()` will allow us to easily show or hide the menu buttons and the **Options** window in an animated fashion. Any logic involved in the showing and hiding animation is encapsulated in these methods, which make it much more convenient to use.

The `showMenuButtons()` method has one parameter (visible) to control whether to show or hide the menu buttons. At the beginning of this method, we not only set many variables that are used to control the overall behavior of the animation, such as duration and easing, but also some other variables whose values obviously depend on the visible flag. After the position, duration, and easing have been computed, we head over and add a couple of actions to both menu buttons. The **Play** button is going to be directly moved to a relative position while the **Options** button does exactly the same but with an added delay prior to its move action. We will now discuss a pretty exciting example of how flexible actions are. We create a new and empty sequence and store it in `seq`. What follows is a conditional `delay()` action, so to say, which is only going to be added to the new sequence if the visible flag is set to `true`.

This means you can create and script actor behaviors in code while also being able to dynamically adjust and put them together as needed at a later time as we just did! Albeit, as a result of the prior condition, we always add a run() action to the sequence. The run() action takes a Runnable which is used in Java to put code that is going to be executed in a separate thread. We use this and the conditional delay() action to call setTouchable() on the **Play** and **Options** buttons which controls whether the buttons receive and respond to touches and mouse clicks. Finally, the sequence() action stored in seq is added as a new action to the stage.

> In this case, we can safely do this to enqueue the sequence() action for execution because the sequence does not modify the stage with the delay() and run() actions.

The showOptionsWindow() method animates the options menu in the same way as described for the menu buttons in showMenuButtons(). The only difference here is that it takes a second flag that can be used to skip the animation.

Now, make the following changes to the MenuScreen class:

```
private Table buildOptionsWindowLayer () {
  ...
  // Make options window slightly transparent
  winOptions.setColor(1, 1, 1, 0.8f);
  // Hide options window by default
  showOptionsWindow(false, false);
  if (debugEnabled) winOptions.debug();
  // Let TableLayout recalculate widget sizes and positions
  winOptions.pack();
  // Move options window to bottom right corner
  winOptions.setPosition(Constants.VIEWPORT_GUI_WIDTH
    - winOptions.getWidth() - 50, 50);
  return winOptions;
}

private void onOptionsClicked () {
  loadSettings();
  showMenuButtons(false);
  showOptionsWindow(true, true);
}

private void onCancelClicked () {
  showMenuButtons(true);
  showOptionsWindow(false, true);
  AudioManager.instance.onSettingsUpdated();
}
```

These changes simply put our animation methods in place where needed. `buildOptionsWindowLayer()` calls `showOptionsWindow()` with both parameters for visible and animated set to `false`. The reason for this is that we want the **Options** window to be hidden at the start like before and we also want this to happen in an instant. The `onOptionsClicked()` and `onCancelClicked()` methods call both show-methods to either show or hide the menu buttons or the **Options** window, respectively.

Using sequences of images for animations

Up until now, all the animations we have created are based on changing attributes, such as the position, color value, and size, of still images. Therefore, our next enhancement is targeted towards the game objects that inhabit the game world of Canyon Bunny. We want to breathe life into the gold coin and bunny head game objects by creating several animations that are built from sequences of individual images. The resulting effect is very similar in comparison to an ordinary flip book where multiple images are perceived as a continuous animation when shown in rapid succession.

Libgdx provides a class called `Animation` that helps us define image sequences and also helps us to pick the right (key) frame from a sequence at a specific time which, for example, depends on the desired frame rate for playback. There is some clever mathematics and state keeping involved for finding the right frame in an efficient way. Luckily, the `Animation` class saves us from having to go down that mathematical road and lets us just do animations the easy way with a variety of extra playback options.

Packing animations using the texture packer

Before we look any further into the `Animation` class, let us first cover a great feature of Libgdx's texture packer that should be used when working with animations. Whenever the texture packer builds a new texture atlas, it always scans the end of each image filename for an underscore followed by a number like `waterfall_03`. `png`. In this case, the number `03` is considered as the frame index of this animation, while the animation itself will be named and referred to as `waterfall` in the texture atlas.

Let us imagine that we have a five frame animation called `waterfall`. So, according to the mentioned pattern for allowing animation frames to be recognized by the texture packer, we would name our image files as follows:

- `waterfall_01.png`

- `waterfall_02.png`

- `waterfall_03.png`

- `waterfall_04.png`

- `waterfall_05.png`

The following short code example further illustrates the line of action to build animations:

```
TextureAtlas atlas = assetManager.get("atlas.pack");
AtlasRegion firstFrame = atlas.findRegion("waterfall");
AtlasRegion thirdFrame = atlas.findRegion("waterfall", 3);
Array<AtlasRegion> allFrames = atlas.findRegions("waterfall");
```

Let us assume that the `waterfall` animation is now available in the texture atlas (`atlas.pack`). To retrieve any given image from a texture atlas, we already know that we can simply call the `findRegion()` method and pass in the original filename without its extension to reference it. The preceding code example shows that you can also do this with an animation to get the first frame or you can pass a second argument to specify a concrete frame index like index number 3 to get the third frame. The next line uses the `findRegions()` method instead of `findRegion()`. Notice the plural "s" in the method's name. This method returns a whole array of frames associated with the supplied name which is stored in the `allFrames` variable for now.

The following lines of code show how new animations are built using the `Animation` class:

```
float fps = 1.0f / 15.0f; // Time between frames in seconds
Animation aniFirst, aniFirstThird, aniAll, aniAllPingpong;
aniFirst        = new Animation(fps, firstFrame);
aniFirstThird   = new Animation(fps, firstFrame, thirdFrame);
aniAll          = new Animation(fps, allFrames);
aniAllPingPong  = new Animation(fps, allFrames,
  Animation.PINGPONG);
```

The constructor of the class takes the time given in seconds that describes the time stepping or delay between the current and the next frame that is to be displayed. In this example, we use a frame rate of 15 frames per second. As the example code shows us further, we can pass in either an arbitrary number of AtlasRegion objects (our individual frames) or an array of those objects to define what frames should be used and in what particular order. Another feature of the Animation class is its play mode.

Choosing between animation play modes

There are six distinct play modes we can choose from:

- NORMAL: This plays the animation once (first frame to last)
- REVERSED: This plays the animation once (last frame to first)
- LOOP: This plays the animation in a loop (first frame to last)
- LOOP_REVERSED: This plays the animation in a loop (last frame to first)
- LOOP_PINGPONG: This plays the animation in a loop (first frame, to last, to first)
- LOOP_RANDOM: This plays the animation in a loop (random frames)

The NORMAL play mode is used as default if it is not explicitly set in the code.

Finally, the animations are now ready to be used and queried for their frames that should be currently displayed according to calculations. These calculations require one input value, which is the so-called state time. The state time is the elapsed time of an animation given in seconds. Usually, game objects keep track of their animation time, as we will see shortly.

```
TextureRegion region = aniAll.getKeyFrame(stateTime);
```

Assuming that the stateTime in the preceding code line yields a value of 0 seconds, the region variable will contain the first frame defined in the aniAll animation.

Animating the game screen

We are now going to animate the gold coin and bunny head game objects. However, before we can start building new animations, some preparations need to take place first, such as adding the actual image files to the project and rebuilding the texture atlas afterwards.

Copy the following files to `CanyonBunny-desktop/assets-raw/images/`:

- `anim_bunny_normal_XX.png` (where XX is 01, 02, 03)
- `anim_bunny_copter_XX.png` (where XX is 01, 02, 03, 04, 05)
- `anim_gold_coin_XX.png` (where XX is 01, 02, 03, 04, 05, 06)

Now, set the `rebuildAtlas` variable to `true` and run the Canyon Bunny desktop application once to let the texture atlas be rebuilt with the newly added images for our animations.

Defining and preparing new animations

The following image depicts all the frames including their indices of the gold coin animation:

The shown frames are meant to be played back in a ping-pong loop (play mode `LOOP_PINGPONG`) for the final animation. We will later refer to it as `animGoldCoin` in the code. The frame progression is as follows: 01, 02, 03, 04, 05, 06, 06, 05, 04, 03, 02, 01, [restart at first frame].

The following image depicts all the frames including their indices of the bunny normal animation:

The shown frames are meant to be played back in a ping-pong loop (play mode `LOOP_PINGPONG`) for the final animation and replace the current still image of the bunny head game object. We will later refer to this animation as `animNormal` in the code. The frame progression is as follows: 01, 02, 03, 03, 02, 01, [restart at first frame].

The following image depicts all the frames including their indices of the bunny copter animation:

The shown frames are meant to be played back as three different animations:

1. The first animation `animCopterTransform` plays all frames once (play mode: NORMAL; frame progression: 01, 02, 03, 04, 05).

2. The second animation `animCopterRotate` plays the last two frames in a ping-pong loop (play mode: LOOP_PINGPONG; frame progression: 04, 05, 05, 04, [restart at first frame]).

3. Lastly, the third animation `animCopterTransformBack` is simply the reverse of the first animation (play mode: REVERSED; frame progression: 05, 04, 03, 02, 01).

Now let us put all these animations in our `Assets` class for later use. Add the following import lines to the `Assets` class:

```
import com.badlogic.gdx.graphics.g2d.Animation;
import com.badlogic.gdx.utils.Array;
```

Then, make the following changes to the same class:

```
public class AssetGoldCoin {
  public final AtlasRegion goldCoin;
  public final Animation animGoldCoin;

  public AssetGoldCoin (TextureAtlas atlas) {
    goldCoin = atlas.findRegion("item_gold_coin");

    // Animation: Gold Coin
    Array<AtlasRegion> regions =
    atlas.findRegions("anim_gold_coin");
    AtlasRegion region = regions.first();
    for (int i = 0; i < 10; i++)
    regions.insert(0, region);
    animGoldCoin = new Animation(1.0f / 20.0f, regions,
      Animation.LOOP_PINGPONG);
```

```
      }
  }

  public class AssetBunny {
    public final AtlasRegion head;
    public final Animation animNormal;
    public final Animation animCopterTransform;
    public final Animation animCopterTransformBack;
    public final Animation animCopterRotate;

    public AssetBunny (TextureAtlas atlas) {
      head = atlas.findRegion("bunny_head");

      Array<AtlasRegion> regions = null;
      AtlasRegion region = null;

      // Animation: Bunny Normal
      regions = atlas.findRegions("anim_bunny_normal");
      animNormal = new Animation(1.0f / 10.0f, regions,
        Animation.LOOP_PINGPONG);

      // Animation: Bunny Copter - knot ears
      regions = atlas.findRegions("anim_bunny_copter");
      animCopterTransform = new Animation(1.0f / 10.0f, regions);

      // Animation: Bunny Copter - unknot ears
      regions = atlas.findRegions("anim_bunny_copter");
      animCopterTransformBack = new Animation(1.0f / 10.0f, regions,
        Animation.REVERSED);

      // Animation: Bunny Copter - rotate ears
      regions = new Array<AtlasRegion>();
      regions.add(atlas.findRegion("anim_bunny_copter", 4));
      regions.add(atlas.findRegion("anim_bunny_copter", 5));
      animCopterRotate = new Animation(1.0f / 15.0f, regions);
    }
  }
```

In regards to the code for the gold coin animation, you may have stumbled upon why we are inserting 10 additional copies of the animation's first frame at the beginning. Well, actually we are cheating here a little bit to achieve an artificial pause of the continuously looped animation that will now display for the first frame for a much longer period of time in comparison to the other times. Unfortunately, there is currently no way to define a per frame duration; so we need to use a trick to create a short pause after a full animation cycle that basically avoids too flashy gold coins in our special case.

Animating the gold coin game object

Now, add the following import line to the `AbstractGameObject` class:

```
import com.badlogic.gdx.graphics.g2d.Animation;
```

Then, add the following lines of code to the same class:

```
public float stateTime;
public Animation animation;

public void setAnimation (Animation animation) {
  this.animation = animation;
  stateTime = 0;
}
```

After that, make the following changes to the same class:

```
public void update (float deltaTime) {
  stateTime += deltaTime;
  if (body == null) {
    updateMotionX(deltaTime);
    updateMotionY(deltaTime);

    // Move to new position
    position.x += velocity.x * deltaTime;
    position.y += velocity.y * deltaTime;
  } else {
    position.set(body.getPosition());
    rotation = body.getAngle() * MathUtils.radiansToDegrees;
  }
}
```

With these additions, we introduce two new common attributes that are shared with every game object in Canyon Bunny, the state time (`stateTime`) and the currently set animation (`animation`), which are going to be used for rendering the game object. We also added a convenience method called `setAnimation()` that allows you to change the current animation as well as reset the state time to 0. This is desirable because in almost every case, we do not want to start somewhere in the middle of a new animation, but instead we want to start right from the beginning at the first frame. The change in the `update()` method simply makes sure that the state time is increased correctly.

Now, add the following import line to the `GoldCoin` class:

```
import com.badlogic.gdx.math.MathUtils;
```

After that, make the following changes to the same class:

```
private void init () {
   dimension.set(0.5f, 0.5f);

   setAnimation(Assets.instance.goldCoin.animGoldCoin);
   stateTime = MathUtils.random(0.0f, 1.0f);

   // Set bounding box for collision detection
   bounds.set(0, 0, dimension.x, dimension.y);

   collected = false;
}

public void render (SpriteBatch batch) {
   if (collected) return;

   TextureRegion reg = null;

   reg = animation.getKeyFrame(stateTime, true);
   batch.draw(reg.getTexture(),
      position.x, position.y,
      origin.x, origin.y,
      dimension.x, dimension.y,
      scale.x, scale.y,
      rotation,
      reg.getRegionX(), reg.getRegionY(),
      reg.getRegionWidth(), reg.getRegionHeight(),
      false, false);
}
```

In the `init()` method, we use the inherited `setAnimation()` method of `AbstractGameObject` to set the `animGoldCoin` animation. Also, the state time is initialized with a random value in the range of `0.0f` to `1.0f`. This is really a special use case here where we want each gold coin to use a different starting frame so that they look much more natural instead of being perfectly synchronized.

The following screenshot is of some gold coins that were initialized using the random state time:

You can recognize the different state times by looking closely at the top-left corner of each gold coin where the little highlight either appears or disappears during the animation.

Animating the bunny head game object

Animating the bunny head is going to take a little more effort as we want to trigger all three of the available animations at certain events. The basic idea of having three animations is to have one standard animation (animNormal) that appears when nothing special is going on. Currently, when a feather power-up is picked up, the bunny head is tinted in an orange color to signalize that it is in the state of being able to fly at that very moment. Now this is where the other three animations come into play. The first animation (animCopterTransform) shows a transformation from a normal bunny to a helicopter bunny by knotting its ears into something rotor-like. The second animation (animCopterRotate) will replace the original color-tinting effect by constantly rotating the knotted rotor ears of the bunny. Finally, there will be a reversed transformation animation (animCopterTransformBack) that unknots the bunny's ears again.

Take a look at the following diagram:

This diagram shows a **state machine** that we will need to implement to correctly change the states and animations of the bunny head game object. It begins with an overall check whether the feather power-up has been picked up (and is still active). Then, subsequent checks will try to find out what the current animation state is to take the correct actions accordingly.

To find out more about (finite) state machines like the one we used in the preceding diagram, check out the wiki article at `http://en.wikipedia.org/wiki/Finite_state_machine`.

Now, add the following import line to the `BunnyHead` class:

```
import com.badlogic.gdx.graphics.g2d.Animation;
```

Then, add the following lines of code to the same class:

```
private Animation animNormal;
private Animation animCopterTransform;
private Animation animCopterTransformBack;
private Animation animCopterRotate;
```

After that, make the following changes to the same class:

```
public void init () {
  dimension.set(1, 1);

  animNormal = Assets.instance.bunny.animNormal;
  animCopterTransform = Assets.instance.bunny.animCopterTransform;
  animCopterTransformBack =
    Assets.instance.bunny.animCopterTransformBack;
  animCopterRotate = Assets.instance.bunny.animCopterRotate;
  setAnimation(animNormal);

  // Center image on game object
  origin.set(dimension.x / 2, dimension.y / 2);

  . . .
}
```

In the `init()` method, we store the references of every animation we are going to use in corresponding local variables for much shorter names. Moreover, the starting animation is set to `animNormal`.

Now, make the following changes to the same class:

```
@Override
public void update (float deltaTime) {
  super.update(deltaTime);
  if (velocity.x != 0) {
    viewDirection = velocity.x < 0 ? VIEW_DIRECTION.LEFT
      : VIEW_DIRECTION.RIGHT;
  }
```

```
    if (timeLeftFeatherPowerup > 0) {
      if (animation == animCopterTransformBack) {
        // Restart "Transform" animation if another feather power-up
        // was picked up during "TransformBack" animation. Otherwise,
        // the "TransformBack" animation would be stuck while the
        // power-up is still active.
        setAnimation(animCopterTransform);
      }
      timeLeftFeatherPowerup -= deltaTime;
      if (timeLeftFeatherPowerup < 0) {
        // disable power-up
        timeLeftFeatherPowerup = 0;
        setFeatherPowerup(false);
        setAnimation(animCopterTransformBack);
      }
    }
    dustParticles.update(deltaTime);

    // Change animation state according to feather power-up
    if (hasFeatherPowerup) {
      if (animation == animNormal) {
        setAnimation(animCopterTransform);
      } else if (animation == animCopterTransform) {
        if (animation.isAnimationFinished(stateTime))
        setAnimation(animCopterRotate);
      }
    } else {
      if (animation == animCopterRotate) {
        if (animation.isAnimationFinished(stateTime))
        setAnimation(animCopterTransformBack);
      } else if (animation == animCopterTransformBack) {
        if (animation.isAnimationFinished(stateTime))
        setAnimation(animNormal);
      }
    }
  }
```

The update() method now contains the logic that is shown in the preceding diagram. One detail that has not been covered yet is how we can find out if an animation is finished. The Animation class provides the isAnimationFinished() method for this purpose.

Now, make the following final changes to the same class:

```java
@Override
public void render (SpriteBatch batch) {
  TextureRegion reg = null;

  // Draw Particles
  dustParticles.draw(batch);

  // Apply Skin Color
  batch.setColor(
    CharacterSkin.values()[GamePreferences.instance.charSkin]
    .getColor());

  float dimCorrectionX = 0;
  float dimCorrectionY = 0;
  if (animation != animNormal) {
    dimCorrectionX = 0.05f;
    dimCorrectionY = 0.2f;
  }

  // Draw image
  reg = animation.getKeyFrame(stateTime, true);

  batch.draw(reg.getTexture(),
    position.x, position.y,
    origin.x, origin.y,
    dimension.x + dimCorrectionX,
    dimension.y + dimCorrectionY,
    scale.x, scale.y,
    rotation,
    reg.getRegionX(), reg.getRegionY(),
    reg.getRegionWidth(), reg.getRegionHeight(),
    viewDirection == VIEW_DIRECTION.LEFT, false);

  // Reset color to white
  batch.setColor(1, 1, 1, 1);
}
```

In the `render()` method, we have removed the color-tinting effect in favor of our new animations. If an animation other than the standard one (`animNormal`) is detected, we will apply correcting values to the width and height for rendering. This is necessary because the standard animation has a different dimension than the others.

You can now run the game to check out all the animations we added throughout this chapter.

Summary

In this chapter we have learned how to manipulate `Actor` objects using the `Actions` class. We discussed and used several complex chains of actions in Canyon Bunny's menu screen which greatly demonstrate the power and flexibility of actions. Furthermore, we now know that the `Interpolation` class can also be used with those actions for added effects.

Apart from that, we have covered the `Animation` class and used the texture packer's support for packing animation frames which makes it easier to handle in the code. In addition to this, we have learned about the different play modes provided by the `Animation` class. Finally, we have implemented a state machine that is able to handle all events to trigger the right bunny head animations at the right time.

A special note from the author to the reader:

Congratulations! I assume that you have just finished reading this book and I really hope you enjoyed it just as much as I did while writing. You should now feel confident enough about using the Libgdx framework to start developing your very own games.

All that's left to say is that I wish you good luck in your future projects that will hopefully make great use of Libgdx.

Index

Symbols

A

U

uiskin.png file 222
UML class diagram 85
Uniform Resource Identifier (URI)
  opening 58
update() method 184, 194, 207, 246, 320, 352,
    357
updateMotionY() method 177-179
updateTestObjects() method 157

V

Variables tab 79
variable time steps 265
Velocity property 240
vertical synchronization (vsync) 92
visible() action 340

W

W 135
water overlay object 145, 146
WebGL
  official website 51

Wind property 240
WorldController class
  about 205, 251, 297
  implementing 91
WorldController method 106
WorldRenderer class
  about 256, 316
  implementing 92, 93

X

X Offset property 240

Y

Y 135
Y Offset property 240

Thank you for buying
Learning Libgdx Game Development

About Packt Publishing

Packt, pronounced 'packed', published its first book *"Mastering phpMyAdmin for Effective MySQL Management"* in April 2004 and subsequently continued to specialize in publishing highly focused books on specific technologies and solutions.

Our books and publications share the experiences of your fellow IT professionals in adapting and customizing today's systems, applications, and frameworks. Our solution based books give you the knowledge and power to customize the software and technologies you're using to get the job done. Packt books are more specific and less general than the IT books you have seen in the past. Our unique business model allows us to bring you more focused information, giving you more of what you need to know, and less of what you don't.

Packt is a modern, yet unique publishing company, which focuses on producing quality, cutting-edge books for communities of developers, administrators, and newbies alike. For more information, please visit our website: www.packtpub.com.

About Packt Open Source

In 2010, Packt launched two new brands, Packt Open Source and Packt Enterprise, in order to continue its focus on specialization. This book is part of the Packt Open Source brand, home to books published on software built around Open Source licences, and offering information to anybody from advanced developers to budding web designers. The Open Source brand also runs Packt's Open Source Royalty Scheme, by which Packt gives a royalty to each Open Source project about whose software a book is sold.

Writing for Packt

We welcome all inquiries from people who are interested in authoring. Book proposals should be sent to author@packtpub.com. If your book idea is still at an early stage and you would like to discuss it first before writing a formal book proposal, contact us; one of our commissioning editors will get in touch with you.

We're not just looking for published authors; if you have strong technical skills but no writing experience, our experienced editors can help you develop a writing career, or simply get some additional reward for your expertise.

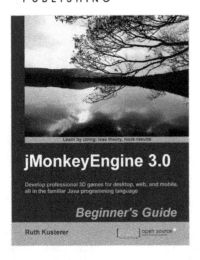

jMonkeyEngine 3.0 Beginner's Guide

ISBN: 978-1-84951-646-4   Paperback: 352 pages

Develop professionla 3D games for desktop, web, and mobile, all in the familiar Java programming language

1. Create 3D games that run on Android devices, Windows, Mac OS, Linux desktop PCs and in web browsers – for commercial, hobbyists, or educational purposes.

2. Follow end-to-end examples that teach essential concepts and processes of game development, from the basic layout of a scene to interactive game characters

3. Make your artwork come alive and publish your game to multiple platforms, all from one unified development environment.

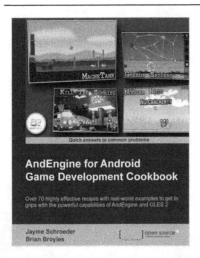

AndEngine for Android Game Development Cookbook

ISBN: 978-1-84951-898-7   Paperback: 380 pages

Over 70 highly effective recipes with real-world examples to get to grips with the powerful capabilities of AndEngine and GLES 2

1. Step by step detailed instructions and information on a number of AndEngine functions, including illustrations and diagrams for added support and results

2. Learn all about the various aspects of AndEngine with prime and practical examples, useful for bringing your ideas to life

3. Improve the performance of past and future game projects with a collection of useful optimization tips

Please check **www.PacktPub.com** for information on our titles

[PACKT] PUBLISHING
open source*
community experience distilled

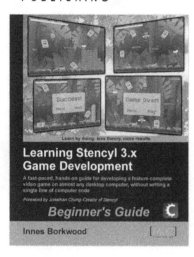

Learning Stencyl 3.x
Game Development

A fast-paced, hands-on guide for developing a feature-complete video game on almost any desktop computer, without writing a single line of computer code

Foreword by Jonathan Chung-Creator of Stencyl

Beginner's Guide C

Innes Borkwood

Learning Stencyl 3.x Game Development: Beginner's Guide

ISBN: 978-1-84969-596-1   Paperback: 336 pages

A fast paced, hands-on guide for developing a feature-complete video game on almost any desktop computer, without writing a single line of computer code

1. Learn important skills that will enable you to quickly create exciting video games, without the complexity of traditional programming languages

2. Find out how to maximize potential profits through licencing, paid-sponsorship and in-game advertising

3. Explore numerous step-by-step tutorials that will guide you through the essential features of Stencyl's powerful game-development toolkit

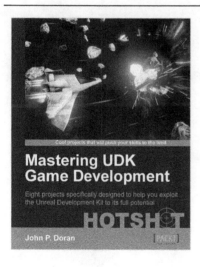

Mastering UDK
Game Development

Eight projects specifically designed to help you exploit the Unreal Development Kit to its full potential

HOTSHOT

John P. Doran

Mastering UDK Game Development

ISBN: 978-1-84969-560-2   Paperback: 290 pages

Eight projects specifically designed to help you exploit the Unreal Development Kit to its full potential

1. Guides you through advanced projects that help augment your skills with UDK by practical example

2. Comes complete with all the art assets and additional resources that you need to create stunning content

4. Perfect for level designers who want to take their skills to the next level

Please check **www.PacktPub.com** for information on our titles

www.ingramcontent.com/pod-product-compliance
Lightning Source LLC
Chambersburg PA
CBHW062044050326
40690CB00016B/2985